THE CAMBRIDGE BIBLE COMMENTARY

NEW ENGLISH BIBLE

GENERAL EDITORS
P. R. ACKROYD, A. R. C. LEANEY, J. W. PACKER

1 SAMUEL

THE FIRST BOOK OF
SAMUEL

COMMENTARY BY

PETER R. ACKROYD

Samuel Davidson Professor of Old Testament Studies
University of London, King's College

CAMBRIDGE
AT THE UNIVERSITY PRESS
1971

Published by the Syndics of the Cambridge University Press
Bentley House, 200 Euston Road, London NW1 2DB
American Branch: 32 East 57th Street, New York, N.Y.10022

© Cambridge University Press 1971

Library of Congress Catalogue Card Number: 77-128636

ISBN
0 521 07965 9 clothbound
0 521 09635 9 paperback

Printed in Great Britain
at the University Printing House, Cambridge
(Brooke Crutchley, University Printer)

GENERAL EDITORS' PREFACE

The aim of this series is to provide the text of the New English Bible closely linked to a commentary in which the results of modern scholarship are made available to the general reader. Teachers and young people have been especially kept in mind. The commentators have been asked to assume no specialized theological knowledge, and no knowledge of Greek and Hebrew. Bare references to other literature and multiple references to other parts of the Bible have been avoided. Actual quotations have been given as often as possible.

The completion of the New Testament part of the series in 1967 provides a basis upon which the production of the much larger Old Testament and Apocrypha series can be undertaken. The welcome accorded to the series has been an encouragement to the editors to follow the same general pattern, and an attempt has been made to take account of criticisms which have been offered. One necessary change is the inclusion of the translators' footnotes since in the Old Testament these are more extensive, and essential for the understanding of the text.

Within the severe limits imposed by the size and scope of the series, each commentator will attempt to set out the main findings of recent biblical scholarship and to describe the historical background to the text. The main theological issues will also be critically discussed.

Much attention has been given to the form of the volumes. The aim is to produce books each of which will be read consecutively from first to last page. The introductory material leads naturally into the text, which itself leads into the alternating sections of the commentary.

The series is accompanied by three volumes of a more general character. *Understanding the Old Testament* sets out to provide the larger historical and archaeological background, to say something about the life and thought of the people of the Old Testament, and to answer the question 'Why should we study the Old Testament?'. *The Making of the Old Testament* is concerned with the formation of the books of the Old Testament and Apocrypha in the context of the ancient near eastern world, and with the ways in which these books have come down to us in the life of the Jewish and Christian communities. *Old Testament Illustrations* contains maps, diagrams and photographs with an explanatory text. These three volumes are designed to provide material helpful to the understanding of the individual books and their commentaries, but they are also prepared so as to be of use quite independently.

P. R. A.
A. R. C. L.
J. W. P.

EDITOR'S PREFACE

The sequel to this commentary on the First book of Samuel will follow the same pattern; inevitably much of what is said here can become fully intelligible only when it is seen in relation to the developments in Israel's life which took place under the rule of David. At many points the reader will find it useful to refer to the fuller discussions of historical, literary and religious questions which may be found in larger books such as those listed at the end of this volume or conveniently in the general volumes noted on p. vi which are to accompany this series of commentaries.

I wish to express my thanks to those who have given me help in the preparation of the commentary, and especially to my colleagues as General Editors of the series, Professor A. R. C. Leaney and the Reverend J. W. Packer; also to my father, the Reverend J. R. Ackroyd, and to Miss Jean Kemble.

To my appreciation of the assistance given by the staff of the Cambridge University Press must be added a note of thanks for permission granted by the Press together with the Oxford University Press to make use of proofs of the N.E.B. text before its publication, thus making possible the publication of this commentary soon after the appearance of the text itself.

P. R. A.

CONTENTS

LIST OF MAPS AND PLAN

MAPS

PLAN

THE FOOTNOTES TO THE
N.E.B. TEXT

The footnotes to the N.E.B. text are designed to help the reader either to understand particular points of detail—the meaning of a name, the presence of a play upon words—or to give information about the actual text. Where the Hebrew text appears to be erroneous, or there is doubt about its precise meaning, it may be necessary to turn to manuscripts which offer a different wording, or to ancient translations of the text which may suggest a better reading, or to offer a new explanation based upon conjecture. In such cases, the footnotes supply very briefly an indication of the evidence, and whether the solution proposed is one that is regarded as possible or as probable. Various abbreviations are used in the footnotes.

(1) Some abbreviations are simply of terms used in explaining a point: *ch(s).*, chapter(s); *cp.*, compare; *lit.*, literally; *mng.*, meaning; *MS(S).*, manuscript(s), i.e. Hebrew manuscript(s), unless otherwise stated; *om.*, omit(s); *or*, indicating an alternative interpretation; *poss.*, possible; *prob.*, probable; *rdg.*, reading.

(2) Other abbreviations indicate sources of information from which better interpretations or readings may be obtained.

Aq.   Aquila, a Greek translator of the Old Testament (perhaps about A.D. 130) characterized by great literalness.

Aram.   Aramaic—may refer to the text in this language (used in parts of Ezra and Daniel), or to the meaning of an Aramaic word. Aramaic belongs to the same language family as Hebrew, and is known from about 1000 B.C. over a wide area of the Middle East, including Palestine.

Heb.   Hebrew—may refer to the Hebrew text or may indicate the literal meaning of the Hebrew word.

Josephus   Flavius Josephus (A.D. 37/8–about 100), author of the *Jewish Antiquities*, a survey of the whole history of his people, directed partly at least to a non-Jewish audience, and of various other works, notably one on the *Jewish War* (that of A.D. 66–73) and a defence of Judaism (*Against Apion*).

Luc. Sept.   Lucian's recension of the Septuagint, an important edition made in Antioch in Syria about the end of the third century A.D.

Pesh. Peshitta or Peshitto, the Syriac version of the Old Testament. Syriac is the name given chiefly to a form of Eastern Aramaic used by the Christian community. The translation varies in quality, and is at many points influenced by the Septuagint or the Targums.

Sam. Samaritan Pentateuch—the form of the first five books of the Old Testament as used by the Samaritan community. It is written in Hebrew in a special form of the Old Hebrew script, and preserves an important form of the text, somewhat influenced by Samaritan ideas.

Scroll(s) Scroll(s), commonly called the Dead Sea Scrolls, found at or near Qumran from 1947 onwards. These important manuscripts shed light on the state of the Hebrew text as it was developing in the last centuries B.C. and the first century A.D.

Sept. Septuagint (meaning 'seventy'); often abbreviated as the Roman numeral (LXX), the name given to the main Greek version of the Old Testament. According to tradition, the Pentateuch was translated in Egypt in the third century B.C. by 70 (or 72) translators, six from each tribe, but the precise nature of its origin and development is not fully known. It was intended to provide Greek-speaking Jews with a convenient translation. Subsequently it came to be much revered by the Christian community.

Symm. Symmachus, another Greek translator of the Old Testament (beginning of the third century A.D.), who tried to combine literalness with good style. Both Lucian and Jerome viewed his version with favour.

Targ. Targum, a name given to various Aramaic versions of the Old Testament, produced over a long period and eventually standardized, for the use of Aramaic-speaking Jews.

Theod. Theodotion, the author of a revision of the Septuagint (probably second century A.D.), very dependent on the Hebrew text.

Vulg. Vulgate, the most important Latin version of the Old Testament, produced by Jerome about A.D. 400, and the text most used throughout the Middle Ages in western Christianity.

[...] In the text itself square brackets are used to indicate probably late additions to the Hebrew text.

(Fuller discussion of a number of these points may be found in *The Making of the Old Testament* in this series)

THE FIRST BOOK OF
SAMUEL

✷　✷　✷　✷　✷　✷　✷　✷　✷　✷　✷　✷　✷

WHAT THE BOOK IS ABOUT

This book tells a story which begins with the birth of a man named Samuel and ends with the death of a king named Saul. It tells how Samuel became a leader in Israel—probably about 1050 B.C.—and was responsible for Saul becoming the first king of Israel. Though the book is named after him, Samuel dies before the end of the book (25: 1), but we can see that in many ways he is presented as the most dominant personality, involved in the events and in some measure controlling them. The title appears stranger still when it is used also for the Second book of Samuel which carries on the story from the accession of David as Saul's real successor through almost to David's death. David's death and the appointment of his successor form the opening part of the First book of Kings (1 Kings 1–2). Yet there is a unity in the two books of Samuel; the appearance of David in the first book provides a clear link with the second, and his relationship to Samuel makes it appropriate that the name of Samuel should have been used to suggest that the developments described in the two books could all be regarded as connected with this outstanding personality.

THE DIVIDED 'BOOK' OF SAMUEL

In reality, the two books are one. At an early date the larger work was divided, and similar divisions have been made in other Old Testament books. Thus, the 'book' of Kings has been divided into two, and the writings of the author we conveniently call 'the Chronicler' have been divided into

I

four—1 and 2 Chronicles, Ezra and Nehemiah. So too the first four (or perhaps five) books of the Old Testament should be regarded as a continuous work divided into smaller, more convenient, units—Genesis, Exodus, etc. The divisions may have been made partly on the basis of length: the two books of Samuel are more or less the same length. But it is clear that considerations of content have also played a part, and the division at the death of Saul marks off the period of Samuel and Saul from that of the first great king, David. It would, however, be a mistake to let the division prevent our reading straight on from the First book to the Second. The division of the commentary on these books into two volumes is dictated by the demands of space; but much that appears in this volume can only be more fully understood as we read its sequel.

THE LARGER WORK TO WHICH THE BOOK OF SAMUEL BELONGS

The division of the 'book' of Samuel into two parts was not first made in the original Hebrew text, but in the later translation of it into Greek. Translations of Old Testament books were made for the use of Greek-speaking Jews, particularly in Egypt but also elsewhere in the Mediterranean area, from about the third century B.C. At that time, the conquests of Alexander the Great, which took place in the period 333–323 B.C., had resulted in the spread of Greek language and culture in the Near East, and Greek became the common language employed for diplomatic and commercial purposes over a very wide area. The Greek translation of the Old Testament is very important because it provides evidence of a sometimes rather different Hebrew text, and helps in our understanding of the way in which the books were handed down. It is often known as the Septuagint, 'the translation made by the Seventy', from a story told in a writing called the Letter of Aristeas. This tells how representatives of all the tribes of Israel (actually seventy-two rather than seventy, six from each tribe) translated the

Law—the first five books of the Old Testament—in Alexandria. It is a legend, but no doubt contains some elements of history. The name Septuagint came to be used for the whole Greek translation; it is abbreviated in N.E.B. as Sept., but often by the Roman numeral LXX.

In the Septuagint, the two books of Samuel are divided, but they are called the first two books of Kingdoms (Reigns), and the two books of Kings which follow are called the third and fourth books of Kingdoms. These Greek names are very appropriate, and they also show clearly that the division between Samuel and Kings is artificial. The death of David, the central figure of 2 Samuel, is in fact described in the opening of 1 Kings, because it there paves the way for Solomon's reign and the building of the temple in Jerusalem. Originally all four books belong together. But we may go further. The book of Ruth, which in the English Bible stands between Judges and 1 Samuel, appears in a different place in the Hebrew Old Testament, in a group of five books known as the five 'Scrolls', the Megilloth; the others are the Song of Songs, Lamentations, Ecclesiastes and Esther. The division between 1 Samuel and Judges is artificial, and Judges is also closely linked with Joshua. We are really dealing with the parts of a much longer work which extends from Joshua to 2 Kings. In the Hebrew Bible these books are given a special title: the Former Prophets. This distinguishes them from a second group of books: the Latter Prophets. The names indicate the position of the books in the Old Testament; the first group is made up of what we often call the 'history books' (though not including Ruth, Chronicles, Ezra, Nehemiah, Esther); the second group has what we call the books of prophecy (Isaiah to Malachi, but omitting Lamentations and Daniel).

The book of Deuteronomy is also closely connected with this large work covering the period from the conquest of Canaan in about 1200 B.C. to the exile in Babylon in the sixth century B.C. So it is sometimes called the 'Deuteronomic

History'; this is a modern title, indicating the nature and purpose of the work in its final form. To understand this, we must look a little more closely at how these books came into being.

HOW DID THE BOOK COME TO BE WRITTEN?

The answer to this question is complex. We know nothing directly concerning those who were responsible. The most we can hope to do is begin from the book as we have it and see what we may deduce about the time when it reached this form, the kind of concerns and interests of the final author(s), and then work back by careful examination of the contents of the book to see what lies behind it.

The first part of the discussion clearly turns on the probability that this book is part of the much larger work mentioned above, covering the whole period from the conquest to the exile. Since the last recorded event in 2 Kings is the release of the captive king of Judah, Jehoiachin, from prison, in 561 B.C., we may say that the final form of the work cannot be earlier than this. Whatever the earlier stages, the last author(s) were working when the northern and southern kingdoms of Israel and Judah had fallen, the one to Assyria in 722 B.C., the other to Babylon in 587 B.C. Part of the population was in exile in Babylonia, part in Palestine, and some scattered elsewhere, in the neighbouring lands, and in Egypt. We know very little indeed about their condition, but we can appreciate that at such a moment of depression and doubt about the future, the writing of a history from the conquest to the exile would be of considerable importance. It might help in answering two questions: What went wrong that the great hopes of the conquest and Davidic periods should come to nothing? How, if there is a time of restoration, can the people so organize their life that the future will be better? The whole work—Deuteronomy to 2 Kings—appears to be concerned with this, and answers the questions in terms of God's promise, his giving of the land of Canaan, his care for his people, and the disobedience of leaders and people to his demands, their turning away to other forms of worship, their failure to conform to certain standards of justice and right. It should not surprise us to find, in the First book of Samuel, some passages in which the emphasis rests on this final consideration of the meaning of judgement and the nature of hope.

But it is not likely that the book was first written at that late date. The later interpreters or editors made use of much already existing material, though it is not easy for us to discover now just what they had at their disposal. There are several possibilities. (1) We could suppose that the final authors made use of a great mass of early material, stories, poems, annals (that is, list of officials, names and the like), and that they built this up into its present complex form. (2) There may have existed already one or more accounts of the period and they may have dovetailed these together, fitting them into a sequence in somewhat the way that in the second century A.D. a Christian named Tatian made up a Gospel harmony, using pieces of the four gospels to create a unified narrative. (3) We might picture the process more in terms of the gathering of stories around certain great figures of the past— stories associated with Samuel, others with Saul, with Jonathan, with David.

Probably we should not assume that any one such approach will solve all the problems; we are dealing with a work whose beginnings lie back in the eleventh century B.C. in the lives of Samuel and Saul; its final form was reached about 500 years later, and the process is almost certainly much too complicated to be unravelled from the information available to us.

In the last century and more, the literary study of the books of the Old Testament has been actively pursued. Although there is no complete agreement about the answers to many of the questions which have to be asked, it is most often believed that in the books with which the Old Testament begins— Genesis to Numbers—two or perhaps three early accounts covering the first stages of the people's life have been woven together. Many scholars believe that these accounts can be traced also in the books Joshua, Judges and Samuel (perhaps even in Kings). It would be natural enough if in the period of David and Solomon, when the kingdom was at the height of its new-found prosperity and unity, an attempt should have been made to set out the story of how this had been achieved, to endeavour to trace the hand of God at work in the events and in the people involved in them. Other such accounts may have been developed later, within the life of both the northern kingdom of Israel and the southern kingdom of Judah. Eventually all this different material, or selections from it, has been welded together to form books something like those which we now have. But it is likely that the process was accompanied by much addition of other material, and revision of emphasis. For in the ancient world, where everything was done by hand, a re-writing of a book may well mark a re-presentation of its material, suited to a new situation, offering a new insight into men's thinking. If we read sensitively, we may detect some of these levels in the material, and gain a deeper understanding of how men lived and thought, not just in the period which is being described, but also when these stories were being re-told and re-interpreted.

THE PURPOSE OF THE BOOK

Why are books written? Clearly the question may be differently answered for each book we consider and for each of the stages through which a book may have passed. For an ancient book, we may recognize the possibility that it was produced to offer an explanation—what led up to the rule of David and Solomon could be related by a professional scribe, working at the court, whose business was to record events from day to day and perhaps also to glorify the ruler under whom he worked. His interpretation of the story would be determined in part by this aim. A book may be written for the sheer joy of telling a story. But though this could be a factor in the preservation of many ancient traditions in Israel, the books which we have in the Old Testament must all be regarded as religious books in the sense that they offer an interpretation in religious terms of what they relate. This does not make them any the less artistic as stories.

If we ask what the purpose is of the First book of Samuel, then clearly we can give only a partial answer. Its purpose can only be fully understood when it is seen as part of the larger work to which it belongs. But within that larger purpose, we can see some of the particular interests which are developed. The author(s) set(s) out to tell us how Israel came to have a monarchy, an institution which for good and ill was to be part of the people's life from the time of Saul to the time of the fall of Jerusalem to the Babylonians in 587 B.C. We are shown how the first king, Saul, was a failure, but the future of the monarchy was secured in the person of David. As the story is told, it is David who is the real centre of interest from chapter 16 onwards. We are also shown how the way was prepared for there to be a single central place of worship, at Jerusalem. This is made clear in 2 Samuel, though the real centrality of Jerusalem was only fully established in the seventh century under king Josiah. But the way towards this is shown, and here we can see how the later reality has influenced the telling of the story. The book opens at the ancient sanctuary of Shiloh; but this is doomed, and the situation remains unclear until David captures Jerusalem (2 Sam. 5) and takes there the Ark, the symbol of the God of Israel. Alongside this runs the theme of the priesthood, and again the story is incomplete here. The priesthood of Eli at Shiloh is equally doomed; but it is Samuel who takes over the succession. The priestly line of Eli may be traced further; but it is eventually under David that we see the establishment of a new priestly line, that of Zadok in Jerusalem.

Kingship, holy place, priesthood—three themes which were eventually to be of fundamental importance in Old Testament thought. They are shown here linked together in the figure of

Samuel with whom the book opens; and with him is linked too that other great line of religious influence which so dominates the period of the monarchy and beyond—the prophetic movement. This was to stand alongside, involved but critical, to flower in the eighth century B.C. into one of the richest religious movements the world has ever known, in the great figures of Amos and Hosea and Isaiah and in their successors over the centuries that followed. Such a flowering cannot be understood without a recognition of where the roots lie; this book is a primary source of information.

HISTORY AND INTERPRETATION

The book as we have it has a long history; we may detect in it some traces of how its content has been affected by the particular interpretations, the particular purposes, of those who were responsible for transmitting and shaping the material. How far does it represent what actually happened, and how clearly can we describe the people involved?

A little earlier the point was stressed that the books of the Old Testament as we have them are all religious books. So we may properly recognize at the outset that the authors at the various stages of the book's composition were not setting out to write history as a modern historian might attempt to do it. They are offering stories and traditions about the past of their own people, and offering them in such a way as to tell us what they believed that past experience to mean. They provide us with a great deal of important information. But where a modern historian offers his interpretation of the past, he is also concerned with sifting the information and assessing its historical value. If he has two accounts of the same event, or two estimates of the same person, he will show why he believes certain elements in these to be reliable, or more reliable, while other elements may be shown to be due to misunderstanding or propaganda or bias. The ancient writer is more likely to set down both accounts, side by side or in an

8

interwoven form; or he may use only one account because it offers what fits best with his own understanding of the past.

An example will illustrate what can happen. For some parts of the books of Samuel we have a parallel account in 1 Chronicles. It is clear that the author of that much later work (probably in the fourth century B.C.) knew the material of the books of Samuel, though we cannot be sure whether he used the books more or less as we know them or whether he was working with a somewhat different 'edition'. We notice that in 1 Chronicles a great deal of what is in the books of Samuel does not appear. For example, the monarchy of Saul is very briefly dismissed. There is a short passage giving the family to which Saul belonged (1 Chron. 9: 35–44); one chapter only (1 Chron. 10) tells of Saul's death at Mount Gilboa—the story told in 1 Sam. 31. But to this story, the later author has added his comment: 'Thus Saul paid with his life for his unfaithfulness...' (1 Chron. 10: 13–14). He has selected part of the story of Saul and has made it the vehicle of a particular judgement, drawing out ideas which may be detected in a less developed form in the 1 Samuel narratives. Similarly 1 Chron. 19–20: 3 uses the same story of David's war against the Ammonites as is found in 2 Sam. 10–12; but whereas in the earlier work there is woven into this story that of David's adultery with Bathsheba, the wife of Uriah the Hittite, in the later work this is entirely absent. We may see the absence of this and some other rather discreditable stories about David as due to the way in which the Chronicler idealizes David to a much greater extent than does the author of 1 and 2 Samuel.

We do not have the same precise evidence when we try to get behind the narratives in the books of Samuel, for we do not possess an earlier form of these narratives with which we can make a comparison. But from the present form which they have, from the selection of events which they offer, from the pictures they present of the various great personages, we may readily recognize that here is an interpretation based on a particular handling of the material. One example may illustrate this. The story of David and Saul as it is told in 1 Sam. 16–31 is clearly written with an eye to the establishment of David as the great king whose name was to live as a pattern of kingship in Israel. But the stories about David are not all of them very creditable; as outlaw and bandit his behaviour was certainly sometimes of very doubtful morality. Even as the stories are told, we may sympathize with Saul's difficulties. And although Saul is depicted as failing as a king, we find stories which show him as a hero, as a noble warrior, as a man of generous impulse. We can imagine a telling of the story which would present him in a very favourable light, and if we had such a story, we might well be able to draw up a more accurate assessment of the relationship between him and David. We must, therefore, in reading be continually aware of the interpretation given to the stories. This interpretation may be by comment, shorter or longer, or, less obviously, by the actual arrangement and linking together of different pieces of material.

It is more difficult when we try to sort out the actual people involved, for here we find that, particularly for great figures like that of Samuel, there is more than will fit together for a neat simple description. Samuel was too great to leave only one impression; around him has gathered a wealth of stories, with different estimates of his achievement. Some of these are probably earlier than others; we have to evaluate them all. The same is true of David. Of the many other characters who appear, we can do no more than try to understand their words and actions; we must set them in the context of the period in which they are described, and endeavour to depict that period on the basis of a careful sorting of the information provided by the biblical material and by such non-biblical sources as are available.

The non-biblical sources are, as so often, somewhat elusive. Some of them are described more fully in *The Making of the Old Testament*. We do not have any documents which mention by name any of the people known to us in 1 and 2 Samuel. We have some knowledge of the kings of Phoenicia, among whom must rank Hiram of Tyre who had close relations with David and Solomon, and established trade relationships with them (2 Sam. 5: 11; 1 Kings 5: 1 ff.).

The Jewish historian Josephus, in his account of this period, makes use of the biblical material and of evidence from Phoenician records. These indicate a king of Tyre named Abibaal who was succeeded by Hiram. The name Hiram may be a shortened form of Ahiram (= 'my kinsman (i.e. my god) is exalted'). Fuller documentary evidence exists for the line of kings at Byblos, a very important coastal city; here we find a ruler named Ahiram in about 1000 B.C. whose name appears inscribed on a great stone sarcophagus, itself probably about 200 years older.

It has for many years been supposed that a clearly fixed date for events in this period was provided by the excavations at the site of the ancient city of Shiloh. A major destruction here was dated to about 1050 B.C., and this date would neatly fit in with the natural supposition that the Philistines would attack and destroy Shiloh after capturing the Ark (see 1 Sam. 4). But a recent re-examination of the evidence and further excavation at the site have shown this to be incorrect. The destruction is to be assigned to the period when the northern kingdom fell into Assyrian hands in the late eighth century B.C. When Jeremiah (7: 12; 26: 6, 9) speaks of the ruins of the Shiloh sanctuary as a warning of what can and will happen to the Jerusalem temple, he is likely therefore to have known the place as it was after that disaster. This revised understanding of the archaeological evidence is a good example of the need for caution.

The general background to this period is one of weakness in Egypt and in the north-eastern and Mesopotamian areas; it was therefore a time during which Palestine was free of external pressures. Already by the time of Solomon, Egyptian pressure began to be felt again as Egypt gave support to opponents of Solomon, and after his death Shishak of Egypt marched through Palestine, claiming that the land was really his (cp. 1 Kings 14: 25 ff.). The route described in Shishak's own account of the march on an inscription at Karnak indicates that not only Judah—as the Old Testament account suggests— but also the northern kingdom of Israel was affected by Egyptian policy; more than fifty places in Israel are mentioned, including Beth-shan and Megiddo, and about one hundred in Judah. But if external pressures were less, there were great internal difficulties and much of the narrative of 1 Samuel is concerned with these. In particular, it was the Philistine threat which affected Israel. Was it to be the Philistines, based on their cities in the coastal plain, who would establish a unified rule over the whole area? They pressed hard into the hill country, establishing garrisons and controlling Israelite movement and military power. At Saul's death, they controlled the important city of Beth-shan at the eastern end of the plain of Jezreel (Esdraelon). It was only with David that the Philistine threat could be fully met (see 2 Sam. 5). But already in the stories of Eli, of Saul, Jonathan and David, we can see both the danger and the movements to meet it.

The general historical outline of the period is clear enough. We shall see some of the historical problems as we read through the book. But how far can we know the detail of the events? Here we have to weigh two opposing factors. On the one hand, we must give proper recognition to the fact that ancient traditions are likely to contain more of actual historical content than was once believed. Stories such as those told by Homer in the *Iliad* contain much more of accurate detail about the period of the Trojan wars than was at one time thought; archaeological discovery has made this clear. Ancient peoples clearly preserved much sound tradition about their own past. On the other hand, we have to recognize that such popular tradition, handed down over centuries, imparts its own twist to the material. It selects, it interprets, it transfers tales told about one area to another or from one person to another;

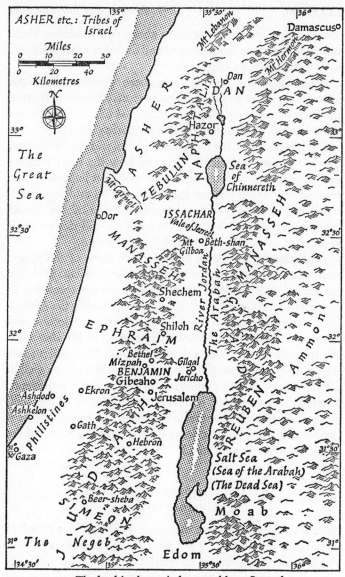

1. The land in the period covered by 1 Samuel
(showing approximate areas of tribal settlement)

13

stories gather around particularly notable personalities. These two points, the one more positive and the other more negative, have to be carefully balanced.

Even where the time lapse between events and written records is likely to be much shorter—as may be true of parts of the David story—we must recognize that selection and interpretation play an important part in producing what is only one way of describing what happened. This means that in the end we find greater interest in discussing how the story is interpreted than merely in trying to discover what happened. The two cannot be fully separated; but since we are studying a book which offers a religious interpretation of a period, we should be doing its authors less than justice if we did not take full account of what they thought the events meant.

Any attempt at writing a consecutive story of the period covered by this book comes up against the problems raised by the variety of its material. Here we have one interpretation of the way the different elements may be related; the Chronicler, as we have seen, provides an alternative selection and assessment. Josephus, the Jewish historian, in his *Antiquities* (v. 10. 1–vi. 14. 9) follows the Samuel order, but offers some dovetailing and reconciling of points of difference, as well as adding some lengthy comments on personalities and events. Later writers up to our own time, with greater or less skill, have made further attempts at ordering and explaining; it is proper that this should be done, but the tentative nature of the results must be kept in mind.

THE FIRST BOOK OF SAMUEL AS A THEOLOGICAL WORK

By a theological work we mean one which sets out to tell us something of what its author believes about God and about the way in which he acts in relation to men. Men's ideas of God do not stand still. We must therefore look at what is said in the light of the way in which beliefs and practices in Israel's

14

religion changed over the years. We must ask: What did men believe at the time about which we are reading? and further: What did those who told the stories believe? In any period the attempt at saying something about God is beset with difficulties, for what may be termed the 'otherness' of God makes all our human language less than adequate. Those who come after us will be critical of the ways in which we express ourselves, and we are right to be critical of what has been said in the past. But we may hope that those who read the theological books of our time will be fair and will try to understand what we were endeavouring to say. So, if we are to be just to this biblical book, we must attempt to see what was really being said, and even where we can see it to be quite inadequate by later standards, we must see what truth it contains. For the Christian reader of the Old Testament, there is always the temptation to dismiss its ideas about God as out of date, as inadequate in comparison with Christian thought at its best. For the Jewish reader, for whom the Old Testament is his Bible, the same difficulty is present; he is aware of the differences of level within the Old Testament and aware too of the ways in which the understanding of God has developed in the course of later Jewish history. Martin Buber, the great Jewish philosopher and theologian of this century, has confessed his total inability to accept that God could have commanded the murder of Agag by Samuel (1 Sam. 15: 10–33): 'I could never believe', he wrote, 'that that was a message from God…it was Samuel who did not understand God.' But we must still ask how far, even with such misunderstanding, there is true insight.

Whatever particular view we take, whether or not we accept a religious interpretation of life, we are still bound to ask questions about meaning. When we consider the world as we know it, we cannot help asking how it is to be understood, what purpose, if any, lies behind it. Whether we use theological language in trying to answer such questions, whether we express our understanding by speaking about God and his purpose or prefer to use philosophical terms of one kind or another, we still have to take seriously what men have said in the past, because it is from them that our ideas derive. The religious tradition which stems from the Bible has been and still is one of the most powerful factors in creating our present-day ways of thinking. A deeper insight into its meaning is part of our equipping ourselves for more adequate thinking and living today.

THE TEXT OF THE BOOK AND ITS INTERPRETATION

The Old Testament was originally written in Hebrew, with only some quite short sections, mainly in Ezra and Daniel, in Aramaic, another language of the Semitic group. Any ancient language presents problems of understanding, and this is particularly true of Hebrew for which we have only a rather limited amount of material. Furthermore—and this is true of all ancient texts which have been frequently copied—there are many points at which the text as we have it may have become corrupt as a result of mistakes made by the scribes. A letter may be misread—and the Hebrew alphabet is such that confusion of letters is rather easy; the manuscript may be accidentally damaged and the next copyist may quite sensibly try to write what he thinks ought to be there. Sometimes, quite understandably, a scribe may have altered the wording to avoid something which he felt to be theologically difficult or perhaps offensive. An example of this is to be seen in 2 Sam. 12: 14. Here the N.E.B. rightly renders: 'You have shown your contempt for the LORD', but adds a footnote to point out that the Hebrew text has 'the enemies of the LORD'. The words 'the enemies of' represent an addition by a pious scribe who felt that the text was theologically undesirable.

Reference has already been made (p. 2) to the Greek translation of the Hebrew text. There are other ancient translations too—into Aramaic and Syriac, both Semitic languages;

and into Latin. The great scholar Jerome in the late fourth century A.D. produced a revised Latin version which came to be known as the Vulgate, that is the 'common', or generally accepted, translation. This was used throughout the Middle Ages and has been particularly revered in the Roman Catholic community. In various ways these translations help us, not only to understand the Hebrew text, but also to see that different forms of the text were once in existence.

All the great Hebrew manuscripts are rather late, from about the ninth century A.D. onwards. But in 1947 and the years that followed, discoveries of manuscripts and fragments were made in the region near the Dead Sea. These are often called the 'Dead Sea Scrolls', or, from the name of the centre of the community from which many of them stemmed, the 'Qumran Scrolls'. Some of these are very old indeed, perhaps of the third century B.C., and certainly of the last two centuries B.C. and the first century A.D. Some important small fragments of the books of Samuel were discovered among them. These reveal a form of text which at some points is closer to the Septuagint, the Greek translation, though at other points the text is different from both the standard Hebrew text and the Greek. Some of these points appear in footnotes to the N.E.B. text. (A note on the abbreviations used in these footnotes appears on pp. xi–xii.) Since at certain points the differences affect our understanding of the text, we shall have to comment on them. But it is important to realize that though some of the differences are just points where one text or another clearly has a form due to a mistake in copying, most of them show different ways in which the material could be understood. If we want to get a full picture of the way in which the material of the books was understood, then we must take account of even quite small differences which lift a curtain on some point in the handing down and interpreting of it. The study of the text, a highly technical aspect of biblical study, is not to be separated from the study of its interpretation. The modern commentator builds upon the work of his predecessors, and among them are those who, in the biblical period itself and after, were responsible for copying and presenting the text.

✳ ✳ ✳ ✳ ✳ ✳ ✳ ✳ ✳ ✳ ✳ ✳ ✳

The birth and call of Samuel

The first three chapters of the book centre on the early part of the story of Samuel, but this is interwoven with judgement on the family of Eli, the priest at the sanctuary of Shiloh. We are led very skilfully by the story-teller from one scene to another; when the story concentrates on Samuel there are reminders of the background of the failure of Eli's sons, and when we turn to the family of Eli, a contrast is drawn with Samuel's growth in wisdom and piety.

AT THE ANNUAL FESTIVAL

1 THERE WAS A MAN from Ramathaim, a Zuphite[a] from the hill-country of Ephraim, named Elkanah son of Jeroham, son of Elihu, son of Tohu, son of Zuph an
2 Ephraimite; and he had two wives named Hannah and Peninnah. Peninnah had children, but Hannah was child-
3 less. This man used to go up from his own town every year to worship and to offer sacrifice to the LORD of Hosts in Shiloh. There Eli's two sons, Hophni and Phinehas, were
4 priests of the LORD. On the day when Elkanah sacrificed, he gave several shares of the meat to his wife Peninnah
5 with all her sons and daughters; but, although[b] he loved Hannah, he gave her only one share, because the LORD had
6 not granted her children. Further, Hannah's rival used to

[a] a Zuphite: *so Sept.; Heb.* Zophim.   [b] *So Sept.; Heb. unintelligible.*

torment her and humiliate her because she had no children.
Year after year this happened when they*a* went up to the 7
house of the LORD; her rival used to torment her.

* The story in chs. 1–3 has to be broken into smaller sections
for the purpose of commentary, but should also be read as a
whole.

1. The family comes *from the hill-country of Ephraim*, in the
central part of Palestine. The actual place is variously named;
here it is *Ramathaim*; in verse 19 and subsequently, 'Ramah'.
There appear to be several places with such names (meaning
'height') and the precise locality cannot be fixed with
certainty; nor can the area of Zuph (see 9: 5) be identified
(for a possible area see map, p. 48). The story begins in very
much the same way as do some of the stories in the book of
Judges, e.g. Samson in Judg. 13: 2 and Micah in Judg. 17: 1. In
one sense this is just one more in that series and it links and
contrasts with the last story (Judg. 21) which reaches its climax
at the annual pilgrimage festival at Shiloh. But a new beginning, marked by the new book, is appropriate in that here is the
story of the man to whom Israel was to owe its monarchy.
That he belonged to a family of some standing is indicated
by the listing of the ancestors of Elkanah.

2. Polygamy was not uncommon in Old Testament times.
It served two very useful purposes. It gave the greater assurance that a man would have a son to keep his name alive;
sometimes, as perhaps here, a second wife was taken simply
because the first wife had no children. It also ensured protection for the women members of the community; as
daughters they came under the protection of father or perhaps
of another male relative, but it was in marriage that they were
best protected. Such a concern is also expressed in the frequent
injunctions to protect the widow who has lost her main
support in society. Hebrew society was male-centred, but it

[a] *So Vulg.; Heb.* she.

had a high regard for the importance of its women, especially in their position as wives and mothers. Prov. 31: 10–31 gives a vivid picture of this. That polygamy created problems is evident; rivalry (so verse 6) between the wives creates much unhappiness.

3. *Shiloh* (see map, p. 13) was an important religious centre. In 3:3 we are told that the Ark, the symbol of God's presence, especially in battle (see chapter 4), was there. Josh. 18: 1 tells that Shiloh was made the centre at some point during the settlement period, but there were other places, for example Shechem (so Josh. 24) and Gilgal (so Josh. 5), which were prominent. It may be that the main religious centre was moved from time to time, or it may be that it was only gradually that there came to be only one centre. Local traditions may have been given a universal application; perhaps Shiloh was originally only the religious centre for the area in which it was situated.

The custom of regular worship is more precisely laid down in later laws (so, for example, in Deut. 16). It is most natural to suppose that *every year* refers to the great autumn festival, known as Tabernacles or Booths from the custom of building small huts of branches, probably as a relic of ancient practices connected with the vine harvest. This is often referred to quite simply as 'the festival'; in later times the spring festival of Passover came to have almost greater prominence.

LORD of Hosts is an important phrase descriptive of God. The form *LORD* always represents in English the use in the original Hebrew of the name of God expressed in the four letters *Y-H-W-H*. Gradually the custom grew up of not pronouncing this name, for it was felt to be too sacred. Probably it was pronounced *Yahweh*—and so it is often written in modern books. In proper names it appears at the beginning or end in forms like *Yehō-* (so *Yehōnāthan*= Jonathan) or *-yāhū* (so *Yirme-yāhū*=Jeremiah). The Jews, to avoid pronouncing it, substituted a title—*Adonai* ('my lord')— or a word suggestive of God such as 'name', for the 'name of God' could be used to stress the actual person and presence of God. The Greek translators followed the practice by rendering Yahweh as *kurios*—lord. This is important, for though this word could be used in a secular manner, for example with reference to the king, it would carry an overtone in Jewish use. When the New Testament uses the title 'Lord' of Jesus, it is clearly suggesting its understanding of Jesus' special nature and place.

The *Hosts* in this phrase have been variously explained. God may be pictured as ruler over the sun, moon and stars, or over the heavenly beings who assemble in his royal court, the 'heavenly host'. Or we may see the understanding of God to be found in chapter 4, as the one who leads his people in battle, the God whom Israel praised for giving them the land of Canaan. Eventually it becomes a title expressing God's power and glory. It is often transliterated in liturgical poems and hymns as Sabaoth, for example, in the great confession of faith known as the *Te Deum*.

The second part of verse 3 introduces the priestly family at Shiloh; the narrator provides here a brief forward look to the story which follows in chapters 2 and 4 in which this priestly family comes under divine judgement. The names *Hophni* and *Phinehas* are possibly of Egyptian origin; the latter is also found for one of the grandsons of Aaron (Exod. 6: 25), and this may be connected with the ancestry of Eli's priestly line (see on 2: 28).

4–5. The customs alluded to are not completely clear. There was evidently a common meal at the time of the sacrificial worship (see verse 9), and there were rules governing the allocation of the portions of meat. We find Samuel giving Saul a special portion at such a feast (9: 23 f.). Hannah is the favourite wife, but she has no child and this puts her in a difficult position. To bear a son to her husband meant keeping alive the family line, and the childless wife was thought in ancient Israel to be in some way under divine displeasure. Many stories, like this one, turn on the theme of how such a woman is blessed with a son (cp. the stories of Abraham and

Sarah, Jacob and his wives, and, in the New Testament, Elizabeth and Mary).

7*a*. Up to this point, the story has been telling what happened each year. The setting is given, and now we move over into what took place on one occasion, the occasion which was to be marked by a change for Hannah which would also bring a change for Israel. ✶

PRAYER AND ANSWER

Once when she was in tears and would not eat, her hus-
8 band Elkanah said to her, 'Hannah, why are you crying and eating nothing? Why are you so miserable? Am I not
9–10 more to you than ten sons?' After they had finished eating and drinking at the sacrifice at Shiloh, Hannah rose in deep distress, and stood before the LORD*a* and prayed to him, weeping bitterly. Meanwhile Eli the priest was sitting on his seat beside the door of the temple of the LORD.
11 Hannah made a vow in these words: 'O LORD of Hosts, if thou wilt deign to take notice of my trouble and remember me, if thou wilt not forget me but grant me offspring, then I will give the child to the LORD for his whole life,
12 and no razor shall ever touch his head.' For a long time she went on praying before the LORD, while Eli watched her
13 lips. Hannah was praying silently; but, although her voice could not be heard, her lips were moving and Eli took
14 her for a drunken woman. He said to her, 'Enough of this drunken behaviour! Go away till the wine has worn off.'
15 'No, sir,' she answered, 'I am a sober person, I have drunk no wine or strong drink, and I have been pouring out my
16 heart before the LORD. Do not think me so degraded, sir; all this time I have been speaking out of the fullness of my

[*a*] and stood...LORD: *so Sept.; Heb. om.*

grief and misery.' 'Go in peace,' said Eli, 'and may the 17
God of Israel answer the prayer you have made to him.'
Hannah said, 'May I be worthy of your kindness.' And 18
she went away and took something to eat, no longer
downcast. Next morning they were up early and, after 19
prostrating themselves before the LORD, returned to their
own home at Ramah. Elkanah had intercourse with his
wife Hannah, and the LORD remembered her. She con- 20
ceived, and in due time bore a son, whom she named
Samuel, 'because', she said, 'I asked the LORD for him.'

* 9–10. *at Shiloh*: the place-name is unnecessary here, and it
is probable that it is an error for 'in the temple-room'
(*lishkāh*), the room in which the special meal was eaten (see
note on verse 18). *and stood before the LORD* is added from Sept.
It was omitted from the Hebrew by accident, presumably because the copyist's eye moved from one occurrence of 'LORD'
to the second (here rendered *to him*). There are many such
small differences between the Hebrew and Greek texts, some
more important than others. *weeping bitterly*: such weeping is
fitting as an accompaniment of a prayer of distress. A fast was so
observed (see the description of the priests weeping in Joel 2:
17), and a psalm which voices distress asks God to 'store every
tear in thy flask' (Ps. 56: 8). Weeping and other such dis-
plays of strong emotion were expressions in Israel of prayer
and praise. Such intense expression may still be seen in worship
in countries where no embarrassment is felt at open display.
   Meanwhile Eli...: in the original text this whole sentence stands in the middle of what appears in N.E.B. as the
preceding sentence. The aside prepares us for the sequel when
Eli's intervention is to be decisive. The customary place of the
priest in the shrine is indicated; from the doorway he could
supervise the coming and going of the worshippers and probably also their sacrifices. We must picture the shrine as being
quite small, but it is called a *temple*, a building constructed

for worship and for the housing of the Ark of God (3: 3). The sketch below shows the plan of a temple of about this period.

11. The story-teller gives only the vow from Hannah's prayer. Such a vow was naturally preceded by the statement of distress and the offering of petition. The kind of language

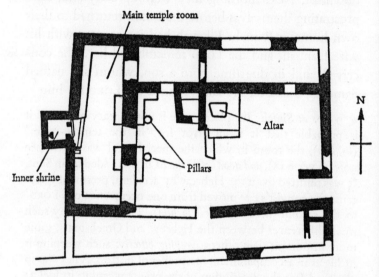

Plan of an ancient shrine. This sketch is based on a temple found at the city of Arad in the Negeb, south of Hebron (mentioned in Judg. 1: 16 and elsewhere). The temples at Shiloh and at Nob may well have been similar in construction. This particular building was about 65 feet long by 50 feet wide.

appropriate to such a prayer may be seen in Ps. 13. *no razor shall ever touch his head:* the story of Samson is similar, and in both cases the vow is life-long. Israel had an institution of this kind in which the vow was for a limited period only. A person making such a vow was called a Nazirite, a 'separated' or 'dedicated' person; Num. 6: 1–8 and 13–21 give the regulations for this practice. Hair as a symbol of strength is very clear in the Samson story; long hair is also associated with dedicated warriors (cp. 'those who had flowing locks' at the opening of the Song of Deborah in Judg. 5, N.E.B. footnote). No further reference is made in the story of Samuel to his having uncut hair, and it is possible that the theme has been added from the Samson tradition; Sept. goes further and refers to abstention from all strong drink (so too in the Samson story, see Judg. 13: 14, and cp. also the injunction concerning John the Baptist in Luke 1: 15).

12. Hannah prayed silently, moving her lips at the words of the prayer. That Eli thought Hannah drunk is a clear indication that at such festivals there was much drinking (alluded to briefly in verses 9–10); Judg. 9: 27ff. describes a vintage festival at which, not surprisingly, the participants became very drunk and spoke foolishly. The point here provides a link with the later descriptions of the evil conditions at the Shiloh temple.

15. *a sober person*: one of strict conduct. The exact meaning of the phrase is not certain.

16. *so degraded*: the text has literally 'a daughter of *belī'al*', a word later regarded as a proper name, applicable to an evil spirit (so 2 Cor. 6: 15). Early commentators explained it as meaning 'without profit'; so 'worthless person'. More recently it has been explained as meaning 'confusion', so 'one who lives in a disorderly manner'; or as 'swallower', equivalent to Sheol, the realm of the dead, which swallows up the dead, and so 'one who belongs to the alien powers of death and disaster'.

17. Eli pronounces a priestly blessing. A full form of such a blessing is given in Num. 6: 24–6: 'The LORD bless you and watch over you...' A blessing was believed to be powerful and effective (cp. Isaac's blessing of Jacob in Gen. 27). *peace* means 'full life', a life richly blessed by God.

18. *kindness*: the name Hannah is the feminine form of the word used here, an example of word-play (see on verse 20). Sept. adds here 'and came into the temple-room'—see the note on verses 9–10—'and ate and drank with her husband'. *no longer downcast*: the meaning of the text is uncertain, but this is what the sense requires. The priestly blessing has given Hannah full assurance.

19. *prostrating themselves*: the crouched position proper to one who comes before God or the king. *remembered:* the word in Hebrew has a wider range of meaning than in English. It does not suggest that God had forgotten her existence for a time, but rather that he acted toward her in kindness. An important priestly function is 'to remember' God, in the sense of 'to invoke his name'. The same sense belongs to the words 'remember' and 'memorial' in the Christian eucharist (see I Cor. II: 24 ff.).

20. *in due time:* or possibly 'at the turn of the year', i.e. in the autumn at about the time of the great annual feast.

Samuel: the name and its explanation present a puzzle. Samuel—*shemū'ēl*—means 'the (his) name is El', i.e. his nature, his person, is El, God. It is a name which glorifies God. The explanation given does not fit this, but corresponds to the name Saul—*shā'ūl*, 'that which has been asked for'. Is this just a case of popular explanation, of which the Old Testament offers many? Or has a feature which belonged originally to the story of Saul, that he was so named because specially requested from God, been transferred to Samuel? Such a transfer would correspond to the declining reputation of Saul in later tradition and the growing reputation of Samuel. The family background and the subsequent story of Samuel have, of course, nothing to do with Saul. What is also remarkable is that other points in the story appear to make the same word-play. In verse 17 the phrase 'prayer you have made' has two words from the same verb 'to ask'; so too verses 27–8 have four such words. The name of the sanctuary, Shiloh, probably has nothing to do with 'asking', but the similarity of sound may have suggested that it too was connected. The Hebrews loved word-play and assonance; their poetry is full of it. The growth of a popular tale, such as this, could very well owe something to the interweaving of words and ideas which appeared to be related. We may compare the word-play on Hannah in verse 18. ✻

THE DEDICATION

Elkanah, with his whole household, went up to make the 21
annual sacrifice to the LORD and to redeem his vow.
Hannah did not go with them, but said to her husband, 22
'When the child is weaned I will come up with him to
enter the presence of the LORD, and he shall*a* stay there
always.' Her husband Elkanah said to her, 'Do what you 23
think best; stay at home until you have weaned him. Only,
may the LORD indeed see your*b* vow fulfilled.' So the
woman stayed and nursed her son until she had weaned
him; and when she had weaned him, she took him up 24
with her. She took also a bull three years old,*c* an ephah of
meal, and a flagon of wine, and she brought him, child as
he was, into the house of the LORD at Shiloh. They 25
slaughtered the bull, and brought the boy to Eli. Hannah 26
said to him, 'Sir, as sure as you live, I am the woman who
stood near you here praying to the LORD. It was this boy 27
that I prayed for and the LORD has given me what I asked.
What I asked I have received; and now I lend him to the 28
LORD; for his whole life he is lent to the LORD.' And they*d*
prostrated themselves there before the LORD.

* Again the annual pilgrimage to Shiloh comes around, and
the final stage of the story is linked back to its opening.

21. *to redeem his vow* : it was Hannah who made the vow, but
by Israelite custom it became her husband's vow if he accepted
it, and the pious Elkanah is naturally portrayed as taking up
what Hannah has promised. For the legal practice involved,
see the account in Num. 30.

[*a*] come up...he shall: *or* bring him up, and he shall come into the
presence of the LORD and... [*b*] *So Sept.; Heb.* his.
[*c*] a bull...old: *so Sept.; Heb.* three bulls. [*d*] *So Pesh.; Heb.* he.

22f. Weaning was celebrated in ancient times as an important moment (see Gen. 21: 8 for a feast at Isaac's weaning); it might well be postponed until a child's second or third year. The mother of the martyrs in 2 Macc. refers to a three-year period of nursing (2 Macc. 7: 27).

24. *child as he was*: literally, 'the child (was) a child'. Some sense can be made of this, but probably there has been an omission of a whole phrase. Sept. has a long, repetitive addition which provides a clue to an original text which might have run: 'They came to the house of the LORD at Shiloh, and the child was with them; so they brought the child in before the LORD...'

26. *as sure as you live*: an oath formula meaning 'I swear that I am...'. A very solemn oath was sworn with invocation of the living God: 'As the LORD lives...' (so, e.g., 14: 39).

27f. On the word-play here, see the note on verse 20. That Hannah vowed Samuel freely to God can be interpreted as meaning that God by giving him to Hannah has asked for him for life-long service.

The conclusion of this part of the story is to be found at 2: 11, after the psalm which follows here. ✳

THE PSALM OF PRAISE

2 Then Hannah offered this prayer:

> My heart rejoices in the LORD,
> in the LORD I now hold my head high;
> my mouth is full of derision of my foes,
> exultant because thou hast saved me.

2
> There is none except thee,
> none so holy as the LORD,
> no rock like our God.

3
> Cease your proud boasting,
> let no word of arrogance pass your lips;

for the LORD is a god of all knowledge:
he governs all that men do.

Strong men stand in mute^a dismay   4
but those who faltered put on new strength.
Those who had plenty sell themselves for a crust,   5
and the hungry grow strong again.
The barren woman has seven children,
and the mother of many sons is left to languish.

The LORD kills and he gives life,   6
he sends down to Sheol, he can bring the dead up again.
The LORD makes a man poor, he makes him rich,   7
he brings down and he raises up.
He lifts the weak out of the dust   8
and raises the poor from the dunghill;
to give them a place among the great,
to set them in seats of honour.

For the foundations of the earth are the LORD's,
he has built the world upon them.
He will guard the footsteps of his saints,   9
while the wicked sink into silence and gloom;
not by mere strength shall a man prevail.

Those that stand against the LORD will be terrified   10
when the High God^b thunders out of heaven.
The LORD is judge even to the ends of the earth,
he will give strength to his king
and raise high the head of his anointed prince.

Then Elkanah went to Ramah with his household, but   11
the boy remained behind in the service of the LORD under
Eli the priest.

[a] in mute: *prob. rdg.; Heb.* obscure.
[b] the High God: *prob. rdg.; Heb.* upon him.

* There are many points of similarity between this psalm and the prayer ascribed to Mary in Luke 1: 46–55. The themes of rejoicing, of the power of God, of the reversal of fortunes, of the prospect for God's people, draw the two together. The prayer of Hannah is really a psalm and might well have stood in the Psalter: in 2 Sam. 22 we have another psalm which does so appear as Ps. 18. Hebrew psalmody is to be found in many parts of the Old Testament.

This is a royal psalm (verse 10). It has been placed here partly no doubt because it seemed suitable to Hannah's position (verse 5); a psalm belonging to a great public occasion could be used as a prayer by an individual worshipper. But the placing of the psalm also stresses what the birth of Samuel means for Israel. A new age begins in which God's will is expressed in power in the monarchy.

1. The psalm is a song of victory. But salvation for Israel was early seen to be much more than military victory. It represented the giving of life in its fullest form, material blessing and security and happiness for all. See Isa. 60 or Zech. 8: 1–8.

2. A favourite psalm theme is that of the unique power and holiness of God, as in Ps. 96. The term *rock* is suggestive of strength and protection, as in the phrase 'my rock and my redeemer' (Ps. 19: 14); the rock which God places in Zion (so Isa. 28: 16) is a symbol of his presence.

3. The opponents of God are warned to keep silent; it is he who controls and judges all things. *knowledge* here suggests God's care and control; Amos 3: 2: 'for you alone have I cared', uses the same word. *governs* paraphrases a word meaning 'measure, estimate'. Another possible rendering of the last clause is ' (wicked) deeds shall not prove firmly founded'; in this case, the sureness of God's action is contrasted with the instability of men's deeds, and such a contrast is to be found echoed in the next verses.

4. The somewhat obscure text speaks of 'the bows of strong men'—the bow being a symbol of warrior strength. The strong are dumb with dismay.

The series of comparisons in verses 4–5 shows that no one of them is to be taken merely literally; together they provide a picture of that reversal of fortunes which is characteristic of the coming of God and of his action in power. See Luke 1: 51–3 for the same theme.

6. It is God alone who has power to give or to withhold life. This is the theme of the Elijah stories (1 Kings 17–18), where the power of Israel's God is contrasted with that of the alien *ba'al*, the title often used for other gods. *Sheol* is the name given to the realm of the dead, a shadowy place of no true life. But death and Sheol are also symbols of distress and weakness. To restore to life means to give full vigour and health and well-being.

7f. Again here the contrasting themes are brought out. It is characteristic of Hebrew thought to emphasize God's protection of the *poor* and *weak*, and we find the prophets especially concerned with a justice which protects those who may easily succumb—the widows, the orphans, the poor. Poverty becomes a symbol of humility and obedience, perhaps largely because wealth becomes one of arrogance, ruthlessness and false trust (cp. the parable of the rich man in Luke 12: 16–21).

8*b* begins a new section of the psalm. The supremacy of God is expressed in his control of the whole created order. This theme is common in royal psalms, where the kingship of God is associated with his creating power: 'The LORD is king. He has fixed the earth firm, immovable' (Ps. 96: 10). The world is pictured as built upon pillars as in Ps. 75: 3, an idea not found in the classic creation narratives in Genesis. Israel had a great wealth of ideas about creation.

9. Another contrast, in which the idea of trust in God as the true source of strength is brought out. 'Neither by force of arms nor by brute strength, but by my spirit' (Zech. 4: 6). *saints* means 'loyal ones'.

10. The first line here may be linked with the end of verse 9, contrasting the implied assurance of God's strength to those

who trust in him with the terrors of those who contend with him. The term *stand against* is a legal term suggesting a court action against God. The next two lines then parallel one another; *when the High God thunders* it is the sign of his activity as *judge even to the ends of the earth.* Whoever inserted the psalm may have seen here an allusion to God's thundering in the battle story of chapter 7. The title *High God* is particularly associated in the Old Testament with God as he reigns at Jerusalem.

The climax of the psalm returns to the theme of victory with which it opened, but the idea of protection and judgement reminds us that the *king*, the *anointed* one (there is no word for *prince*), is the upholder of justice and right. (See the picture of the ideal king of justice in Isa. 11: 1–9.) *head*, literally, 'horn', the symbol of royal power.

The psalm clearly belongs to the period of the monarchy. But here it serves well to point up Samuel's part as the great king-maker, the founder of the new institution. The word used for *anointed* was eventually to become the technical term Messiah (*māshīaḥ*), translated into Greek as Christ (*christos*). It originally denoted simply any anointed ruler (as Saul was anointed, 10: 1), and also an anointed priest (as in Exod. 29: 7).

At the end of the psalm, Sept. adds extra lines found also in Jer. 9: 23–4; they speak of knowledge of God as the source of a man's true pride and emphasize the divine concern with justice. This makes a more precise application of the psalm to human life.

11. The story resumes as Elkanah returns home and Samuel remains as assistant to Eli. The story of Samuel will be picked up again at 2: 18. ✶

THE FAILURE OF ELI'S HOUSE

12 Now Eli's sons were scoundrels and had no regard for the
13 LORD. The custom of the priests in their dealings with the people was this: when a man offered a sacrifice, the priest's

servant would come while the flesh was stewing and 14 would thrust a three-pronged fork into the cauldron or pan or kettle or pot; and the priest would take whatever the fork brought out. This should have been their practice whenever Israelites came to sacrifice at Shiloh; but now under Eli's sons,[a] even before the fat was burnt, 15 the priest's servant came and said to the man who was sacrificing, 'Give me meat to roast for the priest; he will not accept what has been already stewed, only raw meat.' And if the man answered, 'Let them burn the fat first, 16 and then take what you want', he said, 'No, give it to me now, or I will take it by force.' The young men's sin 17 was very great in the LORD's sight; for they brought the LORD's sacrifice into general contempt.

* Against the background of the piety and devotion of Elkanah and Hannah the contrasting picture is now painted of conditions at the Shiloh shrine.

12. The statement about Eli's sons comes in sharp contrast to the preceding words. The second half of verse 11 can really be regarded as introductory to this verse; the description of failure on the part of Eli's family is dovetailed into brief notes about Samuel and his maturing in the service of God. *scoundrels:* 'sons of *belīʿal*' (see note on 1: 16).

13 f. These verses give a description of what was normal and proper practice at that time. No special priestly portion is indicated, but only what happened to come up on the three-pronged fork. Such a method expresses the belief that God himself makes the allocation to the priests. Other information about the practices is given in Lev. 7: 28 ff. and Deut. 18: 3; these passages probably reflect different local custom or different stages of development.

[a] under Eli's sons: *added to help meaning.*

15f. Failure to *burn the fat*, the part of the sacrifice regarded as specially belonging to God, is seen as an even worse crime. The fat should be removed first, and the implication is that these priests at Shiloh had so little regard for proper practice that they even dared to take what they wanted before what should be given to God had been removed.

17. The comment here indicates why this behaviour was thought so reprehensible. If we are to understand the condemnation, we must also appreciate the meaning of the religious practice. What is being described is a sacrificial feast, like that in which Elkanah's family engaged. It is an act of devotion by a whole family at the shrine. It is governed by certain rules. Worship properly conducted is the expression of God's will, and through such worship he mediates his blessing. The practices themselves go back to ancient ways of thinking, and indeed their origins are in most cases impossible to trace. Not to worship properly is to insult God, and, as the last phrase of verse 17 shows, it meant that the shrine at Shiloh would fall into disrepute and the people would have no assurance that God's blessing would be theirs. There is here an attempt to explain the nature of the relationship between God's will to bless and man's response to God's demands. The comment paves the way for the coming disaster to Shiloh. *

SAMUEL AND THE HOUSE OF ELI

18 Samuel continued in the service of the LORD, a mere boy
19 with a linen ephod fastened round him. Every year his mother made him a little cloak and took it to him when she went up with her husband to offer the annual sacrifice.
20 Eli would give his blessing to Elkanah and his wife and say, 'The LORD grant you children by this woman in place of the one for which you asked him.'*a* Then they went home again.

[a] for which...him: *or* which you lent him.

The LORD showed his care for Hannah, and she con- 21
ceived and gave birth to three sons and two daughters;
meanwhile the boy Samuel grew up in the presence of the
LORD.

Eli, now a very old man, had heard how his sons were 22
treating all the Israelites, and how they lay with the
women who were serving at the entrance to the Tent of
the Presence. So he said to them, 'Why do you do such 23
things? I hear from all the people how wickedly you
behave. Have done with it, my sons; for it is no good 24
report that I hear spreading among the LORD's people. If a 25
man sins against another man, God will intervene; but if a
man sins against the LORD, who can intercede for him?'
For all this, they did not listen to their father's rebuke, for
the LORD meant that they should die. But the young 26
Samuel, as he grew up, commended himself to the LORD
and to men.

✳ The interweaving of the Samuel and Eli traditions continues with a sharp contrast between the obedient servant of
God and the declining priestly line.

18. The verse picks up the wording of verse 11 and adds a
little more information. Samuel wears *a linen ephod*; evidently
a short garment. David himself wore such a garment on one
occasion (2 Sam. 6: 14). It appears also to be the name of a cult
object, used to obtain an oracle (see note on verses 28 f.). In
certain late passages (e.g. Exod. 25: 7) it is used of part of the
high priest's outer vestments.

19 reminds us that the pious family of Samuel went
annually to the shrine. The *cloak* is a sleeveless top garment.

20 f. Eli's blessing naturally took effect in the form of
further children; so the dedication of Samuel, the first-born,
did not lead to a loss to the family but to gain. The last phrase

of verse 21 again stresses the closeness of the relationship being welded between Samuel and God.

22. The passage of time is not indicated precisely; Eli is now old (cp. also 4: 15, 18), and it is evident from verse 26 that, though still young, Samuel is already taking an active part in the service of the shrine. The failure of the sons of Eli described in verses 12–17 is now further elaborated with a reference to their immoral conduct. The *Tent of the Presence* is a term appropriate to the time when no sanctuary building existed. It is associated in tradition with the period of Israel's wanderings. A very elaborate, but late, description is given in Exod. 35–40, though the early tent sanctuary was probably quite simple. It is natural that the later traditions of a temple should have incorporated references to the older practice. The exact relationship is far from clear, but Israel rightly saw that religiously there must be a connection, for the God of the temple was the God of the tent sanctuary. The reference to *the women who were serving at the entrance* is closely reminiscent of Exod. 38: 8, and since the whole statement is absent from some of the Greek texts, it is probable that it is a late addition, designed to stress the evil of the condemned priests and perhaps to allude to immoral practices of a kind known at a later time. Such practices are mentioned in 2 Kings 23: 7 as taking place in the seventh century B.C.; in the later Graeco-Roman world, religious prostitution—that is, sexual acts viewed as part of religious practice—was certainly familiar.

24. The last phrase could mean 'cause the LORD's people to sin', suggesting how heavy a weight of responsibility the priests bear. Their failure brings disaster on the whole people.

25. Eli's rebuke contains a strong warning. In wrong doing between man and man, God acts as mediator; much of the law, regarded as God-given, is concerned with this. But if a man sins against God, he comes directly under judgement. The text might be rendered: 'Who (then) can act as mediator for him?' The author of Job makes the same point: 'He is not a man as I am, that I can answer him . . . If only there were one to

arbitrate between us...' (Job 9: 32 f.). It is the recognition that any saving act must come directly from God himself, not from a third party.

The sons of Eli refuse to hear; *the LORD meant that they should die.* The Old Testament often expresses the idea of disobedience in such terms as this, seeing in the outcome in judgement the basic reason for the disobedience. So it is said of Pharaoh that God 'will make him stubborn' (Exod. 7: 3). Hebrew thought attributes as direct intention to God what we should describe as due to secondary causes—man's unwillingness to obey, his freedom to disregard God. But we must also note that in such cases the writers look beyond the stubbornness and see that in the light of subsequent experience there was a wider purpose to be seen. So it is said of Pharaoh: 'I have let you live only to show you my power and to spread my fame throughout the land' (Exod. 9: 16). The rejection of Eli's house was to lead to the establishing of a true and lasting priesthood. ✳

THE REJECTION OF THE HOUSE OF ELI

Now a man of God came to Eli and said, 'This is the word 27 of the LORD: You know that I revealed myself to your forefather when he and his family were in Egypt in slavery[a] in the house of Pharaoh. You know that I chose 28 him from all the tribes of Israel to be my priest, to mount the steps of my altar, to burn sacrifices and to carry[b] the ephod before me; and that I assigned all the food-offerings of the Israelites to your family. Why then do you show 29 disrespect for my sacrifices and the offerings which I have ordained? What makes you resent them?[c] Why do you honour your sons more than me by letting them batten

[a] in slavery: *so Sept.; Heb. om.*   [b] *Or* wear.
[c] What...them?: *so Sept.; Heb.* a dwelling-place.

30 on the choicest offerings of[a] my people Israel? The LORD's word was, "I promise that your house and your father's house shall serve before me for all time"; but now his word is, "I will have no such thing: I will honour those who honour me, and those who despise me shall meet

31 with contempt. The time is coming when I will lop off every limb of your own and of your father's family, so

32 that no man in your house shall come to old age. You will even resent[b] the prosperity I give[c] to Israel; never again

33 shall there be an old man in your house. If I allow any to survive to serve my altar, his[d] eyes will grow dim and his[d]

34 appetite fail, his[d] issue will be weaklings and die off. The fate of your two sons shall be a sign to you: Hophni and

35 Phinehas shall both die on the same day. I will appoint for myself a priest who will be faithful, who will do what I have in my mind and in my heart. I will establish his family to serve in perpetual succession before my anointed king.

36 Any of your family that still live will come and bow humbly before him to beg a fee, a piece of silver and a loaf, and will ask for a turn of priestly duty to earn a crust of bread."'

* There is evident overlap with the story of Samuel in chapter 3 and much to indicate that the present passage is of later origin. It provides an opportunity for a major comment on the meaning of the story; the loss of the Ark (chapter 4) and the fall of Eli's house are major and shattering events. They lie within the larger purpose of God for his people.

27. *man of God:* the phrase is used quite clearly in the sense of 'prophet', as it is also of Samuel, of Elijah and Elisha, and of

[a] *So Targ.; Heb.* to.   [b] You...resent: *prob. rdg.; Heb. obscure.*
[c] *So Targ.; Heb.* he gives.   [d] *So Sept.; Heb.* your.

other named and unnamed prophets. It is not to be regarded as different in sense from the phrase 'messenger' or 'angel of God', though this phrase is used both of prophets and of angelic messengers. The announcing of the divine word, the recall of the past, the condemnation of the present and the foretelling of judgement and promise which we find in this passage are all characteristic of prophetic activity, though there is here a somewhat more sermonizing tone than is usual in the terse oracles of prophets such as Amos and Hosea.

Israel's experience of slavery in Egypt marks the real beginning of her faith and life, and forms a central theme in her religious traditions. It is to this moment that the founding of her institutions is traced.

28. The priesthood of Eli's house is described as ordained from Egypt. The history of the various priestly families in Israel is complicated, partly at least because they are all traced back to the tribe of Levi (Samuel is not here said to be a Levite, but cp. 1 Chron. 6: 33) and especially to Aaron who gradually came to occupy a place of central importance in later thought. The whole of this passage points to a replacement of one priestly line—that of Eli—by another—that of Zadok. The latter came to be fully established in Jerusalem in the time of David and Solomon. Here, Samuel would appear to be the natural successor to Eli; subsequently, however, we find other members of Eli's house (so 14: 3 Ahijah, 22: 20 Abiathar), but eventually Abiathar was exiled and Zadok became the head of the priestly line (1 Kings 1–2).

28f. indicate the nature of priestly functions. The *ephod* appears here to be a cult-object, though the N.E.B. footnote shows that it can be understood as a priestly garment (cp. above on verse 18). 23: 9 indicates an ephod used for obtaining a divine oracle. The *food-offerings*—a term whose meaning is debated—appear to be those portions to which the priests have a right (cp. above on verses 13 f.).

30. The divine promise of a perpetual priesthood in the

house of Eli is reversed because of failure; privilege cannot stand unless there is obedience. Amos says the same about Israel's calling to be a people (Amos 3: 2).

31–4. The terrible judgement is expressed in a series of gradually heightening phrases. None of the family will live to a full age; shortness of life was seen as judgement, long life as a blessing. (For such a picture of blessing, see Isa. 65: 20.) Blessing will be for Israel, not for Eli's family—this is the probable meaning of the very obscure and confused text of verse 32. Even a survivor—possibly an allusion to Ahijah or Abiathar—will be plagued; similar expressions are used of the disaster of exile: 'plagues that dim the sight and cause the appetite to fail' (Lev. 26: 16). The death of Hophni and Phinehas is a sign of this inevitable doom.

35 presents the promise within the judgement. A new and faithful priesthood is to be established, obedient to God's will. This priestly dynasty will endure, associated with the *anointed* king. There is here a clear reference to the priestly dynasty of Zadok which lasted right through the period of monarchy and which continued afterwards to claim the central place. We may note that what is said here of the priestly line is also said of the royal house (13: 14, and see 2 Sam. 7 for a fuller statement).

36. The precise reference of this verse is uncertain, but it is most natural to see an allusion to that much later stage in the history when priests at country sanctuaries, abolished in the reform of king Josiah (621 B.C.; see 2 Kings 22–3), sought office in the one authorized temple in Jerusalem. In much later priestly lists, it seems that the members of other priestly lines which claimed descent from Aaron did acquire some status in the Jerusalem priesthood. So in 1 Chron. 24, the line from Aaron's son Ithamar is traced to Ahimelech who was related to Eli, and this line stands beside the main Zadokite line which claimed descent from Aaron's other son Eleazar.

The commentator here interprets the disaster, and looking back from a later time sees how what must have seemed a dark

moment in Israel's history was meaningful as a time of promise.
The priestly line, whatever its faults were to be, was one of the
institutions by which the tradition of faith and obedience was
maintained. ✳

THE CALL OF SAMUEL

So the child Samuel was in the LORD's service under his 3
master Eli. Now in those days the word of the LORD was
seldom heard, and no vision was granted. But one night 2
Eli, whose eyes were dim and his sight failing, was lying
down in his usual place, while Samuel slept in the temple 3
of the LORD where the Ark of God was. Before the lamp of
God had gone out, the LORD called him, and Samuel 4
answered, 'Here I am', and ran to Eli saying, 'You called 5
me: here I am.' 'No, I did not call you,' said Eli; 'lie
down again.' So he went and lay down. The LORD called 6
Samuel again, and he got up and went to Eli. 'Here I am,'
he said; 'surely you called me.' 'I did not call, my son,' he
answered; 'lie down again.' Now Samuel had not yet 7
come to know the LORD, and the word of the LORD had
not been disclosed to him. When the LORD called him for 8
the third time, he again went to Eli and said, 'Here I am;
you did call me.' Then Eli understood that it was the LORD
calling the child; he told Samuel to go and lie down and 9
said, 'If he calls again, say, "Speak, LORD; thy servant
hears thee."' So Samuel went and lay down in his place.

The LORD came and stood there, and called, 'Samuel, 10
Samuel', as before. Samuel answered, 'Speak; thy servant
hears thee.' The LORD said, 'Soon I shall do something in 11
Israel which will ring in the ears of all who hear it. When 12
that day comes I will make good every word I have
spoken against Eli and his family from beginning to end.

13 You are to*ᵃ* tell him that my judgement on his house shall stand for ever because*ᵇ* he knew of his sons' blasphemies
14 against God*ᶜ* and did not rebuke them. Therefore I have sworn to the family of Eli that their abuse of sacrifices and offerings shall never be expiated.'

15 Samuel lay down till morning and then opened the doors of the house of the LORD, but he was afraid to tell
16 Eli about the vision. Eli called Samuel: 'Samuel, my son',
17 he said; and he answered, 'Here I am.' Eli asked, 'What did the LORD say to you? Do not hide it from me. God forgive you if you hide one word of all that he said
18 to you.' Then Samuel told him everything and hid nothing. Eli said, 'The LORD must do what is good in his eyes.'

✻ Here a different side of the Samuel tradition is opened up. He is called to be a prophet, a messenger of God, to whom a precise experience brings the realization that he is to be the mediator of the word of God to his people. The call may be compared with the experience of Isaiah (Isa. 6) or Jeremiah (Jer. 1: 4–10)

1. *child:* since the same word is rendered 'the young Samuel' in 2: 26, there is no reason to suggest that Samuel was still a child. The word is used for a young person (so too of Jeremiah, 1: 6f.), and may carry the sense of 'inexperienced'. As yet, the divine call has not been felt. *word of the LORD* and *vision* are technical terms belonging to the prophetic literature. It is not clear whether the statement about the rarity of the divine word and the hiddenness of God is to be regarded as a comment by the story-teller on this past period, contrasted with the later time of great prophetic activity, or whether it is a reflection on the low religious ebb of the days of Eli and his sons. It accords

[a] *Prob. rdg.; Heb.* I will.   [b] because: *prob. rdg.; Heb.* in guilt.
[c] against God: *prob. original reading, altered in Heb. to* to them.

well in this latter sense with 2: 12. Now a new era begins, the era of prophecy.

3. Samuel was sleeping in the actual shrine, an appropriate place to receive a divine call; compare Isaiah's temple vision (Isa. 6), and probably also Jacob's vision at Bethel (Gen. 28: 11–18, where 'place' is best understood as meaning 'holy place, sanctuary'). Such connections between prophetic call and temple worship enable us to understand the kind of status which the prophets had in the religious organization of their time. *the lamp of God* would burn all night (see Exod. 27: 20) as a symbol of God's presence, also indicated by the Ark. The experience seems to be set just before dawn.

4–9. The repetition in the story produces a growing tension, and emphasizes the reality of the call experience. The vital comment is made in verse 7 where *to know the LORD* is paralleled by the disclosure of the *word of the LORD*. Samuel had not yet experienced this, but Eli's experience enabled him to recognize what was happening and to indicate the right response. Compare Isaiah's response to the sense of divine compulsion: 'Here am I; send me' (Isa. 6: 8).

10. The story expresses the vivid sense of God's presence by speaking of his actually coming and standing in the shrine. Jacob too experienced God 'standing beside him' (Gen. 28: 13).

11. The message delivered to the newly called prophet is one of doom for the house of Eli. Such a dark message was received by Isaiah (6: 9ff.) and by Amos (7: 15ff.). The 'tingling of the ears' is a common phrase for being struck with horror at the news of disaster or the prospect of it.

12 is probably a verse added to harmonize this story with 2: 27–36.

13. *You are to tell him*: the text has 'I will tell him'. Although the N.E.B. suggestion is easier, since it is clear that this is the message given to Samuel to transmit, the first person form emphasizes that it is God's word. The prophet sometimes speaks about what God has said, and sometimes gives the word of God in the first person. *because*: the Hebrew here may be

lacking some words and perhaps we should render: 'for the guilt of his sons, because...'. *against God:* Jewish writers of the period when the text was being finally fixed (the centuries leading up to A.D. 1000) regarded this passage as containing a 'correction by the scribes'. Such corrections were made to avoid offending the pious worshipper by even the idea of *blasphemies against God.* A simple omission of letters changed the word for God (*'elōhīm*) to the word for 'to them' (*lāhem*). Another example may be found in the story of David and Bathsheba in 2 Sam. 12: 14.

14. The verse could be rendered: 'their guilt can never be expiated by sacrifices or offerings', but N.E.B. is probably better. The statement implies that expiation of sin is normally possible. The dark prospect for Eli's family contrasts with the slight hope held out in 2: 36.

17. *God forgive you...*: the words express a strong oath, pronouncing doom upon Samuel if he conceals the message. The prophet dare not hide the word given to him (cp. Jer. 20: 9 for the burning compulsion of the divine word).

18. Eli's acceptance of the divine judgement is an important point, for it accords well with one of the main themes of the whole historical work in which the books of Samuel belong (see pp. 2 ff.). When disaster came with the fall of Jerusalem in 587 B.C., the acceptance of divine judgement was an essential stage in the development of a new hope for the future. So Eli here accepts that it is God himself who has spoken justly. His reply might be rendered: 'It is the LORD; he must do what he knows to be right.' In the word of judgement, seen as right, Eli is able to recognize the very presence of the God whom he serves.

The call narrative serves to establish Samuel's position; it serves also to reiterate the coming transfer of authority to him from the house of Eli. ✶

THE ESTABLISHED LEADERSHIP OF SAMUEL

As Samuel grew up, the LORD was with him, and none 19
of his words went unfulfilled. From Dan to Beersheba, 20
all Israel recognized that Samuel was confirmed as a
prophet of the LORD. So the LORD continued to appear in 21
Shiloh, because he had revealed himself there to Samuel.*ᵃ*
So Samuel's word had authority throughout Israel.   **4**

* The first stage of the story is drawn to a close and a link
made with the reappearance of Samuel in chapter 7. He plays
no part in the intervening chapters.

19. The presence of God with Samuel assures the truth and
validity of his prophetic message (cp. Jer. 1: 19).

20. *From Dan to Beersheba:* the conventional phrase to
describe the whole area of Israel (see map, p. 13), especially that
of the united kingdom (so 1 Kings 4: 25). Samuel's activity
was in fact limited to a small central area around Ramah. But
just as local leaders described in the book of Judges have been
interpreted as national heroes, so too Samuel, the local seer
(see chapter 9), has come to be understood as a prophet to the
whole people. In the light of the development of the monarchy,
Samuel was seen to be a central character in Israel's history.
prophet: the word used of the great prophets (*nābī'*) is applied
here for the first time to Samuel.

21. The call of Samuel as prophet is seen as providing a basis
for God's continued revealing of himself at Shiloh.

4: 1*a.* is joined in the N.E.B. to the next story, but it is better
to see it as the concluding summary of Samuel's commission
as a prophet. It picks up again the theme of universal authority
stated in 3: 20. *

[a] *Prob. rdg.; Heb. adds* according to the word of the LORD.

The struggle with the Philistines

'THE ARK OF GOD IS TAKEN'

AND THE TIME CAME when the Philistines mustered for battle against Israel,[a] and the Israelites went out to meet them. The Israelites encamped at Eben-ezer and the

2 Philistines at Aphek. The Philistines drew up their lines facing the Israelites, and when they joined battle the Israelites were routed by the Philistines, who killed about

3 four thousand men on the field. When the army got back to the camp, the elders of Israel asked, 'Why did the LORD let us be routed today by the Philistines? Let us fetch the Ark of the Covenant of the LORD from Shiloh to go with

4 us and deliver us from the power of our enemies.' So the people sent to Shiloh and fetched the Ark of the Covenant of the LORD of Hosts, who is enthroned upon the cherubim; Eli's two sons, Hophni and Phinehas, were there with

5 the Ark. When the Ark came into the camp all the Israelites greeted it with a great shout, and the earth rang

6 with the shouting. The Philistines heard the noise and asked, 'What is this great shouting in the camp of the Hebrews?' When they knew that the Ark of the LORD

7 had come into the camp, they were afraid and cried, 'A god has come into the camp. We are lost! No such thing

8 has ever happened before. We are utterly lost! Who can deliver us from the power of these mighty gods? These are the very gods who broke the Egyptians and crushed

9 them in the wilderness. Courage, Philistines, and act like

[a] And...Israel: *so Sept.; Heb. om.*

46

men, or you will become slaves to the Hebrews as they
were yours. Be men, and fight!' The Philistines then gave 10
battle, and the Israelites were defeated and fled to their
homes. It was a great defeat, and thirty thousand Israelite
foot-soldiers perished. The Ark of God was taken, and 11
Eli's two sons, Hophni and Phinehas, were killed.

✻ The whole passage (4: 1*b*–7: 1) is part of the much larger
tradition of the Ark (see also 2 Sam. 6). Judgement comes to
Eli's house, but the capture of the Ark is not the end; with a
grim humour, the story is told of the overthrow of the hostile
forces and of the restoration of the Ark.

1*b*. *The Philistines* were a non-Semitic people who had
settled mainly in the coastal plain shortly after 1200 B.C. as part
of a great movement of so-called 'Sea Peoples'. Some of these
were repulsed by Egypt at that time. Other related groups may
be traced further north at Dor and in the plain of Jezreel as far
as Beth-shan (see 31: 10). Under David we find mercenary
troops called 'Kerethite and Pelethite' guards (2 Sam. 8: 18).
The second of these names is probably a variant of 'Philistine';
the former suggests Crete (Caphtor in Amos 9: 7) as their
place of origin. Traces have been found of their settlement also
in Cyprus. They are recognizable in ancient pictures by their
tall head-dress. (See *Old Testament Illustrations* in this series.)

The main Philistine settlement was in five cities, mentioned
in 6: 17: Ashdod, Ashkelon, Ekron (more correctly Aqqaron),
Gath, Gaza (see map, p. 48). It was from these that they threatened the Israelite areas, especially that of Dan, as indicated in
the Samson stories of Judg. 13–16. The name Philistia, in its
Latin form *Palestina*, was used by the Romans to describe the
whole province in the second century A.D., and hence came
to be a name used for the land.

Nothing in the preceding chapters points to an imminent
Philistine threat, and this suggests that this section was originally quite independent of what now precedes it. The attack is

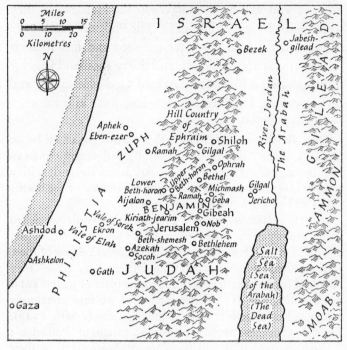

2. The central area (mainly 1 Samuel 1–19)

likely to have come up the valleys from the coastal plain into the central highlands. The map above shows possible locations of the places mentioned. *Aphek* is a name applied to several places; it must here refer to one which occupied a strategic position at the entrance to the hill-country. *Eben-ezer* appears again in 7: 12.

2 f. Defeat by the Philistines suggests the absence of God's favour; the text actually means: 'Why did God defeat us...?' The *Ark* is here given a longer title referring to the *Covenant*. This points to one understanding of its function, namely as container of the covenant tablets (see Deut. 10: 1 ff.). Other passages in these chapters speak simply of the Ark, as a symbol

48

of God's presence and particularly associated with him as leader of Israel's armies. As a symbolic object, it is related to Israel's idea of 'holy war', that is, war regarded as a religious function directed against the enemies of God. Its use in such a context is seen from Num. 10: 35 f. where the Ark is addressed in short poetic sayings expressing its warlike function, and in 2 Sam. 11: 11 where we find that the Ark is on campaign with Israel. Ps. 24, with its welcome to the 'LORD of Hosts', may be seen as a victory song of the God of the Ark. God's presence is believed to ensure victory, but he is independent of the Ark. On *LORD of hosts*, see 1: 3.

4. *enthroned upon the cherubim:* or perhaps 'above the cherubim', another picture of God as king and as victor. An ivory plaque from Megiddo dating from about this period shows a victorious king on a throne supported by winged lions with human heads (compare Solomon's throne in 1 Kings 10: 18–20). These creatures are *cherubim* and later we find such figures in the most holy part of the Jerusalem temple as protectors of the Ark (1 Kings 6: 19–28) and as bearers of the invisible, imageless deity.

5. The Ark is welcomed by Israel *with a great shout*, both a battle cry and a religious shout, appropriate to acclaiming the appearance of God himself. Ps. 95 opens with a call for 'a shout of triumph to the Rock of our salvation'. The *earth* was brought into a state of commotion, a picture often used in the psalms to express the awe created by God's advent (so, e.g., Ps. 97: 3–5).

6. *Hebrews:* the name sometimes used of Israel by other peoples. It is connected in the Old Testament with an ancestor Eber (Gen. 10: 21, 25); a popular explanation suggested that they were so called because they came from 'beyond the River', i.e. the Euphrates (cp. Josh. 24: 2). The word is likely to be connected with the name *Habiru* which appears in various forms in ancient texts, most often to describe lawless bands, vagrants and mercenaries.

6*b*–8. The discovery that the Ark, and therefore Israel's God, has come out to war against them brings panic on the Philistines, such a panic as was produced in Canaan at the approach of Israel (so Deut. 7: 20). This is the God who overthrew Egypt. It is idle to ask whether the Philistines knew of Israel's own religious traditions, for the point of the story rests rather in the awe which is created. For this reason it is probably better in these verses to translate: 'God has come into the camp' and 'this mighty God', although some plural forms are used. For recognition of God's power by aliens, see also the reaction of the sailors in Jonah 1.

9–10. The Philistines encourage one another and are victorious. Is God then unable to save his people? This is a question often posed in the Old Testament, above all in relation to the disaster of exile in Babylon. *thirty thousand:* the numbers in battle stories are often very large. To some extent we may suppose a symbolic use of numbers to suggest the greatness of disaster or of victory (so in 15: 4).

11. The capture of the Ark and the death of Eli's sons brings down the curtain on the first act. All is dark. ✶

'GLORY HAS DEPARTED'

12 A Benjamite ran from the battlefield and reached Shiloh on the same day, his clothes rent and dust on his head.
13 When he arrived Eli was sitting on a seat by the road to Mizpah, for he was deeply troubled about the Ark of God. The man entered the city with his news, and all the people
14 cried out in horror. When Eli heard it, he asked, 'What does this uproar mean?' The man hurried to Eli and told
15 him. Eli was ninety-eight years old and sat staring with
16 sightless eyes; so the man said to him, 'I am the man who has just arrived from the battle; this very day I have escaped from the field.' Eli asked, 'What is the news, my
17 son?' The runner answered, 'The Israelites have fled

from the Philistines; utter panic has struck the army; your two sons, Hophni and Phinehas, are killed, and the Ark of God is taken.' At the mention of the Ark of God, Eli fell 18 backwards from his seat by the gate and broke his neck, for he was old and heavy. So he died; he had been judge over Israel for forty years. His daughter-in-law, the wife 19 of Phinehas, was with child and near her time, and when she heard of the capture of the Ark and the deaths of her father-in-law and her husband, her labour suddenly began and she crouched down and was delivered. As she lay 20 dying, the women who attended her said, 'Do not be afraid; you have a son.' But she did not answer or heed what they said. Then they named the boy Ichabod,[a] 21 saying, 'Glory has departed from Israel' (in allusion to the capture of the Ark of God and the death of her father-in-law and her husband); 'Glory has departed from Israel,' 22 they said, 'because the Ark of God is taken.'

✻ 12. *his clothes rent and dust on his head:* as signs of mourning for the disaster.

13. *by the road to Mizpah:* the text is not at all clear. Mizpah is a name given to several different places, so that it is possible that there was such a place on the road running west towards the battlefield. The best-known place of this name lies south, in the wrong direction (see map, p. 13). The Hebrew word here is actually a verb meaning 'watching out'. Since Eli was by now blind, this could only mean that he was anxiously awaiting news. It seems most probable that he was sitting outside the shrine, by the road-side, waiting for news, tense in his anxiety for the Ark. So he would hear from a distance the people when they *cried out in horror.* The 'gate' mentioned in verse 18 would then be the temple gate.

[a] *That is* No-glory.

17. *the runner:* strictly, the 'bearer of news', a word more often used of good news than bad.

18. The shock killed Eli, and his story concludes with the statement that he had been *judge over Israel for forty years*. This puts him alongside the leaders of the book of Judges of whom similar statements are made. Nothing, however, in the other Eli traditions really makes him appear like these heroic military leaders; he might rank with the so-called 'minor judges' of Judg. 10: 1–5 and 12: 8–15 for whom no military acts are claimed. Here again it seems that in this chapter we are dealing with material quite separate from chapters 1–3, material perhaps linked with the book of Judges.

19. The shock brings on premature labour-pains for Phinehas' widow. *she crouched down:* the normal birth position in the ancient world, with the use of a birth-stool (so Exod. 1: 16).

21. *they named the boy:* the Hebrew text actually has a singular form 'she named', and with this we may compare the story of Rachel's death at the birth of Benjamin whom she named Ben-oni, 'son of my ill luck' (Gen. 35: 16–18). The woman is too distressed to hear a word of encouragement, but able to utter a prophetic word as she names her son. *Ichabod:* 'No-glory'. The name is explained in the text. *Glory* is a word often used to express the very presence of God. Thus Ezekiel speaks of 'the glory of the LORD' leaving the Jerusalem temple when it is doomed to disaster (e.g. Ezek. 10: 18). The loss of the Ark is the loss of his presence. *has departed:* a word used of exile. To later readers the parallel with the situation in the time of the Babylonian exile would be evident.

As the story now stands, following on chapters 1–3, it gives a picture of God's judgement on the house of Eli, precisely corresponding to the oracle of 2: 34. But, bearing in mind that the book of Samuel as we have it is made up of many different elements, we may ask whether this is what the story originally meant. The failure of Eli's house is not indicated; the story is about the Ark, captured but still powerful. When Phinehas'

widow with her dying breath speaks of lost glory, it is because
of the Ark and her father-in-law and her husband; the priestly
house shares that glory now lost. Here we seem to have a
different estimate of Hophni and Phinehas; their death is not
seen as the result of sin, but as part of an overall plan by which
the God of Israel shows his supremacy and power over all his
enemies. 'The Lord who sits enthroned in heaven laughs them
to scorn' (Ps. 2: 4). The story which follows brings out the
real meaning of his apparent willingness to submit to alien
force. ✻

GOD IN EXILE REVEALS HIS POWER

After the Philistines had captured the Ark of God, they **5**
brought it from Eben-ezer to Ashdod; and there they ²
carried it into the temple of Dagon and set it beside
Dagon himself. When the people of Ashdod rose next ³
morning, there was Dagon fallen face downwards before
the Ark of the LORD; so they took him and put him back
in his place. Next morning when they rose, Dagon had ⁴
again fallen face downwards before the Ark of the LORD,
with his head and his two hands lying broken off beside
his platform; only Dagon's body*ᵃ* remained on it. This is ⁵
why from that day to this the priests of Dagon and all who
enter the temple of Dagon at Ashdod do not set foot upon
Dagon's platform.

Then the LORD laid a heavy hand upon the people of ⁶
Ashdod; he threw them into distress and plagued them
with tumours,*ᵇ* and their territory swarmed with rats.*ᶜ*
There was death and destruction all through the city.*ᵈ*
When the men of Ashdod saw this, they said, 'The Ark of ⁷

[a] *Prob. rdg., cp. Sept.; Heb.* only Dagon.
[b] *Or, as otherwise read,* haemorrhoids.   [c] *Or* mice.
[d] and their territory...city: *so Sept.; Heb.* Ashdod and its territory.

the God of Israel shall not stay here, for he has laid a
8 heavy hand upon us and upon Dagon our god.' So they
sent and called all the Philistine princes together to ask
what should be done with the Ark. They said, 'Let the
Ark of the God of Israel be taken across to Gath.' They
9 took it there, and after its arrival the hand of the LORD
caused great havoc in the city; he plagued everybody,
high and low alike, with the tumours which broke out.
10 Then they sent the Ark of God on to Ekron. When the
Ark reached Ekron, the people cried, 'They have brought
the Ark of the God of Israel over to us, to kill us and our
11 families.' So they summoned all the Philistine princes
and said, 'Send the Ark of the God of Israel away; let it
go back to its own place, or it will be the death of us all.'
There was death and destruction all through the city; for
12 the hand of God lay heavy upon it. Even those who did
not die were plagued with tumours; the cry of the city
went up to heaven.

✻ There are two separate elements here: (1) the overthrow of
the alien god; (2) the plaguing of the Philistines with disease.
The latter element has a grim humour about it.

1. *Ashdod:* one of the five Philistine cities (see on 4: 1;
6: 17).

2. *Dagon:* the name is Semitic and means 'corn'. The deity
is known as father of Baal from north Canaanite ritual texts
from Ras Shamra (ancient Ugarit, on the Syrian coast), where
a temple was dedicated to him. The Ras Shamra texts give us
insight into some of the forms of Canaanite religion and
mythology. It would appear that the Philistine settlers adopted
the religion of the land to which they came, no doubt
combining it with practices and beliefs of their own. This
story suggests that Dagon was represented in human form in

54

the shrine at Ashdod. The conquered God's symbol, the Ark, is placed beside Dagon. There was also a shrine to Dagon at Gaza (Judg. 16: 23) where Samson also won a notable victory over the Philistines. (The older view that Dagon was represented partly as a fish is erroneous.)

3 f. The superior power of Israel's God is shown by Dagon's image prostrating itself. This is followed by the shattering of the figure, leaving only the torso on the podium.

5 is a curious antiquarian note, purporting to explain a particular religious custom of the Ashdod shrine. Such explanations are not uncommon in the Old Testament; for example, the story of Jacob's contest at the Jabbok purports to explain why Israelites do not eat a particular thigh sinew (Gen. 32: 32). It is often very doubtful whether such popular traditions preserve correct information; the customs explained may well be very much more ancient, their true origin now lost.

6. *death and destruction* (also in verse 11): could be rendered 'utter panic'.

The text of this verse is in some disorder. The Hebrew text lacks some essential words and N.E.B. supplements from Sept. We must note, however, that in the Hebrew there is no mention of *rats* until 6: 4, and it is therefore possible that the longer text represents an attempt at reconciling two elements in the story—the plague *tumours* and the *rats*. Possibly there were two forms of the tale told about the Philistine misfortunes; in the final forms of the text, both Hebrew and Greek, these have been combined into one somewhat confused story. Such a combining of elements is often to be found in Old Testament and other stories; the popular handing down of traditions results in the growth of different forms which a later story-teller may think it best to bring together.

What was the nature of the disease? *tumours* or *haemorrhoids* (the Hebrew text itself offers an alternative at certain points in the narrative, the latter word being thought improper for public reading) probably denote 'plague-boils', symptoms of bubonic plague; the rapid spread of the disease through Philistia and later into the Judaean area would fit this well. *rats* or *mice*— the word denotes small rodents—indicate a different kind of disaster, not unlike some of those associated with the Exodus in Exod. 8–10. We could suppose that the rats brought the plague; a similar suggestion has been made for the disaster to the Assyrians in the time of Isaiah in 2 Kings 19: 35 (Isa. 37: 36). It may be doubted if the evidence warrants such a conclusion. The real point in both passages is that God is depicted as mocking his enemies and bringing them low.

7. The disaster is recognized as being brought by Israel's God, present in the Ark.

8. *princes*: the word (*seren* or *sōren*) is used only of the Philistine lords. This suggests that we have here a genuine Philistine word. It is thought likely that the same word appears as a loan-word in Greek as *tyrannos*, 'lord'.

8–12. Consultation among the leaders results in the Ark being sent from Ashdod to Gath and from Gath to Ekron; but the same calamities follow and the whole of Philistia is in a desperate state. The story-teller skilfully pictures only these stages in the Ark's movements; the subsequent narrative suggests that Ashkelon and Gaza were not exempt. It is in reality a terrible triumphal procession for the Ark and so for God.

12. *the cry of the city went up to heaven*: since the next chapter sees Philistia released from disaster, and this can only be understood as by God's will, we may see these words as indicating the willingness of God to hear even those who are described as his enemies. A much later writer, the author of the book of Jonah, had to remind his own people that God heeds the prayers and repentance of even the most hated of peoples (see Jonah 4). ✳

THE PHILISTINES SEEK RELEASE

When the Ark of the LORD had been in their territory for **6**
seven months, the Philistines summoned the priests and **2**
soothsayers and asked, 'What shall we do with the Ark of
the LORD? Tell us how we ought to send it back to its own
place.' They answered, 'If you send the Ark of the God of **3**
Israel back, do not let it go without a gift, but send it back
with a gift for him by way of indemnity; then you will be
healed and restored to favour; there is no reason why his
hand should not be lifted from you.' When they were **4**
asked, 'What gift shall we send back to him?', they
answered, 'Send five tumours modelled in gold and five
gold rats, one for each of the Philistine princes, for the same
plague afflicted all of you*a* and your princes. Make models **5**
of your tumours and of the rats which are ravaging the
land, and give honour to the God of Israel; perhaps he will
relax the pressure of his hand on you, on your god, and on
your land. Why should you be stubborn like Pharaoh and **6**
the Egyptians? Remember how this god made sport of
them until they let Israel go. Now make a new wagon **7**
ready with two milch-cows which have never been
yoked; harness the cows to the wagon, and take their
calves from them and drive them back to their stalls. Then **8**
take the Ark of the LORD and put it on the wagon, place
in a casket, beside it, the gold offerings that you are
sending to him as an indemnity, and let it go where it
will. Watch it: if it goes up towards its own territory to **9**
Beth-shemesh, then it is the LORD who has done us this
great injury; but if not, then we shall know that his

[a] *So some MSS.; others* them.

hand has not touched us, but we have been the victims of chance.'

10 The men did this. They took two milch-cows and harnessed them to a wagon, shutting up their calves in the
11 stall, and they placed the Ark of the LORD on the wagon together with the casket, the gold rats, and the models of
12 their haemorrhoids. Then the cows went straight in the direction of Beth-shemesh; they kept to the same road, lowing as they went and turning neither right nor left, while the Philistine princes followed them as far as the territory of Beth-shemesh.

✻ There seems to be more than one element in the story: (1) the provision of an indemnity, an offering to remove the anger of Israel's God; (2) a scheme to discover whether the disaster is really to be attributed to him. The two are harmonized in the present narrative, but in reality they represent somewhat different approaches to the theme.

2. *priests and soothsayers:* religious officials whose task was to show the divine will by various means. In Israel, priestly decisions took the form of 'directives'; the word used, *tōrāh*, means this, but is often rendered 'law' and was eventually used for the whole body of Israel's laws and traditions in the first five books of the Old Testament. The story assumes that God can make his will known to an alien people through their own normal religious procedures. Thus a directive is given to the king of Babylon through various consultings of omens (Ezek. 21: 21). *to its own place:* meaning just 'home' or perhaps 'to its proper sanctuary'.

3. *do not let it go without a gift:* an *indemnity*, an offering in acknowledgement of guilt. The word for *indemnity* can also mean 'guilt'.

4f. The indemnity is to express both the whole community, *five tumours modelled in gold and five gold rats,* one for each prince (but see also verse 18), and also the nature of the affliction suffered. This is on the ancient principle of 'like cures like'. Moses made a bronze snake to heal those suffering from snake-bite (Num. 21: 6–9). *honour:* or 'glory', i.e. 'acknowledge God for who he is'.

6. *stubborn:* the word used in the Exodus narratives of Pharaoh (see note on 2: 25). The Hebrew word comes from the same root as 'glory' in verse 5; perhaps there is an intentional word-play. *made sport of them:* the idea of God mocking his enemies (cp. Ps. 2: 4) underlies this whole story.

7–9 introduce the second theme, designed to discover whether it really is Israel's God who has brought disaster. What has so far been said, both in chapter 5 and the opening of chapter 6, assumes that it can only be he.

7. *a new wagon* is used because new objects were believed to have greater sanctity and so greater effectiveness. In the binding of Samson, 'fresh bowstrings' and 'new ropes' were tried (Judg. 16: 7, 11). Similarly the *milch-cows* had *never been yoked*; in addition they were separated from their young. This will make it clear that only a divine power could drive the wagon away from Philistia towards the city of Beth-shemesh (see map, p. 48), possibly a border city. The discovery in the excavations of the city of much Philistine pottery belonging to this period suggests such a border position, with close trade relationships.

8. *casket:* the meaning is uncertain, possibly 'saddle-bag'.

9. *victims of chance:* literally 'just something that happened', i.e. unconnected with the capture of the Ark.

10–12. When the instructions are carried out, all is well. The Ark is taken straight up into the hills, away from Philistine territory, to Beth-shemesh. The Ark has now begun a journey which will eventually bring it to its true resting place, Jerusalem. Another aspect of God's will in letting the Ark go captive is now becoming plain, and the theme of the Ark takes its place alongside the movement towards a true royal dynasty and a true priestly line. *

THE ARK JOURNEYS HOME

13 Now the people of Beth-shemesh were harvesting their
wheat in the Vale, and when they looked up and saw the
14 Ark they rejoiced at the sight of it. The wagon came to the
farm of Joshua of Beth-shemesh and halted there. Close
by stood a great stone; so they chopped up the wood of
the wagon and offered the cows as a whole-offering to the
15 LORD. Then the Levites lifted down the Ark of the LORD
and the casket containing the gold offerings, and laid
them on the great stone; and the men of Beth-shemesh
offered whole-offerings and shared-offerings that day to
16 the LORD. The five princes of the Philistines watched all
this, and returned to Ekron the same day.

17   These golden haemorrhoids which the Philistines sent
back as a gift of indemnity to the LORD were for Ashdod,
18 Gaza, Ashkelon, Gath, and Ekron, one for each city. The
gold rats were for all the towns of the Philistines governed
by the five princes, both fortified towns and open settle-
ments. The great stone*a* where they deposited the Ark of
the LORD stands witness on the farm of Joshua of Beth-
shemesh to this very day.

19   But the sons of Jeconiah did not rejoice with the rest of
the men of Beth-shemesh when they welcomed the Ark of
the LORD, and he struck down seventy of them.*b* The
people mourned because the LORD had struck them so
20 heavy a blow, and the men of Beth-shemesh said, 'No one

[a] The great stone: so Sept.; Heb. Abel-haggedolah.
[b] But...seventy of them: prob. rdg., cp. Sept.; Heb. And he struck
down some of the men of Beth-shemesh because they had welcomed
the Ark of the LORD; he struck down seventy men among the people,
fifty thousand men.

is safe in the presence of the LORD, this holy God. To whom can we send it, to be rid of him?' So they sent this 21 message to the inhabitants of Kiriath-jearim: 'The Philistines have returned the Ark of the LORD; come down and take charge of it.' Then the men of Kiriath- 7 jearim came and took the Ark of the LORD away; they brought it into the house of Abinadab on the hill and consecrated his son Eleazar as its custodian.

* The Ark as symbol of the presence of God is a source of both blessing and danger. The Philistines watch it go with relief; Israel welcomes it home. But its holiness is dangerous.

13. *harvesting their wheat:* the time is probably May. *in the Vale:* the valley of Sorek (see map, p. 48), mentioned in the Samson story (Judg. 16: 4), a rich, fertile valley above which Beth-shemesh lies on the southern hillside. The valley forms one of the main entries into the hill country from the coastal plain.

14. *the farm of Joshua:* verse 18 explains why this name is remembered. For 'farm' we may perhaps better substitute 'field', the piece of land belonging to his family, where he was harvesting and where *a great stone* offered a suitable place for sacrifice. In the early period, altars could be so improvised, as also by Gideon (Judg. 6: 21) and Saul (14: 33). Later regulations were much stricter.

15. Mention of *the Levites* is unexpected. At a later time the Levites appear as the only authorized bearers of the Ark (so 1 Chron. 15: 2); probably a later scribe felt it necessary to mention the proper procedure as he knew it, and to imply that the stone was not really used as an altar but only as a resting-place for the Ark. In 7: 1 it is the 'men of Kiriath-jearim' who carry it, and there is no mention of Levites in 2 Sam. 6.

A sacrificial act is necessary both because of the holiness of the Ark and because of its safe return. *whole-offerings* are those completely burnt as sacrifice; *shared-offerings* are those of which only a part is dedicated and the remainder eaten.

16. The watching Philistines acknowledge by their witness the supremacy of Israel's God. So Ezekiel depicts the nations as witnesses of God's saving power (Ezek. 39: 7).

17–18 a adds a note about the sacred objects sent by the Philistines. That there were five model tumours is made clear by the list of cities. But the number of *gold rats* is not here precisely stated; probably a much larger number, one for every walled town and open village is intended, again indicating variety in the tradition. We are not told what became of these objects. Verse 15 might be thought to suggest that they were sacrificed, but it is more probable that they were kept as sanctuary treasures.

18 b tells that the *great stone* is still to be seen in token of this return of the Ark. Such great rocks are often mentioned in ancient stories; the story, handed down independently, may have come to be associated with an outstanding landmark. The 'sarcophagus of basalt' associated with king Og was probably a great natural boulder (Deut. 3: 11). The Hebrew (cp. N.E.B. footnote) has a proper name Abel-haggedolah; this could be a relic of another story, telling of disaster, for the name could have been thought to mean 'great mourning'. Mourning is mentioned in relation to the next incident.

19. The Hebrew text here has what may be another confused remnant of another story which from its mention of 50,000 victims as well as *seventy* suggests a much magnified disaster. Sept. offers a coherent wording. The important point is to realize the danger which attends the Ark, a danger felt also by Israel (cp. also 2 Sam. 6: 6–8 for another such story of disaster).

6: 21–7: 1. An appeal to Kiriath-jearim, an important place much nearer Jerusalem. It was formerly a Gibeonite city called Baalah (cp. Josh. 9: 17; 15: 9), its exact position not certain (see map, p. 48). Possibly part of 7: 2 should be joined here to indicate a twenty-year stay of the Ark. Ps. 132, which celebrates the taking of the Ark to Jerusalem, may allude to this place in verse 6: 'the region of Jaar'; this is the singular, meaning 'forest', which appears in the plural in Kiriath-jearim, 'town of the forest thickets'.

Thus the Ark is in safe custody, with the son of Abinadab consecrated as guardian, and there it remains (see 7: 2) until the time of David (2 Sam. 6). That the house is *on the hill* may suggest that it was kept in a holy place.

The story told in these chapters is part of the story of the Ark, and tells in reality of God's control over the destiny of his own people and of other nations. Just as it might have seemed that God was powerless when his people were in slavery in Egypt, so here he seemed to be weak; but his arm was strong to deliver, then as now, and to bring the nations to recognize him (so 6: 5, 16). Later the people needed to recall such a story, as a reminder that the supremacy of Babylon in 587 B.C. did not mean that God had lost control. One of the psalmists, tracing how Jerusalem came to be God's sanctuary and David his chosen king, could say:

'He forsook his home at Shiloh,
the tabernacle in which he dwelt among men;
he surrendered the symbol of his strength into captivity
    and his pride into enemy hands;
he gave his people over to the sword
    and put his own possession out of mind.
Fire devoured his young men,
and his maidens could raise no lament for them;
his priests fell by the sword,
and his widows could not weep.

Then the Lord awoke as a sleeper awakes,
like a warrior heated with wine;
he struck his foes in the back parts
and brought perpetual shame upon them.' (Ps. 78: 60–6)✻

Samuel judge over Israel

2 So FOR A LONG WHILE the Ark was housed in Kiriath-
   jearim; and after some time, twenty years later, there
   was a movement throughout Israel to follow the LORD.
3 So Samuel addressed these words to the whole nation: 'If
   your return to the LORD is whole-hearted, banish the
   foreign gods and the Ashtaroth from your shrines; turn to
   the LORD with heart and mind, and worship him alone,
4 and he will deliver you from the Philistines.' The Israelites
   then banished the Baalim and the Ashtaroth, and worshipped the LORD alone.
5   Samuel summoned all Israel to an assembly at Mizpah,
6 so that he might intercede with the LORD for them. When
   they had assembled there, they drew water and poured it
   out before the LORD and fasted all day, confessing that
   they had sinned against the LORD. It was at Mizpah that
   Samuel acted as judge over Israel.
7   When the Philistines heard that the Israelites had assembled at Mizpah, their princes marched against them. The
   Israelites heard that the Philistines were advancing, and
8 they were afraid. They said to Samuel, 'Do not cease to
   pray for us to the LORD our God to save us from the power
9 of the Philistines.' Thereupon Samuel took a sucking lamb,
   offered it up complete as a whole-offering and prayed
   aloud to the LORD on behalf of Israel; and the LORD
10 answered his prayer. As Samuel was offering the sacrifice
   and the Philistines were advancing to battle with the
   Israelites, the LORD thundered loud and long over the

Philistines and threw them into confusion. They fled in
panic before the Israelites, who set out from Mizpah in 11
pursuit and kept up the slaughter of the Philistines till they
reached a point below Beth-car. There Samuel took a 12
stone and set it up as a monument between Mizpah and
Jeshanah,*a* naming it Eben-ezer,*b* 'for to this point', he
said, 'the LORD has helped us.' Thus the Philistines were 13
subdued and no longer encroached on the territory of
Israel; and the hand of the LORD was against them as long
as Samuel lived. The cities they had captured were 14
restored to Israel, and from Ekron to Gath the borderland
was freed from their control. Between Israel and the
Amorites peace was maintained. Samuel acted as judge in 15
Israel as long as he lived, and every year went on circuit 16
to Bethel and Gilgal and Mizpah; he dispensed justice at all
these places, returning always to Ramah. That was his home 17
and the place from which he governed Israel, and there he
built an altar to the LORD.

* Samuel reappears in a new guise, as a judge over all Israel,
bringing victory and peace for his people. He also acts as a
priest.

2. The first part of this verse (see above) is probably better
regarded as a link phrase in the Ark story, though now it also
provides an introduction to a new phase in the Samuel story.
It could be rendered: 'Now time passed after the moment
when the Ark was housed in Kiriath-jearim, namely twenty
years...' The natural sequel would be a new story of the
Ark, perhaps the one which tells of David bringing it to
Jerusalem (2 Sam. 6).

The turning of Israel to God in loyalty is a theme repeatedly

[a] *Prob. rdg.* (*cp. 2 Chron. 13: 19*); *Heb.* the tooth.
[b] *That is* Stone of Help.

used in the book of Judges. A period of religious unfaithfulness is there followed by disaster, and this in its turn leads to repentance and appeal to God. A deliverer appears and, after victory, peace and loyalty are assured. The story here is built on a similar pattern, though its style is more formal and the battle scene is more theological than military. One of the many traditions of the Philistine period may have been used, and the result is a narrative of theological significance.

3 sets out the theme of renewing the covenant by forsaking other gods and confessing loyalty to the LORD alone. This is the central theme of Deuteronomy, and we may see here the application of the theology of that book to the interpretation of Israel's experience. *Ashtaroth*, a plural word used generally for 'goddesses' though in the singular it denotes the important Canaanite goddess 'Ashtart, connected with Babylonian Ishtar, a goddess of fertility and war (see also on 31: 10).

4. *Baalim*, another plural for 'gods'; the singular is used as a title 'lord, husband', for a god, even sometimes for Israel's God. It is associated particularly with a great Canaanite deity, Hadad, a god of storm and king of the gods.

5. *Mizpah* (see map, p. 13) appears as an important religious and political centre here and again in 10: 17. *intercede:* an important prophetic function—so too in verse 8—and one especially associated with Samuel. Ps. 99: 6 and Jer. 15: 1 both give special place to him in this capacity. Abraham as prophet is described as an intercessor (Gen. 20: 7); so too is Moses (Exod. 17: 8–13).

6. *drew water:* the pouring out of water as an act of worship appears here to mark a repentance ritual. We may compare Lam. 2: 19: 'pour out your heart like water', a metaphor in a passage calling for penitent appeal to God. Such purification by repentance makes Israel fit to be used by God. *Samuel acted as judge:* the verb means both 'to judge' and 'to establish someone's rights', i.e. to deliver. So the 'judges' are deliverers. Both senses are appropriate here.

66

7. The inference seems to be that the Philistines took advantage of Israel's involvement in a religious celebration to make an attack. Israel's fear is expressed in an appeal to Samuel for unceasing intercession (verse 8).

9f. The answer to the Philistine attack comes not in military action but in the offering of sacrifice and prayer. At that very moment *the LORD thundered.* Thunder as the voice of God (so here paraphrased in the word *loud*) is a common idea both in Israel and elsewhere; Ps. 29 has some vivid pictures. God's voice produces *panic*; the Philistines are defeated before Israel has even moved.

So many of the stories in this book, and in other Old Testament narrative books, turn on warfare and the slaughter of great numbers, that we find them somewhat distasteful. We need to remember first that these are ancient hero tales, concerned with the past glories of a people's life; every community has such traditions. But we need also to see that in the Old Testament these stories are used not to exult in war and to lord it over defeated enemies; they are used to express the confidence that it is God who gives victory, salvation. War may be understood as 'holy war' in the sense that it is believed that God fights with and through the people consecrated to him. (On consecration for war, cp. 21: 5.) The enemies of Israel are seen as the enemies of God; they cease to be merely real peoples, they become symbols of all that is opposed to God. The New Testament takes up this battle theme: 'our fight is not against human foes, but against cosmic powers...' (Eph. 6: 12). Ancient Israel had a strong national sentiment; but it also saw that to believe in the one God who controls all life means to believe in promise and hope for all nations.

11. *Beth-car* is otherwise entirely unknown.

12. *Jeshanah* is not in the Hebrew text, though implied by Sept. If this is correct, it lies somewhat north of Jerusalem, in what appears to be the wrong locality. It is better to assume an unknown place, 'the tooth' or 'the crag'; *Eben-ezer* too is unknown, probably a name given to a great stone in one of

the valleys leading to the coastal plain. *Eben-ezer* appeared in
4: 1. It is probably not the same place, but the story of
victory is designed in some measure to answer the disaster of
chapter 4. So, the writer appears to say, the site of defeat
became the site of victory. '*for to this point*': a slight emendation would give: 'this is the witness that...'

13. The statement that the Philistines were subdued during
the whole life of Samuel does not fit with the evidence of
subsequent chapters, e.g. 13 and 14. The story has built up the
picture of Samuel as judge into that of one who gave peace to
Israel for the whole period of his activity. This now serves to
underline the lack of faith shown by Israel in asking for a king
in chapter 8.

14. The border territory in fact came under Israelite control
only in the time of David. This and the reference to peace with
the Amorites, a name for the earlier inhabitants of Canaan,
seem to be part of the magnification of Samuel's position as
judge.

15–17 suggest an older tradition of Samuel as active only in
a more restricted area in the central part of the land, with his
home at Ramah. That *he built an altar* suggests a priest who
gave directives to inquirers. But even here, since the three
places mentioned all feature as notable centres (*places* perhaps
means 'holy places', see note on 3: 3), it is probable that there
has been some enlargement of Samuel's function. *Bethel*
('house of God') is well known as a cult-centre; its foundation-
legend is in Gen. 28: 11 ff. (see map, p. 48). *Gilgal* ('stone-circle')
is a name used for several places; we might think of a site near
Shiloh, but the writer is probably thinking of the great
religious centre near Jericho (see map, p. 48 and cp. Josh. 4:
19–5: 12).

This chapter provides a clear example of the way in which
an author whose concerns are primarily theological makes use
of elements of ancient tradition, but so transforms them that
he presents what is not history but an interpretation of the
meaning of history. ✳

Saul anointed king

'A KING LIKE OTHER NATIONS'

WHEN SAMUEL grew old, he appointed his sons to be **8**
judges in Israel. The eldest son was named Joel and 2
the second Abiah; they acted as judges in Beersheba. His 3
sons did not follow in their father's footsteps but were
intent on their own profit, taking bribes and perverting
the course of justice. So all the elders of Israel met, and 4
came to Samuel at Ramah and said to him, 'You are now 5
old and your sons do not follow in your footsteps; appoint
us a king to govern us, like other nations.' But their request 6
for a king to govern them displeased Samuel, and he
prayed to the LORD. The LORD answered Samuel, 'Listen 7
to the people and all that they are saying; they have not
rejected you, it is I whom they have rejected, I whom they
will not have to be their king. They are now doing to you 8
just what they have done to me*a* since I brought them up
from Egypt: they have forsaken me and worshipped other
gods. Hear what they have to say now, but give them a 9
solemn warning and tell them what sort of king will
govern them.' Samuel told the people who were asking 10
him for a king all that the LORD had said to him. 'This will 11
be the sort of king who will govern you', he said. 'He will
take your sons and make them serve in his chariots and
with his cavalry, and will make them run before his
chariot. Some he will appoint officers over units of a 12
thousand and units of fifty. Others will plough his fields

[a] to me: *so Sept.; Heb. om.*

and reap his harvest; others again will make weapons of
13 war and equipment for mounted troops. He will take
your daughters for perfumers, cooks, and confectioners,
14 and will seize the best of your cornfields, vineyards, and
15 olive-yards, and give them to his lackeys. He will take a
tenth of your grain and your vintage to give to his
16 eunuchs and lackeys. Your slaves, both men and women,
and the best of your cattle*a* and your asses he will seize and
17 put to his own use. He will take a tenth of your flocks, and
18 you yourselves will become his slaves. When that day
comes, you will cry out against the king whom you have
chosen; but it will be too late, the LORD will not answer
19 you.' The people refused to listen to Samuel; 'No,' they
20 said, 'we will have a king over us; then we shall be like
other nations, with a king to govern us, to lead us out to
21 war and fight our battles.' So Samuel, when he had heard
22 what the people said, told the LORD; and he answered,
'Take them at their word and appoint them a king.'
Samuel then dismissed all the men of Israel to their homes.

* Chapters 8–15 of the book present the story of how Israel
came to have her first king, Saul. The story of Saul continues
thereafter, but always in subordination to the younger figure
of David. The chapters present many problems, literary and
historical. Most obvious is the contrast between passages in
which kingship is seen as an act of rebellion against God and
others in which it is considered a divinely ordained institution.
It is not unlikely that from the very outset there would be
division of opinion; the old tribal organization, the local
heroes, the priests and prophets, provided a certain kind of life
for the community. Kingship, as this chapter shows, could
bring many undesirable features. But such criticism would

[a] your cattle: *so Sept.; Heb.* your picked men.

gain added force in the light of experience. In 722 B.C. the northern monarchy of Israel came to an end; in 587 the Davidic house ceased to rule in Judah. Was not this a sign that kingship was evil?

No simple answer can be given. Different parts of the material say different things. They would add up to the judgement: kingship has existed for 400 years; it cannot have existed solely by accident, and much that is associated with it is good; it must be a divinely appointed institution. But the history shows that kings can lead the whole people astray from obedience to God; kingship is a human institution, under divine judgement. Such a double estimate needs to be kept in mind. A similar judgement is found on the temple at Jerusalem.

1. No date is given; the continued activity of Samuel in Saul's reign suggests that we should not try to put the materials in precise order. As with Eli, the sons of an approved leader are found to be deficient.

2. Their names warrant a better response: *Joel*—'Yahweh is God', *Abiah*—'Yahweh is my father'. *Beersheba* (see map, p. 13) is at the southern edge of the country (see on 3: 20). Here again Samuel's activity has been re-interpreted to make him judge over all Israel.

3. The failure is of the kind frequently condemned by the prophets, e.g. in Amos 5: 7, 10–12. It is a misuse of the office of judge, just as Eli's sons misused the priestly position.

4. *elders*: literally 'bearded men', i.e. full adult members of the community. But the term is often used, as here, to denote representatives. Later in the chapter, it is the whole people which is involved (so verses 10, 19, 21; so too in the sequel 10: 17).

5. Two reasons are given for the request for a king: the failure of Samuel's sons in his old age, and the desire to be like other nations. The former theme is like that of Eli; it is not mentioned again in this narrative (but see also 12: 2). The latter theme suggests a failure by Israel to acknowledge her

distinctive place as 'people of God'. Kingship was already known to Israel. There were kings of city-states in Canaan, like Adoni-bezek of Jerusalem (Judg. 1: 5); they were rulers of small areas surrounding the cities. There were also kings of peoples more like Israel; Gen. 36: 31–9 lists kings of Edom 'before there were kings in Israel'.

6f. Kingship is here understood as belonging only to God. To reject God's spokesman is to reject God; the theme is expounded in John 15: 18–16: 4. Gideon answers those who offer him rule: 'I will not rule over you, nor shall my son; the LORD will rule over you' (Judg. 8: 23). The idea has been developed into a short sermon (verses 7–9) on the people's repeated disloyalty and apostasy, right back to the moment of deliverance from Egypt.

9. *what sort of king will govern:* elsewhere the expression is: 'the nature of monarchy' (so 10: 25 where N.E.B. has 'the nature of a king'). The word used is that rendered 'custom' in 2: 13; it expresses what is proper or normal. Here, however, it clearly has a derogatory tone.

11–17 lists a whole range of evils which may be associated with the monarchy. Examples of some of these may be found in the stories of the kings which follow in 1 and 2 Samuel and 1 and 2 Kings. It is clear that if kings were to rule and to provide government and protection for the people, some of the things here noted would be necessary. But that kings often misused power is also clear. The prophetic criticism of kings brings this out again and again (e.g. Elijah in the Naboth case, 1 Kings 21). Deut. 17: 14–20 has a short 'kingship law' which clearly has close links in style with this chapter; it warns of evils and legislates for right practice.

12. *thousand, fifty:* normal names for any units.

13. *perfumers:* possibly a euphemism for 'concubines'.

14. *lackeys:* the bad sense of this word is not necessarily implied: 'servants' would avoid this. *eunuchs:* though the term had this meaning, it is often used more generally for 'court officers'.

16. *your cattle*: the Hebrew has 'your picked men'. The two words sound much alike; the difference could perhaps be due to copying at dictation.

It is often asked whether the evils listed in these verses reflect kingship as it was experienced over the centuries, and so belong later in the monarchy, or indicate practices known at an early date. It is quite clear that such practices as the military provisions, the possession of royal lands, the tithing of produce, the imposition of forced labour, are all familiar from city-states long before Israel's time. But the finding of similar criticisms elsewhere does not mean that this passage has not been influenced by the experience of Israel's subsequent history. Saul and David (at least at first) were not kings of that kind. Israel seems at first to have had a kingship unlike that of the city-states, and more like an extension into more permanent forms of the 'judge' type of institution. Only in the latter years of David and more particularly with Solomon and the successors in the divided kingdoms do we find the political and economic disadvantages described here.

18. The king chosen by Israel—as permitted by God—is not like a foreign ruler who invades and from whom God will save. He is from now on a part of Israel's life.

20. Three functions of kingship are here drawn out. The emphasis rests on order and security.

22. The dismissal of Israel allows a new story to be introduced in 9: 1–10: 16. Only at 10: 17 do we return to the themes of this chapter. The whole of this chapter must be understood in its relationship to the narratives which follow in which a different picture is given of the origins of the monarchy. ✳

SAUL IS LED TO SAMUEL

There was a man from the district of Benjamin, whose **9** name was Kish son of Abiel, son of Zeror, son of Bechorath, son of Aphiah a Benjamite. He was a man of substance, and had a son named Saul, a young man in his 2

prime; there was no better man among the Israelites than
he. He was a head taller than any of his fellows.

3   One day some asses belonging to Saul's father Kish had
strayed, so he said to his son Saul, 'Take one of the servants
4 with you, and go and look for the asses.' They crossed the
hill-country of Ephraim and went through the district of
Shalisha but did not find them; they passed through the
district of Shaalim but they were not there; they passed
through the district of Benjamin but again did not find
5 them. When they had entered the district of Zuph, Saul
said to the servant with him, 'Come, we ought to turn
back, or my father will stop thinking about the asses and
6 begin to worry about us.' The servant answered, 'There
is a man of God in the city here, who has a great reputation,
because everything he says comes true. Suppose we go
there; he may tell us something about this errand of ours.'
7 Saul said, 'If we do go, what shall we offer him? There is
no food left in our packs and we have no present for the
8 man of God, nothing at all.' The servant answered him
again, 'Wait! I have here a quarter-shekel of silver. I can
10[a] give that to the man, to tell us what we should do.' Saul
said, 'Good! let us go to him.' So they went to the city
9 where the man of God was. (In days gone by in Israel,
when a man wished to consult God, he would say, 'Let us
go to the seer.' For what is nowadays called a prophet used to
11 be called a seer.) As they were going up the hill to the city
they met some girls coming out to draw water and asked,
12 'Shall we find the seer there?' 'Yes,' they said, 'the seer is
ahead of you now; he has just[b] arrived in the city because

[a] *Verses 9 and 10 transposed.*   [b] the seer...just: *prob. rdg.; Heb.*
he is ahead of you, hurry now, for he has today...

there is a feast at the hill-shrine today. As you enter the 13
city you will meet him before he goes up to the shrine
to eat; the people will not start until he comes, for he has
to bless the sacrifice before the company can eat. Go up
now, and you will find him at once.' So they went up to 14
the city, and just as they were going in, there was Samuel
coming towards them on his way up to the shrine.

* 1. The story begins like that of Samuel (1: 1), Micah
(Judg. 17: 1), and others. No connections are made with what
precedes. Saul is a hero like any of the judges, chosen from the
tribe of Benjamin. *a man of substance:* the list of ancestors
indicates a family of standing. To have property (like that of
Job, 1: 1–3) gives a man position and influence in the community. The opposite is 'idle men', literally 'empty men',
i.e. those who have no property (Judg. 11: 3). The family home
was at Gibeah (10: 26), about five miles north of Jerusalem
(map, p. 48).

2. *a young man in his prime...no better man:* the chronology
is very uncertain; Saul is said to be 'fifty years old when he
became king' and is described as having a grown son,
Jonathan (see note on 13: 1f.). Again we must recognize
different elements in the material, not exactly fitting together.
Better may indicate moral quality, but the phrases following
suggest superiority of physical appearance. So too David is
'handsome' (16: 12). Physical strength and good appearance
are seen as divine gifts. On the name Saul, see on 1: 20.

3. *asses:* actually 'she-asses'. In Zech. 9: 9, the she-ass
appears in connection with a royal figure. Is there a concealed
reference here? Saul searches for asses, associated with
royalty: he finds kingship.

4f. The places mentioned are not precisely known; what is
important is that Saul arrives in *the district of Zuph* (cp. 1: 1).

6. *a man of God:* a 'prophet'. We may note that no name
is given until verse 14. It is possible that a story of Saul's

75

anointing by an unnamed prophet has been ascribed to Samuel. Such an explanation would have the advantage of overcoming the difficulty that Samuel appears both as a prominent judge on circuit and also as an obscure local seer, the sort of man whom one would consult about a relatively small matter.

7. *what shall we offer him?* It was clearly normal to pay a small fee to a prophet when a question was put. Thus the wife of Jeroboam took a present of food to Ahijah the prophet (1 Kings 14: 3). Micah condemns prophets who give a message according to the amount of the payment (Mic. 3: 5); he does not question the practice of paying. *a quarter-shekel* would be about 3 gm in weight; its value is impossible to assess.

9. This verse is clearly a comment subsequently added to the text. Its position before verse 10 is unsatisfactory, but N.E.B.'s position after verse 10 is not much better. Since it annotates the word 'seer' in verse 11, it should probably be regarded as a marginal note to this verse which has subsequently been copied into the text. It sets out to explain a change of name. At a later time the commonly used word was 'prophet' (*nābī'*) of which the meaning seems to be 'spokesman' or 'one who is called'. At an earlier stage, 'seer' was used. 'Seer' may translate one of two Hebrew words, the one used here (*rō'eh*) which is used several times by the Chronicler (e.g. of Samuel in 1 Chron. 9: 22), and the one used in Amos 7: 12 (*ḥōzeh*). 1 Chron. 29: 29 uses all three terms. By the time of Amos, it is clear, 'prophet' and 'seer' were used interchangeably, and in the prophetic books we find the use of the two verbs meaning 'to see' and words like 'vision' (from the second) as normal descriptions of prophetic activity. At an earlier stage a distinction could probably have been made between all these, but exactly what sort of distinction is no longer clear; seers may have been the recipients of visionary experiences or have been regarded as able to see the future, where prophets are seen rather as spokesmen, though also in this narrative as ecstatics.

11. *up the hill:* if the city is Ramah, which is nowhere
stated, then its name ('high') suggests that it was on a hill.
Verse 12 could imply that this is not the seer's home town
anyway. The mention of a 'hill-shrine' points to a higher
position, above the city. For protection, cities were often
built on hills, and gradually as buildings decayed and fell the
level of building rose. This is why modern archaeologists in
Palestine and elsewhere are often able to dig down through
different layers of a city and uncover its history in some
measure. The phrase *up the hill* here could, however, simply
mean the slope leading up to the city-gate. The girls are
coming down this slope to the spring.

12. *hill-shrine:* a *bāmāh* or high-place. It is not made clear
whether this is inside or outside the city.

13. Here again we see that the functions of priest and
prophet are closely linked. The word rendered *sacrifice* is the
same as that rendered 'feast' in verse 12; for this is an occasion
like those described in chapters 1 and 2 when the worshippers
eat together at the shrine. *the company*: literally 'those who have
been summoned'. As appears in the next section, this is a
special occasion in which those summoned are really honouring
Saul, though they are not aware of the reason for this.

14. *going in:* literally 'coming into the heart of the city',
but perhaps we should emend to 'coming into the middle of
the gateway' (so verse 18). ✲

THE HONOURING OF SAUL

Now the day before Saul came, the LORD had disclosed 15
his intention to Samuel in these words: 'At this same time 16
tomorrow I will send you a man from the land of
Benjamin. Anoint him prince over my people Israel, and
then he shall deliver my people from the Philistines. I have
seen the sufferings of[a] my people and their cry has reached
my ears.' The moment Saul appeared the LORD said to 17

[a] the sufferings of: *so Sept.; Heb. om.*

Samuel, 'Here is the man of whom I spoke to you. This
18 man shall rule my people.' Saul came up to Samuel in the
gateway and said, 'Would you tell me where the seer
19 lives?' Samuel replied, 'I am the seer. Go on ahead of me
to the hill-shrine and you shall eat with me today; in the
morning I will set you on your way, after telling you
20 what you have on your mind. Trouble yourself no more
about the asses lost three days ago, for they have been
found. But what is it that all Israel is wanting? It is you
21 and your ancestral house.' 'But I am a Benjamite,' said
Saul, 'from the smallest of the tribes of Israel, and my
family is the least important of all the families of the tribe
22 of Benjamin. Why do you say this to me?' Samuel then
brought Saul and his servant into the dining-hall and gave
them a place at the head of the company, which numbered
23 about thirty. Then he said to the cook, 'Bring the portion
24 that I gave you and told you to put on one side.' So the
cook took up the whole haunch and leg and put it before
Saul; and Samuel said, 'Here is the portion of meat*a* kept
for you. Eat it: it has been reserved for you at this feast to
which*b* I have invited the people.' So Saul dined with
25 Samuel that day, and when they came down from the
hill-shrine to the city a bed was spread on the roof for
26 Saul, and he*c* stayed there that night.

∗ 15. *had disclosed his intention*: to the prophet, God reveals his
secret counsel. This is a prophet's privilege (so Amos 3: 7;
Jer. 23: 22).

[a] the portion of meat: *prob. rdg.; Heb.* what is left over.
[b] to which: *so Vulg.; Heb.* saying.
[c] a bed…and he: *so Sept.; Heb.* he spoke with Saul on the roof and
they…

16. *prince:* literally 'leader', 'one who stands in front'. It is noticeable that this narrative uses this term, not 'king'. The same word is used of David in 13: 14; 25: 30 and elsewhere.

The promise is that he will be anointed—as a king would be—to deliver Israel from *the Philistines*. This indicates a tradition separate both from that of chapter 7, in which Samuel has already delivered Israel, and from chapter 11, where Saul's action is against the Ammonites. Saul was engaged in prolonged warfare with the Philistines, but did not succeed in driving them out of Israelite territory. Only David succeeded in that. The latter half of this verse is very reminiscent of the Exodus traditions (cp. Exod. 3: 7).

17. Samuel's inspired recognition of Saul as deliverer is like his recognition of David (16: 12). His foreknowledge of the object of Saul's search is like Ahijah's knowledge of the reason for the visit of Jeroboam's wife (1 Kings 14: 1–6). *shall rule:* again the word used is not 'be a king' but 'have authority'.

19f. *what you have on your mind:* the meaning of this is obscure. It could refer to anxiety about the asses, but this is immediately disposed of. It is more likely that we should see here a suggestion that, though Saul does not yet know it, the series of apparent chances by which he has been brought to Samuel mark out a special future. Only thus can we understand the strange sequel: *But what is it that all Israel is wanting? …you and your ancestral house. is wanting* is a noun meaning 'something desired'; it is used in Hag. 2: 7 of that which all the nations treasure, in a passage often interpreted as referring to the coming of the Messiah. Did the word perhaps have a hint of royal status?

21. Saul's disclaimer is like Gideon's in a similar situation (Judg. 6: 15). Such a confession of inadequacy serves to heighten the wonder of the gift of divine power (cp. also Moses and Jeremiah for a similar hesitation: Exod. 4: 1–17; Jer. 1: 6).

22. The answer given by Samuel to Saul's disclaimer is to show him to the place of honour at the feast. *dining-hall:* the

room for sacrificial feasts (1: 9, 18), an indication that there was here a sanctuary building as at Shiloh.

24. Saul is given an enormous special portion, as was Benjamin when honoured in Egypt (Gen. 43: 34). *at this feast*: the word indicates an appointed time, i.e. the moment of Saul's being honoured in anticipation of his anointing.

Although no further detail is given about this meal, it could be that it is thought of as initiating a covenant relationship between the new ruler and representatives of his people before God. We also observe the establishing of a close bond between Samuel and Saul. ✳

SAUL THE ANOINTED LEADER

At dawn Samuel called to Saul on the roof, 'Get up, and I will set you on your way.' When Saul rose, he and Samuel
27 went out together into the street. As they came to the end of the town, Samuel said to Saul, 'Tell the boy to go on.' He did so, and then Samuel said, 'Stay here a moment, and I will tell you the word of God.'

10   Samuel took a flask of oil and poured it over Saul's head, and he kissed him and said, 'The LORD anoints you prince over his people Israel; you shall rule the people of the LORD and deliver them from the enemies round about them. You shall have a sign[a] that the LORD has anointed
2 you prince to govern his inheritance: when you leave me today, you will meet two men by the tomb of Rachel at Zelzah in the territory of Benjamin. They will tell you that the asses you are looking for have been found and that your father is concerned for them no longer; he is anxious about you and says again and again, "What shall I do
3 about my son?" From there go across country as far as the

[a] The LORD anoints...sign: *so Sept.; Heb. om.*

terebinth of Tabor, where three men going up to Bethel to
worship God will meet you. One of them will be carrying
three kids, the second three loaves, and the third a flagon
of wine. They will greet you and will offer you two 4
loaves, which you will accept from them. Then when you 5
reach the Hill of God, where the Philistine governor[a] [b]
resides, you will meet a company of prophets coming
down from the hill-shrine, led by lute, harp, fife, and
drum, and filled with prophetic rapture. Then the spirit 6
of the LORD will suddenly take possession of you, and you
too will be rapt like a prophet and become another man.
When these signs happen, do whatever the occasion 7
demands; God will be with you. You shall go down to 8
Gilgal ahead of me, and I will come to you to sacrifice
whole-offerings and shared-offerings. Wait seven days
until I join you; then I will tell you what to do.' As Saul 9
turned to leave Samuel, God gave him a new heart. On
that same day all these signs happened. When they reached 10
the Hill there was a company of prophets coming to meet
him, and the spirit of God suddenly took possession of
him, so that he too was filled with prophetic rapture.
When people who had known him previously saw that 11
he was rapt like the prophets, they said to one another,
'What can have happened to the son of Kish? Is Saul also
among the prophets?' One of the men of that place said, 12
'And whose sons are they?' Hence the proverb, 'Is Saul
also among the prophets?' When the prophetic rapture 13
had passed, he went home.[c] Saul's uncle said to him and 14
the boy, 'Where have you been?' Saul answered, 'To look

[a] Or garrison.   [b] So Sept.; Heb. governors, or garrisons.
[c] Prob. rdg.; Heb. to the hill-shrine.

for the asses, and when we could not find them, we went
15 to Samuel.' His uncle said, 'Tell me what Samuel said.'
16 'He told us that the asses had been found', said Saul; but
did not repeat what Samuel had said about his being
king.

* 26*b*. N.E.B. begins a new section at 10: 1; but the introduction to the anointing starts here.

27. Samuel arranges to be alone with Saul so that he may
now disclose fully what has already been hinted.

10: 1. Anointing is with olive oil, and the kiss is a sign of
homage (cp. Ps. 2: 11 'tremble, and kiss the king'). A similar
description is given of the anointing of Jehu by a prophet
(2 Kings 9: 6). The N.E.B. footnote makes clear that a
substantial part of this verse was accidentally omitted at some
stage from the Hebrew text; the copyist's eye jumped from
one occurrence to another of a word translated first as *anoints
you* and second as *has anointed you. prince* and *rule*: see the notes
on 9: 16 and 17. *his inheritance*: an expression commonly used,
especially in Deuteronomy, to describe the relationship between God and *his people*. The poem in Deut. 32 makes this
clear: 'but the LORD's share was his own people,
          Jacob was his allotted portion. (32: 9)

The whole section 32: 8–27 provides a poetic review and
interpretation of Israel's history.

2. Three signs are given. The first is to take place *by the
tomb of Rachel*; according to Jer. 31: 15 this is near Ramah,
probably on the border of Benjamin south of Bethel. Later
the traditional site was located at Bethlehem. *Zelzah* is
unknown. It is indeed very uncertain whether the word is
really a place-name. The word is very similar to that translated
'take possession' in verses 6 and 10; perhaps it suggests that
these two men were divinely possessed. Since both the other
signs involve men engaged in religious activities, this would

seem very probable. The *tomb* could well have been a place for religious activity. '*What shall I do about my son?*' Possibly the story-teller sees a deeper meaning in these words: Saul's father, as yet unaware of what has happened, nevertheless looks forward to something unknown.

3. *terebinth of Tabor:* a turpentine tree which may reach 30 to 40 feet in height. Such trees are in the Old Testament associated with holy places or leaders. *Tabor* here might be an error for 'Deborah'; we may compare Gen. 35: 8 which refers to an oak near Bethel associated with Deborah, Rebecca's nurse. The words for 'oak' and 'terebinth' are very similar. The Tabor mentioned in other passages (e.g. Josh. 19: 12) appears to be too far north.

3 f. The offerings are being taken to the shrine at Bethel. The greeting of Saul and the presentation of gifts to him may be intended to suggest acknowledgement of his, as yet undisclosed, position; offerings intended for God are given instead to his coming representative. Possibly the details of the numbers and the offerings have some symbolic meaning now lost to us.

5. *Hill of God:* presumably an ancient holy place. The word for 'hill' is 'Gibeah'. In 13: 3 a *Philistine governor* is found at Geba, and in that chapter the two names are probably confused at some points. Gibeah is named as Saul's home (10: 26), and the sequel here suggests that what happened took place not far from his own locality. The reference to the *Philistine governor* (or 'garrison') here may be a gloss from 13: 3. *a company of prophets:* the group is associated with the *hill-shrine.* Music is elsewhere mentioned as an accompaniment of prophecy in the story of Elisha (2 Kings 3: 15). The stories of Elisha in 2 Kings give us, in fact, a considerable amount of information about prophetic groups and their functions. We see them in relation to a leader, who is the 'father' of the group; they are often described as 'the sons of the prophets'. The powerful possession by what is here called *prophetic rapture* is seen both in groups and in individuals. It is seen as

something contagious, an overpowering of men by the divine spirit which can overtake even a bystander (see also 19: 18–24). Wild, uncontrolled behaviour has often, in fact, been a characteristic of religion. What is of most interest is the way in which this is interpreted and the way in which it developed in Israel. This group of prophets provides a sign for Saul of that divine power which will enable him to save God's people. Nothing in the story directly suggests that the prophets were the centre of rebellion against the Philistines; their allegiance to the LORD may well, however, have made them intense nationalists.

6. *the spirit of the LORD will suddenly take possession of you, and you...will...become another man:* so too the spirit of the LORD 'clothed itself with' Gideon, and he was empowered to act (Judg. 6: 34—so N.E.B. footnote). The divine spirit, literally 'wind' or 'breath', may rest upon a man and he becomes something new. The word used suggests catastrophic experience. This is a vivid way of describing the sense of power which overtakes such a person.

7. *do whatever the occasion demands:* like other heroes so empowered, Saul will know when the moment for action comes; the presence of God will both assure and guide.

8. This verse appears to bear no relation to the present narrative. It was clearly added here to harmonize this story with the one related in chapter 13 where Saul's unwillingness to wait for Samuel brings judgement upon his kingship. The addition does, however, serve to point forward to Saul's rejection; the compiler is fully aware of the tragedy of Saul.

9. This verse seems to anticipate the effect of the three signs, but perhaps we should understand it as pointing to Saul's sense of encouragement as he leaves Samuel. *a new heart:* or 'a different disposition' in the sense of a courageous spirit.

10. Only the final sign is now related in detail, and this provides the occasion for a short explanatory passage.

11. The acquaintances of Saul see a new person and comment: '*Is Saul also among the prophets?*' They recognize what

has happened, but apparently express surprise at such a show
of divine power in Saul.

12. The question: '*And whose sons are they?*' is very obscure,
but must in some way relate to the concept of a prophetic
band as a group of 'sons' who have a father, their leader. The
question actually runs: 'And who is their father?' and the basic
meaning of the question may be: 'Who is their interpreter?'
since the word 'father' appears in a number of passages to
suggest this. Joseph is to be 'father' or 'counsellor' to Pharaoh
(Gen. 45: 8); Micah asks the Levite to be 'priest and father'
to him (Judg. 17: 10). The questioner here wanted to know
the meaning of the ecstatics' behaviour and hence, presumably,
to understand Saul's place among them.

The saying: '*Is Saul also among the prophets?*' is said to have
become a *proverb*. Another explanation is given of its origin in
19: 18–24. We cannot therefore assume that we know either
its origin or its precise meaning. Two main lines have been
followed: (1) Is Saul, the man of standing, likely to have been
connected with these low, ill-behaved prophetic bands? This
assumes a later critical attitude to the bands of prophets, as in
the story of Micaiah and the false prophets in 1 Kings 22. The
fact that Samuel uses this group as a sign may, however,
suggest that he was himself their leader, their father; he
appears as leader of the group in chapter 19. It seems unlikely
that anyone would regard as of low value an institution so
closely connected with Samuel. (2) Is Saul, who was to be
rejected as king and possessed of an 'evil spirit' (16: 14), to be
regarded as a member of the prophetic order? This, though
quite likely, again would appear to be a later explanation. A
further possibility is that the question asks quite simply
whether Saul is really a permanent member of the group; the
subsequent withdrawal of the prophetic spirit indicates that he
was not. We have to acknowledge that, as with many
proverbial sayings, we do not have the original meaning; we
can only try to understand what such a saying was subsequently thought to mean.

13. The prophetic inspiration of Saul was only temporary, and then he *went home*. The text has 'to the hill-shrine', and there seems no good reason why this may not be correct.

14–16. If it is correct, then was *Saul's uncle* or 'kinsman' an official at the shrine? He appears to know nothing of the search for the asses. If he was an official at the shrine to which Saul went—for what purpose is not stated—then his inquiries would be understandable, though he was evidently not able to discover the full truth. He clearly knew Samuel. ✳

SAUL CHOSEN BY LOT

17 Meanwhile Samuel summoned the Israelites to the LORD
18 at Mizpah and said to the people, 'This is the word of the LORD the God of Israel: I brought Israel up from Egypt; I delivered you from the Egyptians and from all the
19 kingdoms that oppressed you; but today you have rejected your God who saved you from all your misery and distress; you have said, "No,*a* set up a king over us." Now therefore take up your positions before the LORD tribe
20 by tribe and clan by clan.' Samuel then presented all the
21 tribes of Israel, and Benjamin was picked by lot. Then he presented the tribe of Benjamin, family by family, and the family of Matri was picked. Then he presented the family of Matri, man by man,*b* and Saul son of Kish was picked;
22 but when they looked for him he could not be found. They went on to ask the LORD, 'Will the man*c* be coming back?' The LORD answered, 'There he is, hiding among the bag-
23 gage.' So someone ran and fetched him out, and as he took his stand among the people, he was a head taller than anyone
24 else. Samuel said to the people, 'Look at the man whom

[a] said, "No: *so many MSS.; others* said to him.
[b] Then...by man: *so Sept.; Heb. om.*   [c] *So Sept.; Heb.* a man.

the LORD has chosen; there is no one like him in this whole nation.' They all acclaimed him, shouting, 'Long live the king!' Samuel then explained to the people the nature of a 25 king, and made a written record of it on a scroll which he deposited before the LORD; he then dismissed them to their homes. Saul too went home to Gibeah, and with him 26 went some fighting men*a* whose hearts God had moved. But there were scoundrels who said, 'How can this 27 fellow deliver us?' They thought nothing of him and brought him no gifts.

✻ This section is linked with chapter 8. It shows the same hostile attitude to kingship, the demand for a king being seen as a rejection of God.

17. *Mizpah:* cp. 7: 5 (see map, p. 13).

18. The past history of God's saving power is again rehearsed as in 8: 8. God is the saviour, not the king.

19. To ask for a king is to reject God; so too in 8: 7. The text here uses the word *king* as in chapter 8 and not 'prince' as in the preceding narrative. This verse may also be compared with 8: 19. *today:* emphasizes that disobedience is now. So in Deut. 5: 3 the ancient covenant is seen as being made with Israel 'today' (N.E.B.: 'this day').

19–21. A procedure is followed which enables a choice to be made by lot, understood to be divinely controlled. By a gradual process of elimination, first the *tribe* and *clan* (two terms which appear not to be distinguished here; the second is more often used of military divisions), and then the *family* within the chosen tribe, is presented, and finally the individuals in the chosen family. The procedure is presumably one in which the representative or the individual is brought before the shrine, and in some way the indication is given whether the one presented is chosen or rejected. A similar procedure is

[a] *So Sept.; Heb.* with him went the army.

described in Josh. 7: 16–18. The repetitiveness of the text has understandably led to an omission in the Hebrew in verse 21. *Matri:* the name does not appear in Saul's family tree in 9: 1.

21–2 introduces a new theme, that of the reluctant chosen one. We may compare Saul's disclaimer in 9: 21. The question: '*Will the man be coming back?*' is obscure; Sept. has: 'Did the man come hither?' *the baggage:* suggests that warriors are assembled ready for war (cp. 30: 24).

23. The theme of great height is found also in the other story (9: 2). The suggestion has been made that in these verses there is a relic of yet another story in which the choice must fall on the most distinguished man. When none is found adequate, it is asked whether there is not one more. Such a theme is to be found in the choice of David in 16: 11. The idea of unique appearance is developed in verse 24.

24. '*Long live the king!*': the normal acclamation of the king (so also 1 Kings 1: 25, 34), with a shout like that in worship and at the arrival of the Ark (4: 5).

25. *the nature of a king:* almost identical with the phrase used in 8: 9. It was presumably thought to be a catalogue of warnings like that in chapter 8. The term may originally have meant the statutes governing royal power, like those in Deut. 17: 14–20. The written document is *deposited before the LORD*, i.e. in the shrine as a continual witness of the nature of kingship in Israel. Such a document may be intended in the 'warrant' referred to at the anointing of Joash in 2 Kings 11: 12.

26 f. may be a separate element, perhaps linked to 10: 1–16; it indicates that Saul found both glad acceptance and loyalty (cp. 14: 52), and also reluctance to believe that such a man could be a divinely appointed deliverer. This opposition has nothing to do with Samuel's objections to kingship; it shows a lack of faith in the divine choice. The story of Moses also contains the theme of disbelief (cp. Exod. 14: 11 f.). *gifts:* the tribute due to the newly appointed king. For the last words of verse 27 ('But he was silent', N.E.B. footnote to 11: 1) see note on 11: 12 f. ✳

88

SAUL THE HEROIC DELIVERER

About a month later[a] Nahash the Ammonite attacked and **11**
besieged Jabesh-gilead. The men of Jabesh said to Nahash,
'Come to terms with us and we will be your subjects.'
Nahash answered them, 'On one condition only will I 2
come to terms with you: that I gouge out your right eyes
and bring disgrace on Israel.' The elders of Jabesh-gilead 3
then said, 'Give us seven days' respite to send messengers
throughout Israel and then, if no one relieves us, we will
surrender to you.' When the messengers came to Gibeah, 4
where Saul lived, and delivered their message, all the
people broke into lamentation. Saul was just coming from 5
the field driving in the oxen, and asked why the people
were lamenting; and they repeated what the men of
Jabesh had said. When Saul heard this, the spirit of God 6
suddenly seized him. In his anger he took a pair of oxen 7
and cut them in pieces, and sent messengers with the
pieces all through Israel to proclaim that the same would
be done to the oxen of any man who did not follow Saul
and Samuel into battle. The fear of the LORD fell upon the
people and they came out, to a man. Saul mustered them 8
in Bezek; there were three hundred thousand men from
Israel and thirty thousand from Judah. He[b] said to the men 9
who brought the message, 'Tell the men of Jabesh-gilead,
"Victory will be yours tomorrow by the time the sun is
hot."' The men of Jabesh heard what the messengers
reported and took heart; and they said to Nahash, 10
'Tomorrow we will surrender to you, and then you may
deal with us as you think fit.' Next day Saul drew up his 11

[a] *So Sept.; Heb.* But he was silent.   [b] *So Sept.; Heb.* They.

men in three columns; they forced their way right into the enemy camp during the morning watch and massacred the Ammonites while the day grew hot, after which the survivors scattered until no two men were left together.

12   Then the people said to Samuel, 'Who said that Saul should not reign over us? Hand the men over to us to be

13 put to death.' But Saul said, 'No man shall be put to death on a day when the LORD has won such a victory in Israel.'

14 Samuel said to the people, 'Let us now go to Gilgal and

15 there renew our allegiance to the kingdom.' So they all went to Gilgal and invested Saul there as king in the presence of the LORD, sacrificing shared-offerings before the LORD; and Saul and all the Israelites celebrated the occasion with great joy.

✷ 1. *About a month later:* this time-link is found in Sept. and other ancient texts, though it is not clear whether it should be regarded as connected with 10: 17–27 or perhaps rather with 9: 1–10: 16. What follows may be seen as the fulfilment of Samuel's words in 10: 7: 'do whatever the occasion demands'. But most probably the story in this chapter should be treated as an originally quite independent hero tale in which Saul appears just like one of the great 'judges'. *Nahash the Ammonite:* the royal family in Ammon was to be troublesome again to David (so 2 Sam. 10); but according to that narrative, Nahash himself became a loyal friend of David. Ammonite–Israelite relationships are also the cause of Jephthah's campaigns (Judg. 11). *Jabesh-gilead:* an important town east of Jordan (see map, p. 48). The hard-pressed inhabitants were forced to offer to submit to Ammonite terms. An earlier connection between Gibeah and Jabesh-gilead is found in the story in Judg. 19–21, esp. 21: 8–14.

2. The harsh terms of the treaty offered are said to be

designed to *bring disgrace on Israel.* A similar provocation is found in the story of Ammon in 2 Sam. 10. The statement expresses the belief in the unity of the tribes and their responsibility for each other: disgrace to one place is disgrace to all. Compare the claim for the preciousness of one city, Abel-beth-maacah, in 2 Sam. 20: 19. To *gouge out* eyes is a barbarity known to have been practised by Assyrians and Babylonians (cp. 2 Kings 25: 7).

3. Whether or not the willingness of Nahash to let the city appeal for help is likely to be historical—and on the face of it, it seems improbable—the real point is that the Ammonites see Israel as totally impotent, having no 'saviour'.

4. *broke into lamentation:* not to be taken as just helpless distress, but as an appeal to God for help (see on 1: 10).

6. *the spirit of God suddenly seized him:* the same expression as is used in 10: 6, 10. The spirit is here seen to empower Saul for saving action. It is described also in terms of great *anger.*

7. Saul is inspired to perform a 'symbolic action'; the cutting up of the oxen is an expression of his resolve that anyone who fails to respond will be treated accordingly. Such 'symbolic actions' were frequently performed by the prophets: thus Jeremiah broke a jar as a symbol of God's breaking, i.e. judgement, of Judah (Jer. 19: 10ff.). This is not just a picturesque illustration; it is understood as part of the judgement. The prophet, as it were, puts the judgement in train. A similar, even more gruesome, symbolic action is described in Judg. 19: 29f. *and Samuel:* probably an addition, since the story here really concentrates only on the divine inspiration of Saul. *The fear of the LORD:* that awe at the divine power which can produce both panic and wholehearted response. *to a man:* or possibly 'as one man' (so N.E.B. in Judg. 20: 1).

8. *Bezek:* the nearest rallying point west of Jordan, opposite the approach to Jabesh-gilead (see map, p. 48). The numbers, 300,000 and 30,000, represent a conventional view that Judah is one tenth of Israel (see Isa. 6: 13). The figures in Sept. and Josephus are even more exaggerated. As in the stories of the

judges, what may well originally have been a relatively localized action is magnified into a campaign by all Israel.

10. *we will surrender:* literally, 'we will come out', a neat ambiguity, for it can mean both 'surrender' and 'come out to attack'. The second half of the verse is humorously ironical.

11. *three columns:* a military formation commonly adopted, as, for example, by Gideon (Judg. 7: 16), and as in 13: 17. *the morning watch:* the dawn watch, a good moment for attack. A sequel to Saul's deliverance of Jabesh-gilead is to be found in 31: 11–13; 2 Sam. 2: 4–7.

12f. is another fragment of the tradition found in 10: 26f., skilfully placed here. Saul's victory provides the real answer to the objections raised against him. The Hebrew text at 10: 27 'but he was silent' (see N.E.B. footnote to 11: 1) makes good sense as an introduction to the most effective answer which can be given to Saul's critics.

14. *renew our allegiance:* the tradition here associates the origins of kingship with Gilgal (cp. 10: 8; 13: 7 ff.). The text represents an attempt at harmonizing the various divergent statements about the origins of the monarchy. A change of a single letter would give: 'let us consecrate the kingdom', i.e. 'declare it holy'.

15. As this narrative ends, we are to see Saul's heroic exploit as providing the basis for his kingship. Like Gideon and Jephthah, he has delivered his people from the enemy and this leads to the establishment of a more permanent rule.

At this point, we may pause to consider the origins of Israel's monarchy. We can see at least three different types of tradition about this vital stage of the historical development. (1) Saul, the inspired hero of Jabesh-gilead, is acknowledged by the people. (2) Saul, the young warrior searching for lost asses, is anointed and inspired by prophetic spirit. (3) Saul, the distinguished member of the tribe of Benjamin, is picked by lot to be king in response to the wishes of the people, as a concession made by God to their demands. There may be remnants too of other traditions, e.g. in 10: 26f. and 11: 12f.

It should occasion no surprise that an event of such importance has evoked different and indeed irreconcilable stories. We
do less than justice to the material if we simply attempt to
harmonize them into one account. Great events in every
community call forth rich traditions, expressive of the many
different points from which an event may be viewed. The
traditions as now woven together have a certain unity, resting
in the conviction of the overruling purpose of God; but it is a
unity built up while preserving the diversity of the materials.

Israel naturally asked: Why did kingship appear at this
moment? The question is variously answered: political needs,
the Philistine pressure particularly, necessitated a new system,
a more unified control. Other nations already had kings, and
earlier heroes had already occupied positions which were
those of kings in everything but name. Above all, the actual
fact of the monarchy was a present one to those who told the
stories, though by the time of their final shaping, monarchy
had come to an end in the Babylonian exile. Such an institution
was seen to be both good and evil. It therefore could be
explained in terms of divine action, but also in terms of
human aspirations and human disobedience. God both gives
kingship and presents criticism of it as an institution liable to
failure; such criticism is particularly associated with prophets,
from Samuel to Ezekiel. To the later community kingship
seemed a failure, for the kings were seen to be those who led
their people to disaster. But it was also known to be a source of
blessing; the king was God's chosen, the mediator of God's
blessing, his anointed, the 'lamp of Israel' (2 Sam. 21: 17). So
Israel came to think of the future in terms of an anointed one,
a Messiah, a chosen ruler of the Davidic line, but truly obedient
to God as even David himself had not always been. Such a
confidence is expressed in later writings; we find it reflected in
the New Testament. It is expressed in the idealization of David.

Kingship for Israel was an institution rich in theological

93

meaning. The kingship of God (see here 8: 7 and such psalms as 47, 96–8), his rule over Israel and over all nations, was an idea of great significance in the development of Old Testament thought. What God does in establishing his rule and his justice is seen to be expressed in human terms in the activity of the king; the true king upholds justice and right, and is a source of blessing to his people (see Isa. 11: 1–9 and Ps. 72 for pictures of the ideal king). ✶

SAMUEL'S FAREWELL

12 Then Samuel thus addressed the assembled Israelites: 'I have listened to your request and installed a king to rule

2 over you. And the king is now your leader, while I am old and white-haired and my sons are with you; but I have

3 been your leader ever since I was a child. Here I am. Lay your complaints against me in the presence of the LORD and of his anointed king. Whose ox have I taken, whose ass have I taken? Whom have I wronged, whom have I oppressed? From whom have I taken a bribe, to turn a

4 blind eye? Tell me, and I will make restitution.' They answered, 'You have not wronged us, you have not oppressed us; you have not taken anything from any

5 man.' Samuel then said to them, 'This day the LORD is witness among you, his anointed king is witness, that you have found my hands empty.' They said, 'He is witness.'

6 Samuel said to the people, 'Yes, the LORD is witness,*a* the LORD who gave you Moses and Aaron and brought your

7 fathers out of Egypt. Now stand up, and here in the presence of the LORD I will put the case against you and recite*b* all the victories which he has won for you and for

[a] is witness: *so Sept.; Heb. om.* [b] and recite: *so Sept.; Heb. om.*

your fathers. After Jacob and his sons[a] had come down to 8
Egypt and the Egyptians had made them suffer,[b] your
fathers cried to the LORD for help, and he sent Moses and
Aaron, who brought them out of Egypt and settled them
in this place. But they forgot the LORD their God, and he 9
abandoned them to Sisera, commander-in-chief of Jabin
king of[c] Hazor, to the Philistines, and to the king of
Moab, and they had to fight against them. Then your 10
fathers cried to the LORD for help: "We have sinned, we
have forsaken the LORD and we have worshipped the
Baalim and the Ashtaroth. But now, if thou wilt deliver
us from our enemies, we will worship thee." So the LORD 11
sent Jerubbaal and Barak,[d] Jephthah and Samson,[e] and
delivered you from your enemies on every side; and you
lived in peace and quiet.

'Then, when you saw Nahash king of the Ammonites 12
coming against you, although the LORD your God was
your king, you said to me, "No, let us have a king to rule
over us." Now, here is the king you asked for; you chose 13
him, and the LORD has set a king over you. If you will 14
revere the LORD and give true and loyal service, if you do
not rebel against his commands, and if you and the king
who reigns over you are faithful to the LORD your God,
well and good; but if you do not obey the LORD, and if 15
you rebel against his commands, then he will set his face
against you and against your king.[f]

'Stand still, and see the great wonder which the LORD 16

[a] and his sons: *so Sept.; Heb. om.*
[b] and the Egyptians...suffer: *so Sept.; Heb. om.*
[c] Jabin king of: *so Sept.; Heb. om.*
[d] *So Sept.; Heb.* Bedan.   [e] *So Luc. Sept.; Heb.* Samuel.
[f] *So Sept.; Heb.* your fathers.

17 will do before your eyes. It is now wheat harvest; when I
call upon the LORD and he sends thunder and rain, you
will see and know how wicked it was in the LORD's eyes
18 for you to ask for a king.' So Samuel called upon the
LORD and he sent thunder and rain that day; and all the
19 people were in great fear of the LORD and of Samuel. They
said to Samuel, 'Pray for us your servants to the LORD
your God, to save us from death; for we have added to all
our other sins the great wickedness of asking for a king.'
20 Samuel said to the people, 'Do not be afraid; although you
have been so wicked, do not give up the worship of the
21 LORD, but serve him with all your heart. Give up[a] the
worship of false gods which can neither help nor save,
22 because they are false. For his name's sake the LORD will
not cast you off, because he has resolved to make you his
23 own people. As for me, God forbid that I should sin
against the LORD and cease to pray for you. I will show
24 you what is right and good: to revere the LORD and
worship him faithfully with all your heart. Consider what
25 great things he has done for you; but if you persist in
wickedness, you shall be swept away, you and your king.'

* Although Samuel appears again in the narratives that
follow, this chapter really contains both a summing up of
Israel's fortunes to his day and a reflection on the meaning of
her history. It is a sort of last will and testament, containing
comment on the past and warning and exhortation for the
future. Formal speeches, of which this chapter provides a good
example, punctuate the story as it is told in the books from
Joshua to 2 Kings. The period of the judges begins with one
(Judg. 2: 6–3: 6); here that period in effect comes to an end.

[a] Give up: *so Targ.; Heb. obscure.*

1. The installation of the king provides a moment for pause and reflection. What does the new office mean? What is Israel to learn from it and from its subsequent history?

2. *your leader*: literally, 'walking in front of you', perhaps a military metaphor, but more probably one linked to the idea of the king as shepherd of his people. For this picture applied to Joshua, see Num. 27: 17. Kings in the ancient world were often described as 'shepherds'. An inscription praising the Assyrian king Adad-nirari (about 800 B.C.) runs: 'He whose shepherding they made (to be) as good for the people of Assyria as (is) the plant of life and whose throne they founded securely.' Ezekiel condemns Israel's rulers as bad shepherds, and promises a New David, a true shepherd (so Ezek. 34, and especially verse 23). The shepherd metaphor is used of Jesus in the New Testament (see John 10: 1 ff.). *and my sons are with you*: the theme mentioned in 8: 1–5, though no adverse comment is here made on the sons. Samuel is depicted in extreme old age, looking back over the experiences of a lifetime. His death is noted only in 25: 1. This passage sees the whole complex Samuel tradition as one; from his dedication and call, Samuel has been the true, divinely designated leader.

3. As if standing in a law-court, and with the use of legal language, Samuel invites the laying of charges of injustice. Specific examples illustrate the absolute standard of right; no theft, no oppression, no bribery can be imputed to the true judge of Israel. This is done *in the presence of the LORD and of his anointed king*. The declaration of Samuel's probity of character stands before God and his earthly representative as a perpetual witness. The whole statement may be compared with the so-called 'memorial of Nehemiah' (the main part of the book of Nehemiah) in which Nehemiah's faithfulness is set before God as a 'memorial', a continual reminder: 'Remember for my good, O God, all that I have done for this people' (Neh. 5: 19). *to turn a blind eye*: Sept. has a 'bribe or sandal(s)', probably an allusion to a legal device for evading proper responsibility. So Amos 2: 6 and 8: 6 speak of judicial

corruption with a reference to 'a pair of shoes'. Ruth 4: 7 and Deut. 25: 9 both refer to a sandal in connection with legal actions, though the precise nature of the customs involved is obscure. Comparable customs are known from Mesopotamia.

4 f. affirms the innocence of Samuel, solemnly ratified by the people. By these verses, the memory of Samuel is kept clear for all time.

6. *witness:* the wording of verse 5 is picked up and provides a starting-point for a sermon on the meaning of the people's experience of God and their disobedience. He is *witness* as the great deliverer of his people.

7. The people *stand up* to hear the indictment spoken against them; so the people stood to hear Ezra read and expound the law, the story of God's dealings with them (Neh. 8: 5). *put the case against you:* again, in the sermon, legal terms are used.

8–11 provides a short summary of historic experience. It begins as such presentations usually do (cp. 8: 8) with slavery in Egypt and deliverance by Moses and Aaron. Settlement in Canaan was followed by disobedience, and the preacher refers to examples of the oppressors described in the book of Judges. A similar summary appears there in Judg. 10: 10–16. *Sisera* appears in Judg. 4–5; *the Philistines* in Judg. 13–16 (and also briefly in 3: 31); the *king of Moab* in Judg. 3: 12–30. Israel's repentance and appeal are also summarized. For *Baalim* and *Ashtaroth* see notes on 7: 3 f. The deliverers are also listed: *Jerubbaal* (Gideon) appears in Judg. 6–8; *Barak* in Judg. 4–5; *Jephthah,* who delivered from the Ammonites, in Judg. 10: 17–12: 7; *Samson* in Judg. 13–16. The name *Barak* is not in the Hebrew text; this has a muddled form 'Bedan', which could possibly contain a relic of 'Gideon', added after *Jerubbaal* to explain that this hero had two names. More interesting is the name *Samson,* for which the Hebrew text has 'Samuel'. It is easy to see why *Samson* was substituted, for it would be odd for Samuel to refer to himself; but the Hebrew is likely to be correct and the sermon here alludes to Samuel's victory over *the Philistines* described in chapter 7. This shows that here we have a later sermon, put into the mouth of Samuel and used by the compiler to illustrate his point.

12. Now the sermon is brought to the point with a reference to *Nahash*. But we observe that the use made of the Nahash story is different from that which we find in chapter 11. Here it has been understood as interwoven with the theme of chapter 8 and of 10: 17–25, so as to suggest that it was the Ammonite threat which brought about Israel's demand for a king. We see here a writer who unifies the various elements of the tradition in a different manner.

13. *asked for:* Saul's name is not mentioned, but there is here the same word-play as in 1: 20. *you asked for; you chose:* Hebrew style is often repetitive, particularly in the rhythmic prose which appears in sermon-like passages such as this and such as are common in Deuteronomy. But the wording here is awkward and it is more probable that the text has preserved two alternatives side by side; such a procedure can often be suspected. The theme here again is of the king, *asked for* in lack of faith, but granted by God.

14. *king who reigns over you:* people and king are to be faithful. Judgement will fall on both in case of rebellion (verse 15).

15. *against your king:* N.E.B. footnote indicates that there are alternatives here. Possibly the texts we have are shortened forms of a longer: 'against you and against your king to destroy you like your fathers'.

These verses, 13–15, really provide a summary of Israel's life under the monarchy.

16. *Stand still:* almost exactly as in Exod. 14: 13 at the crossing of the Sea: 'Have no fear; ...stand firm and see the deliverance that the LORD will bring you this day.' The theme of not fearing appears here in verse 20: 'Do not be afraid'. What God has done at the exodus is what he does for each generation when men have faith and wait upon his wonderful acts.

17. *thunder and rain* in late May, the time of the *wheat harvest*, is a wonder which reveals God's power. So the people will again learn faith. If God's saving power is so great, then to ask for a king shows lack of trust. For this wonder, cp. also 7: 10, where thunder as God's voice brings panic to the Philistines.

18. God's action now brings fear, almost panic, to Israel, and leads to a renewed confession of failure by the people (verse 19). It is clear that the sense of the presence of God in judgement is an experience that brings awe; so Isaiah shrinks from the presence of the holy God, the judge (Isa. 6: 5).

20. Awe at God's presence is right, but not a fear that prevents right action. God saves and forgives, but a right relationship is only possible with him if he is accepted as sole lord. This is what the Old Testament means when it speaks of God as 'jealous' (so, e.g., Exod. 20: 5). Total allegiance is one of the basic themes of the covenant relationship between God and Israel. The commandments in Exod. 20 and Deut. 5 place side by side the statement of God's deliverance of his people from Egypt and the absolute: 'You shall have no other god to set against me.'

21. *false gods:* they are without power, a theme often emphasized in the psalms (e.g. 115: 4–7) and in the unnamed prophet of the exile (often called 'the Second Isaiah', e.g. Isa. 41: 29—'mere nothings'). The word here translated *false* is used to describe the earth in its state of chaos in Gen. 1: 2.

22. *For his name's sake:* because God is God, he will not reject Israel. This is a theme common in Deuteronomy, and especially developed by Ezekiel. Israel in exile could not claim deliverance for any merits of her own; she could only put her faith in God, who will save because it is his nature to do so. This in Ezekiel is linked with God's honour; if the nations see Israel rejected, they may be so misguided as to suppose that God is impotent. He will act lest such a disastrous misunderstanding occur; then both Israel and the nations will

know that he really is God (cp. Ezek. 36: 22–32 for a full exposition of this).

23. Samuel's function as intercessor is again emphasized (cp. verse 19 and also 7: 8f.); to fail to intercede would be a sin against God. This shows why it was a matter of such distress to Jeremiah to be forbidden by God to perform this normally essential function of a prophet (e.g. Jer. 14: 11).

24f. *swept away:* perhaps an allusion to the exile of 587 B.C. The sermon ends in exhortation to faithfulness and warning of the consequences of evil. Such alternating of promise and warning is found in the great sermons of Deuteronomy (e.g. chapters 28 and 30); blessing and curse accompany the establishing or re-establishing of the covenant relationship.

The whole chapter looks back to the time of Samuel and offers an interpretation of the whole section in chapters 1–11. The various elements are drawn together; warning and promise are given. The re-enactment of the covenant relationship is urged. When the final form of the work was read, it was a time of exile; the disasters had now come on king and people. The rightness of divine judgement was now plain for all to see. But alongside judgement the promise stood and the future was open. The position of Samuel, to whom the statement of these truths is credited, stands assured; he was the great prophet who could see at the beginning of the monarchy both its strength and its weakness. The weakness is immediately made plain in the narrative that follows.   *

THE CHOSEN KING REJECTED

Saul was fifty years[a] old when he became king, and he **13** reigned over Israel for twenty-two[b] years. He picked **2** three thousand men from Israel, two thousand to be with him in Michmash and the hill-country of Bethel and a

[a] fifty years: *prob. rdg.; Heb.* a year.   [b] *Prob. rdg.; Heb.* two.

thousand to be with Jonathan in Gibeah[a] of Benjamin; and he sent the rest of the people home.

3 Jonathan killed the Philistine governor[b] in Geba, and the news spread among the Philistines that the Hebrews were in revolt.[c] Saul sounded the trumpet all through the land;

4 and when the Israelites all heard that Saul had killed a Philistine governor and that the name of Israel stank among the Philistines, they answered the call to arms and

5 came to join Saul at Gilgal.[d] The Philistines mustered to attack Israel; they had thirty thousand chariots and six thousand horse, with infantry as countless as sand on the sea-shore. They went up and camped at Michmash, to the

6 east of Beth-aven. The Israelites found themselves in sore straits, for the army was hard pressed, so they hid themselves in caves and holes and among the rocks, in pits and

7 cisterns. Some of them crossed the Jordan into the district of Gad and Gilead, but Saul remained at Gilgal, and all the

8 people at his back were in alarm.[e] He waited seven days for his meeting with Samuel, but Samuel did not come to

9 Gilgal; so the people began to drift away from Saul. He said therefore, 'Bring me the whole-offering and the shared-offerings', and he offered up the whole-offering.

10 Saul had just finished the sacrifice, when Samuel arrived,

11 and he went out to greet him. Samuel said, 'What have you done?', and Saul answered, 'I saw that the people were drifting away from me, and you yourself had not come as

[a] Geba *in verse 3.*   [b] *Or* garrison.
[c] that...revolt: *prob. rdg.; Heb. has* saying, Let the Hebrews hear *after* through the land.
[d] they answered...Gilgal: *or* they were summoned to follow Saul to Gilgal.
[e] but Saul...in alarm: *or* but Saul was still at Gilgal, and all the army joined him there.

you had promised, and the Philistines were assembling at
Michmash; and I thought, "The Philistines will now 12
move against me at Gilgal, and I have not placated the
LORD"; so I felt compelled to make the whole-offering
myself.' Samuel said to Saul, 'You have behaved foolishly. 13
You have not kept the command laid on you by the LORD
your God; if you had, he would have established your
dynasty over Israel for all time. But now your line will 14
not endure; the LORD will seek a man after his own heart,
and will appoint him prince over his people, because you
have not kept the LORD's command.'

Samuel left Gilgal without more ado and went on his 15
way. The rest of the people followed Saul, as he moved
from Gilgal towards the enemy.*a* At Gibeah of Benjamin
he mustered the people who were with him; they were
about six hundred men. Saul and his son Jonathan and the 16
men they had with them took up their quarters in Gibeah*b*
of Benjamin, while the Philistines were encamped in
Michmash. Raiding parties went out from the Philistine 17
camp in three directions. One party turned towards
Ophrah in the district of Shual, another towards Beth- 18
horon, and the third towards the range of hills overlooking
the valley of Zeboim and the wilderness beyond.

✻ The establishment of Saul is immediately followed by a
story indicating his rejection; the compiler is paving the way
for David, the founder of the great dynasty which was to last
until 587 B.C. Underlying this story and those that follow, we
may detect traditions of the heroic exploits of Saul and
Jonathan, now written up to show that it was not to be in them
that Israel's full nationhood would be built.

[a] and went on...enemy: *prob. rdg., cp. Sept.; Heb. om.*
[b] *So Targ.; Heb.* Geba.

1. The books of Kings introduce each reign with much fuller statements about age and length of rule. The brief summary for Saul is more like those for the so-called 'minor' judges (Judg. 10: 1–5; 12: 8–15); 'minor' because no full story is given of their achievements, such as are told of the 'major' judges like Gideon. The verse lacks a note of Saul's age. The best Sept. manuscripts omit the whole verse; some others have 'thirty years old', which makes the responsible position of Jonathan in verse 2 difficult, though perhaps there was originally no connection between this summary and the statements of that verse regarding the conflict with the Philistines. *fifty years old* is based on two considerations: that Saul had a grandson before his death (2 Sam. 4: 4), and that the text may contain a misunderstood abbreviation for the numeral. The length of reign is also uncertain. *twenty-two* is an easy correction of the Hebrew 'two', but Acts 13: 21 and Josephus give Saul a forty-year reign (*Antiquities*, VI. 14. 9 has eighteen years before Samuel's death and twenty-two after, though X. 8. 4 has only twenty years altogether). This looks like an assimilation to the pattern found in Judges and in 4: 18 for Eli; it places Saul among the 'judges'.

2. A contrast is drawn between the whole of Israel assembled for war, or for the election of Saul, and the establishment of a standing army of 3,000. The statement that Saul was at *Michmash* does not easily fit with the subsequent Philistine encampment there (verse 5). Perhaps we should regard verse 2 as a separate fragment concerned with Saul's military organization (see also 14: 52).

3. Jonathan's exploit here is similar to that related in detail in 13: 23–14: 23. It appears that the compiler, introducing a story to show Saul's rejection, has made use of a familiar element in the Jonathan tradition; the result is a certain repetitiveness. We note here the confusion of the names *Gibeah* (verse 2) and *Geba* (as also in chapter 14), a confusion which makes the precise detail of the narratives difficult to follow (see map, p. 48).

The text in this verse is somewhat out of order, but N.E.B. offers the most probable rearrangement and emendation. *Hebrews* here, as in 4: 6, is used to describe Israel as viewed by her enemies. The sounding of *the trumpet* marks the summons to arms to all Israel, which again suggests the presence of different elements in these verses.

4. *the name of Israel stank*: an odd phrase, occurring in almost identical form in 2 Sam. 10: 6 where an Ammonite insult to David brings retribution. It appears that the murder of the *Philistine governor* (or the wiping out of the garrison, as in chapter 14) is pictured as an insult which provokes revenge. *the call to arms*: the word used regularly suggests the actual summons to battle (cp. N.E.B. footnote); it means 'to be called out'. The people assemble at Gilgal, the holy place (see map, p. 48).

5. The size of the Philistine force is certainly exaggerated; but such exaggeration serves to emphasize that Saul should have had absolute faith in God and not have acted presumptuously (see verses 7–11). *Michmash*: see note on verse 2 and map, p. 48. The Philistines had evidently pressed far into Saul's Benjamite territory. *Beth-aven*, 'house of iniquity'. In some passages in Hosea, it appears to be a derogatory name for Beth-el ('house of El', see map, p. 48); in 1 and 2 Kings Bethel is especially associated with the worship of the northern kingdom, regarded by the Judaean compilers as apostate (see 1 Kings 12: 26 ff.).

6f. The picture of these verses is of a people hard pressed by their enemies, taking refuge in the remote places or crossing the Jordan to safety. Similar escape was sought in the time of Gideon (Judg. 6: 1 ff.) and at Jerusalem's fall in 587 B.C. (Jer. 40: 11 f.).

7. N.E.B. footnote is based on a different understanding of the word rendered *were in alarm*.

8. *his meeting with Samuel*: this should perhaps be rendered 'the meeting which Samuel had arranged'. It links with 10: 8, but, as we have seen, that verse is clearly an addition designed

to anticipate the story of Saul's rejection which is given here.

Saul appears in a tragic light. He is faced with an urgent situation. The army is drifting away in fear; Samuel does not come at the appointed time. So Saul acts as seems best, but his action shows a lack of faith, and this reveals his unfitness to be king. We may compare Ahaz' lack of faith in a political emergency and Isaiah's judgement of him (Isa. 7: 1–17). The true king must be one who is not deceived by external events into distrust of the God whose anointed he is.

10. At the very moment that the sacrifice was completed, *Samuel arrived*; the story dramatically presents the inevitable judgement.

11 f. Saul's excuses (cp. the similar excuse in 15: 15) appear to spring from a pious concern. How could he face the enemy if the proper offerings had not been made and the favour of God sought for the enterprise? So too Ahaz refused to act, not wishing to impose upon God (Isa. 7: 12). But obedience and faith are what God demands.

13 f. Obedience would have saved Saul's *dynasty*. Now his *line will not endure*; Jonathan, the natural successor, the hero of chapter 14 and no doubt of other stories (cp. 2 Sam. 1: 23 in David's lament at his death), will not succeed his father. God will choose the line of David, not named here but known to the reader to be the one which will endure. Again the writer points forward to what is to come. Obedience is equally laid upon the Davidic line and equally becomes the touchstone of that dynasty's enduring life.

15. Here again the Hebrew text lacks a long phrase, omitted because the copyist's eye passed from one occurrence of the name *Gilgal* to another. With this verse, the story of the conflict with the Philistines is resumed, and in verses 16–18 further indications are given of the Philistine pressure on Israel. After the judgement pronounced by Samuel, there would seem to be little prospect of success. But the story evidently continues in chapter 14, and so we see that we are dealing with a

different tradition; here Saul and Jonathan are heroic warriors, victorious with only *six hundred* (cp. Gideon's three hundred, Judg. 7) against a vast enemy. It is clear that the condemnation of Saul has been superimposed on a story which told of his heroism. This double estimate of Saul shows how ancient traditions favourable to him have been preserved but reshaped.

18. The places named suggest raids to north, west and probably east (i.e. towards *the wilderness*), though the identity of *the valley of Zeboim* is not clear (see map, p. 48).

The indication in this passage of a conflict between Saul and Samuel may well reflect both earlier and later ideas. The new institution of monarchy might be expected to be unwelcome to the upholders of older ways; Samuel perhaps in some parts of the tradition represents the older, conservative views. In later times, the right to offer sacrifice was denied to the ruler; king Uzziah (Azariah) was condemned for entry into the temple to burn incense (2 Chron. 26: 16–21). Saul's action would be viewed as impious, though at an early time it would not have been so regarded. There is here a complex interweaving of earlier and later ideas. ✳

PHILISTINE SUPREMACY

No blacksmith was to be found in the whole of Israel, for 19 the Philistines were determined to prevent the Hebrews from making swords and spears. The Israelites had to go 20 down to the Philistines for their ploughshares, mattocks, axes, and sickles*[a]* to be sharpened. The charge was two- 21 thirds of a shekel for ploughshares and mattocks, and one-third of a shekel for sharpening the axes and setting the goads.*[b]* So when war broke out none of the followers of 22 Saul and Jonathan had either sword or spear; only Saul and Jonathan carried arms.

[a] and sickles: *so Sept.; Heb.* and ploughshares.
[b] one-third...the goads: *prob. rdg.; Heb. obscure.*

❋ A short piece of archaeological information, probably indicating that at this time the Philistines had a monopoly of iron and iron-working, though iron is not specifically mentioned here. The transition from bronze implements to iron did not take place all at once, but iron tools became more frequent in the levels belonging to this period which are exposed in archaeological excavations. There is some evidence to suggest that iron-working came from Asia Minor; the Philistines may have gained control of it, or have brought it with them when they settled.

21. *two thirds of a shekel:* 'a pim' or 'payim' (a dual form), a word of which the meaning was quite unknown until weights inscribed with the word were discovered. From their size, the value could be assessed at about ⅔ shekel (about 8 gm). These weights are of stone or of bronze and vary in shape. One discovered in Jerusalem has the word 'pim' on one side and on the other 'belonging to Zechariah, son of Jair'. ❋

JONATHAN'S HEROIC EXPLOIT

23 Now the Philistines had posted a force to hold the pass of
14 Michmash; and one day Saul's son Jonathan said to his armour-bearer, 'Come, let us go over to the Philistine
2 post beyond that ridge'; but he did not tell his father. Saul, at the time, had his tent under the pomegranate-tree at Migron on the outskirts of Gibeah; and he had about six
3 hundred men with him. The ephod was carried by Ahijah son of Ahitub, Ichabod's brother, son of Phinehas son of Eli, the priest of the LORD at Shiloh. Nobody knew that
4 Jonathan had gone. On either side of the pass through which Jonathan tried to make his way over to the Philistine post stood two sharp columns of rock, called Bozez*a* and
5 Seneh;*b* one of them was on the north towards Michmash,

[a] *That is* Shining.   [b] *That is* Bramble-bush.

and the other on the south towards Geba. Jonathan said to 6
his armour-bearer, 'Now we will visit the post of those
uncircumcised rascals. Perhaps the LORD will take a hand
in it, and if he will, nothing can stop him. He can bring us
safe through, whether we are few or many.' The young 7
man answered, 'Do what you will, go forward; I am
with you whatever you do.' 'Good!' said Jonathan, 'we 8
will cross over and let them see us. If they say, "Stay 9
where you are till we come to you", then we will stay
where we are and not go up to them. But if they say, 10
"Come up to us", we will go up; this will be the sign that
the LORD has put them into our power.' So they showed 11
themselves to the Philistines, and the Philistines said,
'Look! Hebrews coming out of the holes where they have
been hiding!' And they called across to Jonathan and the 12
young man, 'Come up to us; we have something to show
you.' Jonathan said to the young man, 'Come on, the
LORD has put them into the power of Israel.' Jonathan 13
climbed up on hands and feet, and the young man followed
him. The Philistines fell in front of Jonathan, and the
young man, coming behind him, dispatched them. In that 14
first attack Jonathan and his armour-bearer killed about
twenty of them, like men cutting[a] a furrow across a half-
acre field. Terror spread through the army in the field and 15
through the whole people; the men at the post and the
raiding parties were terrified; the very earth quaked, and
there was panic.

* 23. The geographical setting is brought out by this
statement and those of 14: 4f., though the confusion of Geba

[a] like men cutting: *so Pesh.; Heb.* as in half of.

and Gibeah again leaves uncertainty. A small outpost is stationed to give warning of attack and to defend *the pass* into the valley occupied by the main Philistine force.

14: 1. *beyond that ridge:* the text is not quite clear. Perhaps we should read the almost identical word for 'pass', i.e. 'beyond' or 'in the pass'. Jonathan's absence passed unnoticed until later (verse 17).

2. Meanwhile Saul's tiny force of 600 is at Gibeah, the centre of command being *under the pomegranate-tree at Migron*. Trees of various kinds, no doubt local landmarks, are often mentioned in connection with leaders (cp. note on 10: 3). *Migron* is mentioned in Isa. 10: 28, but north of Michmash and therefore wrongly situated for this story. Perhaps the name is an error for the 'threshing-floor' which would be outside the town and convenient as an assembly point.

3. The Shiloh priestly line is shown to be still active; we may note that this story has no place for Samuel. The *ephod* appears as the sacred object associated with priestly status (cf. on 2: 28). *Ahijah* is great-grandson of Eli, *son of Ahitub, Ichabod's brother*; the latter's name commemorates the loss of the Ark (4: 21 f.). *Ahijah* is possibly to be identified with Ahimelech (see 21: 1, 9 ff.), since the divine title 'melech', king, could be an alternative to the divine name 'jah', Yahweh (Ahijah= 'Yahweh is brother'; Ahimelech= 'melech (God as king) is brother'). The family history is not easy to follow, and the chronology also is by no means simple. How many years have elapsed since chapter 4? The reference to the priestly family here points forward to verse 18 and the narrative of verses 36–46.

4 f. The precise topographical data are interesting, but the reason for their mention is not clear. Probably we should see this as a comment designed to point out to the reader that the site of the exploit is well known and can still be identified. The two *columns of rock, Bozez* and *Seneh*, have names which may have had stories attached to them in addition to this one, but their names 'Shining' (or 'Slippery') and 'Bramble-bush' (so N.E.B. footnotes) are not given any precise application here.

Seneh is a variant spelling of the word used for the burning bush in Exod. 3: 2; since we are about to have a remarkable example of divine action, we might suppose that the name (and *Bozez* too?) was thought to suggest this, but the point is not made explicit.

6. *uncircumcised rascals:* no word for *rascals* appears in the text, but clearly the expression is intended to be scornful. Circumcision was known to other peoples besides the Israelites, but for them it became a special mark of their membership of the people of God (cp. Gen. 17 for one explanation of the origin and meaning of the practice). The Philistines who did not practise it are here a particular object of derision (cp. David's lament in 2 Sam. 1: 20). Mockery of one's enemies is a way of expressing confidence of victory; the prophets often use such a style in judgement both of Israel and of other nations. So Isaiah mocks the Assyrian conqueror (Isa. 37: 22–9 = 2 Kings 19: 21–8).

Jonathan expresses the confidence that victory belongs to God; if he undertakes the exploit through him, success is assured. *nothing can stop him. He can bring us safe through...*: could be rendered 'nothing can stop him from gaining the victory, whether by few or many'. Compare David's words to the Philistine giant in 17: 45 ff.

9f. The *sign* that God has chosen to act is set out by Jonathan; the words which God will put into the enemy's mouth will show his intention. By such a sign Abraham's servant found a wife for Isaac (Gen. 24: 12 ff.).

11. The Philistine response is also a mocking saying (see on verse 6).

12. The Philistine words are confident, but ironically they offer the assurance that Jonathan needs. Victory is now certain.

13. It is idle to ask how two men climbing up on hands and feet could overcome so large an opposing company. The essence of the story—brought out further in verse 15—is that God himself went into the attack and so the enemy was panic-stricken. *The Philistines fell* as they suddenly recognized

a supernatural power before them. This is comparable to the dismay felt at the arrival of the Ark (4: 7f.), and we may also compare the dismay and collapse of Jesus' opponents, vividly portrayed in John 18: 6: 'When he said, "I am he", they drew back and fell to the ground.' The words, 'I am he', commonly used by the Second Isaiah of God (e.g. 43: 25), express the real presence of God himself. The biblical narratives often make a theological statement by describing events in terms of direct intervention by God.

14. The vivid picture here continues the clearly supernatural victory. It is as if the remaining soldiers in the post just stood impotently by as Jonathan and his armour-bearer cut a line straight through.

15. The consequence of such *panic* in the outpost is universal terror; the contagion of fear spread, and even *the...earth quaked*. God himself has come to the conquest of his enemies, as so often in earthquake and storm (cp. also 4: 5 and 7: 10). *panic:* literally 'divine terror', a phrase which draws out the point that it is at the very presence of God that his enemies are terrified.

What has been said earlier about the overthrow of Israel's enemies needs to be borne in mind here (see on 7: 9f.). The writer of the story is much more interested in the supremacy of God and his power to deliver than in the detail. To him a victory over the uncircumcised Philistines is a victory for God. ✳

THE BATTLE SCENE

16 Saul's men on the watch in Gibeah of Benjamin saw the
17 mob of Philistines surging to and fro[a] in confusion; so he ordered the people to call the roll and find out who was missing; and they called the roll and found that Jonathan
18 and his armour-bearer were absent. Saul said to Ahijah, 'Bring forward the ephod', for it was he who carried the

[a] to and fro: *so Sept.; Heb.* and he went thither.

ephod at that time before Israel.*a* But while Saul was still   19
speaking, the confusion in the Philistine camp was in-
creasing more and more, and he said to the priest, 'Hold
your hand.' Then Saul and all his men with shouting made   20
for the battlefield, where they found the enemy fighting
one another in complete disorder. The Hebrews who up   21
to now had been under the Philistines, and had been with
them in camp, changed sides*b* and joined the Israelites
under Saul and Jonathan. All the Israelites in hiding in the   22
hill-country of Ephraim heard that the Philistines were in
flight, and they also joined in and set off in hot pursuit.
The LORD delivered Israel that day, and the fighting   23
passed on beyond Beth-aven.

Now the Israelites on that day had been driven to   24
exhaustion. Saul had adjured the people in these words:
'A curse be on the man who eats any food before nightfall
until I have taken vengeance on my enemies.' So no one
ate any food. Now there was honeycomb*c* in the country-   25
side; but when his men came upon it, dripping with honey   26
though it was, not one of them put his hand to his mouth
for fear of the oath. But Jonathan had not heard his father   27
lay this solemn prohibition on the people, and he stretched
out the stick that was in his hand, dipped the end of it in
the honeycomb, put it to his mouth and was refreshed.
One of the people said to him, 'Your father solemnly   28
forbade this; he said, "A curse on the man who eats food
today!"' Now the men were faint with hunger. Jonathan   29

[a] 'Bring forward...Israel: *so Sept.; Heb.* 'Bring forward the Ark of
God', for the Ark of God was on that day and the sons of Israel.
[b] changed sides: *so Sept.; Heb.* round and also.
[c] Now...honeycomb: *prob. rdg.; Heb.* All the land went into the
forest, and there was honey.

said, 'My father has done the people nothing but harm;
30   see how I am refreshed by this mere taste of honey. How
much better if the people had eaten today whatever they
took from their enemies by way of spoil! Then there
would indeed have been a great slaughter of Philistines.'

* 16f. The watchmen see the unexplained panic, and Saul,
deducing that some one of his own people is involved, checks
on those who are with him. *call the roll:* perhaps too formal an
expression for a word which implies any appropriate form of
checking.

18. Now the preparatory statement of verse 3 is picked up.
Saul needs to consult God, through the *ephod*, to discover
what he should do. Evidently the *ephod* is here understood as
providing a holder for the sacred lot. In Exod. 28: 30 this
sacred lot, called 'Urim and Thummim' (two obscure terms;
see also verses 40f.), is put in the breast-piece fastened upon
the ephod worn by the high priest. The context here clearly
demands such a sense. The next verse reveals that a further
increase of panic among the Philistines makes the consultation
unnecessary; it is as if God thus shows his will by direct means.
The Hebrew text is quite evidently corrupt here (see N.E.B.
footnote for a translation of it), but its mention of the 'Ark of
God' raises a problem. Underlying the present corrupt text,
there may be a tradition conflicting with other elements in
1 Sam. and suggesting that the Ark was in Saul's hands at this
time. Or might we suppose that this symbol of God's presence
and power was not a unique object as was later believed? If
Saul called for the Ark, it would mean that he was about to
attack, as verse 20 indicates.

20. *with shouting:* the word could mean simply 'they were
mobilized for the attack', but a battle shout would, of course,
further increase the enemy's panic. Just as in Gideon's attack
on the Midianites (Judg. 7: 22), it is implied that God himself
causes the enemy to fight among themselves.

114

21 f. Evidently there were Hebrew mercenaries fighting for the Philistines (compare David's position in chapters 27 and 29); at such a moment they not surprisingly change sides, and the victory brings a new hope also to those who have taken refuge in the hills.

23. It is God's victory, not Israel's. For *Beth-aven* see note on 13: 5.

24. A new aspect of the battle appears here, and one which does not quite fit with the picture of success. Is it perhaps an element from another tradition of the Philistine wars? Saul's action is appropriate in an extreme situation; Israel, fighting a holy war, is to be sanctified for the service of God by fasting (cp. on 21: 5).

25 f. Some confusion has occurred in the text here, partly because the word meaning *honeycomb* is identical with a word meaning 'forest' or 'thicket'. What is being stressed is on the one hand the refreshing nature of the honey (cp. verse 29)— Canaan is often described as a 'land flowing with milk and honey'—and on the other hand the obedience of the people to the oath.

27. It is made clear that Jonathan's infringement of the oath is unwitting, but this is no excuse, as the sequel shows (verses 36 ff.).

29 f. To impose an oath on an army was a proper proceeding; that it went wrong in this instance is just one more indication of Saul's tragedy. Why should Jonathan criticize? Are his words perhaps designed to avert the evil consequences of the infringement? Or is the story-teller introducing another comment on Saul's unfitness to be king, this time in the words of his own son? ✳

THE DIRE CONSEQUENCES OF WRONG ACTION

They defeated the Philistines that day, and pursued them 31 from Michmash to Aijalon. But the people were so faint with hunger that they turned to plunder and seized sheep, 32

cattle, and bullocks; they slaughtered them on the bare
33 ground, and ate the meat with the blood in it. Someone
told Saul that the people were sinning against the LORD by
eating their meat with the blood in it. 'This is treason!'
34 cried Saul. 'Roll a great stone here at once.' He then said,
'Go about among the people and tell them to bring their
oxen and sheep, and let each man slaughter his here and
eat it; and so they will not sin against the LORD by eating
meat with the blood in it.' So as night fell each man came,
35 driving his own ox, and slaughtered it there. Thus Saul
came to build an altar to the LORD, and this was the first
altar to the LORD that Saul built.

36 Saul said, 'Let us go down and make a night attack on
the Philistines and harry them till daylight; we will not
spare a man of them.' The people answered, 'Do what you
think best', but the priest said, 'Let us first consult God.'
37 So Saul inquired of God, 'Shall I pursue the Philistines?
Wilt thou put them into Israel's power?'; but this time
38 he received no answer. So he said, 'Let all the leaders of the
people come forward and let us find out where the sin
39 lies this day. As the LORD lives, the deliverer of Israel, even
if it lies in my son Jonathan, he shall die.' Not a soul
40 answered him. Then he said to the Israelites, 'All of you
stand on one side, and I and my son Jonathan will stand
on the other.' The people answered, 'Do what you think
41 best.' Saul said to the LORD the God of Israel, 'Why hast
thou not answered thy servant today? If this guilt lie in
me or in my son Jonathan, O LORD God of Israel, let the
lot be Urim; if it lie in thy people Israel,[a] let it be
Thummim.' Jonathan and Saul were taken, and the people

[a] Why hast...thy people Israel: *so Sept.; Heb. om.*

were cleared. Then Saul said, 'Cast lots between me and 42
my son Jonathan'; and Jonathan was taken. Saul said to 43
Jonathan, 'Tell me what you have done.' Jonathan told
him, 'True, I did taste a little honey on the tip of my stick.
Here I am; I am ready to die.' Then Saul swore a great 44
oath that Jonathan should die. But the people said to Saul, 45
'Shall Jonathan die, Jonathan who has won this great
victory in Israel? God forbid! As the LORD lives, not a
hair of his head shall fall to the ground, for he has been at
work with God today.' So the people ransomed Jonathan
and he did not die. Saul broke off the pursuit of the 46
Philistines because they had made their way home.

* 31. The pursuit route must be traced west and south-west
from the battle area (see map, p. 48).

32. *blood* is the symbol of life, and its consumption was
strictly forbidden in Israel's law. The origin of the prohibition
is certainly very ancient; for a similar point see on 2: 17.

33f. Saul's piety is made clear. Such an infringement of the
divine law will bring disaster; it must be checked at once.
The *great stone*, like that in 6: 14, is to be an altar; the animals
must be properly killed and the blood poured out according to
the prescribed custom. One set of laws governing this is to be
found in Deut. 12: 15ff.

35. The conclusion to this section points to Saul's establishing of *an altar*, no doubt still pointed out as a landmark
associated with his name; presumably there were other altars
too which tradition linked with him. Such religious acts are
recorded as indications of a ruler's character; Saul is seen as a
good ruler, caring for the religious needs of his people.

This first element in the narrative could well be a quite
independent section, not originally connected with the battle.
Or it could offer an alternative explanation of the breach
between God and Israel indicated in the next verses and now

replaced by the Jonathan story. Again we see the compiler building the traditions together to suit his overall purpose.

36 brings us back to the war and to a proposed new surprise attack by night on the Philistines. It sounds like a different story. The people's ready response encounters priestly caution; no battle can be successful without divine sanction. But there is irony in this, for God will not answer.

37f. The lack of answer to a properly directed inquiry can only point to an infringement of a divine command. Sins 'raise a barrier between you and your God' (Isa. 59: 2). On another occasion (28: 6) we are told of the various mechanisms available for consultation —'dreams', 'Urim' (the lot, cp. verse 41), 'prophets'. The questions addressed are so couched as to be answerable with 'Yes' or 'No' (cp. the similar questions in 23:9ff.); this suggests the use of the lot by which such an answer could be obtained.

39 is again ironical, for Saul in mentioning Jonathan anticipates the conclusion of the story.

40f. show the method of consulting *Urim* and *Thummim* (see on verse 18).

43. When the lot indicates Jonathan, he recognizes that the taste of honey was an infringement which could not be overlooked; the smallness of the action does not alter its seriousness. The death penalty (so verse 39) is necessary, so that the offending member of the community is removed and the community itself purified and restored to right relationship. The story of Achan in Josh. 7 makes the same point: one man's sin brings disaster upon the whole people.

44. Saul, like his son, does not shrink from the rigour of the law, tragic though it would be for Jonathan—surely the successor to the throne—to die. The oath formula invokes disaster upon the one who swears if he fails to carry it out.

45. The people's appeal is based on the practical point that Jonathan's victory clearly indicates divine favour. There is thus a conflict of two principles: divine favour in victory, divine displeasure at infringement of a holy war ruling. How can

such a conflict be resolved? A similar conflict of principle in
2 Sam. 14: 4–11 is between the law of blood revenge and
preserving the name of a family. *the people ransomed Jonathan:*
we are not told how. Probably it was by some action, sacrificial or substitutionary, which enabled his release. Or did
someone else die in his place?

46. The outcome is still serious; the enemy has escaped.

In this chapter the central figure is Jonathan; as popular hero
of an exploit, he is acclaimed by the people. Yet over-
shadowing this is the tragic figure of Saul as he is now presented; so willing to do all that is right, but unable to avoid the
coming disaster. *

SAUL'S REIGN—A SUMMARY

When Saul had made his throne secure in Israel, he fought 47
against his enemies on every side, the Moabites, the
Ammonites, the Edomites, the king[a] of Zobah, and the
Philistines; and wherever he turned he was successful.[b] He 48
displayed his strength by defeating the Amalekites and
freeing Israel from hostile raids.

Saul's sons were: Jonathan, Ishyo[c] and Malchishua. 49
These were the names of his two daughters: Merab the
elder and Michal the younger. His wife was Ahinoam 50
daughter of Ahimaaz, and his commander-in-chief was
Abner son of his uncle Ner; Kish, Saul's father, and Ner, 51
Abner's father, were sons[d] of Abiel.

There was bitter warfare with the Philistines throughout 52
Saul's lifetime; any strong man and any brave man that he
found he took into his own service.

[a] *So Sept.; Heb.* kings.   [b] *Or* he found ample provision.
[c] *So Luc. Sept.; Heb.* Ishvi (Ishbosheth *in 2 Sam. 2: 8*; Eshbaal *in
1 Chron. 8: 33*).
[d] *Prob. rdg.; Heb.* son.

✻ Although Saul's reign does not end until the close of the book, this marks the clear point at which his downfall is sealed. Chapter 15 tells of his rejection (see also chapter 13), and this is followed by the appearance of David, his real successor. So it is logical to look at Saul's reign here and assess its value. The judgement is a remarkably positive one, another reminder that the story of this period could be viewed from various angles.

47. Saul's kingdom is described as secure and victorious over all enemies; similar statements are made about David in 2 Sam. 8. The extent of Saul's activities is not covered by the actual narratives now brought together in these chapters. For some of the peoples mentioned, see map, p. 13. *Zobah*: an Aramaean kingdom north of Damascus. On the Amalekites, see 15: 2. *he was successful*: 'victorious' is certainly the right sense here, but the Hebrew has a word meaning 'he acted wickedly', a word almost identical to that rendered 'victorious'. By a minute change, a copyist has suggested Saul's total failure. N.E.B. footnote: 'found ample provision' is an alternative rendering less appropriate to the context.

49. *Ishyo*: elsewhere named Eshbaal (1 Chron. 8: 33) and Ishbosheth (2 Sam. 2: 8). This last is not a real name, but is produced by putting the word for 'a shameful thing' (i.e. 'an alien god') in place of the title *ba'al* which means 'lord' or 'husband' and was used as a title for deities. It was used quite properly for Israel's God, but in time its association with Canaanite religion suggested its impropriety. Hos. 2: 16 reflects this change of view. The older forms of such names are preserved in the Chronicler. *Ishyo* is short for Ishyahu or Eshyahu; the name means either 'man of Yahweh (God)' or 'Yahweh exists'. Another son, Abinadab, appears in 31: 2; Saul's daughters appear in the David narrative in chapter 18.

50f. Other family and official details are given. *Abner* was subsequently to play an important part. *Ner* was perhaps the uncle mentioned in 10: 13; the family history is linked to 9: 1. David and Solomon are given much fuller lists of officials (2 Sam. 8: 16ff.; 1 Kings 4: 2ff.).

52. Saul's military policy is noted (see also 13: 2) in positive terms, contrasting with the negative view of 8: 11. The Philistine menace was the most serious, ultimately to bring about Saul's defeat and death (chapter 31). ✳

SAUL'S LAST CHANCE

Samuel said to Saul, 'The LORD sent me to anoint you king **15** over his people Israel. Now listen to the voice of the LORD. This is the very word of the LORD of Hosts: "I am resolved 2 to punish the Amalekites for what they did to Israel, how they attacked them on their way up from Egypt." Go 3 now and fall upon the Amalekites and destroy them, and put their property under ban. Spare no one; put them all to death, men and women, children and babes in arms, herds and flocks, camels and asses.' Thereupon Saul called 4 out the levy and mustered them in Telaim. There were two hundred thousand foot-soldiers and another ten thousand from Judah.*a* He came to the Amalekite city 5 and halted for a time in the gorge. Meanwhile he sent 6 word to the Kenites to leave the Amalekites and come down, 'or', he said, 'I shall destroy you as well as them; but you were friendly to Israel when they came up from Egypt.' So the Kenites left the Amalekites. Then Saul cut 7 the Amalekites to pieces, all the way from Havilah to Shur on the borders of Egypt. Agag the king of the Amalekites 8 he took alive, but he destroyed all the people, putting them to the sword. Saul and his army spared Agag and 9 the best of the sheep and cattle, the fat beasts and the lambs*b*

[a] *Prob. rdg.; Heb.* ten thousand with the men of Judah.
[b] the fat beasts and the lambs: *so Targ.; Heb. obscure.*

and everything worth keeping; they were unwilling to destroy them, but anything that was useless and of no value they destroyed.

✴ Saul's final rejection is presented in the story of a great battle against the Amalekites. The story is theological rather than historical, and probably belongs to a relatively late date. But it is presented as a last opportunity for Saul to justify his anointing as king by total obedience.

2. *Amalekites:* a people from ancient times, occupying areas to the south, between Judah and Egypt. A great defeat of Amalek by Israel is related in Exod. 17: 8 ff., culminating in a pronouncement of perpetual hostility. This is alluded to also in Deut. 25: 17–19, and it is on this passage that the present story appears to depend.

3. *put their property under ban:* this is part of the conception of war as a holy enterprise, directed not simply against the enemies of Israel but against the enemies of God. So Exod. 17: 16 states it: 'the LORD is at war with Amalek generation after generation'. For such an understanding of war, see note on 7: 9 f. It is to result in total destruction. The Moabite Stone, an inscribed pillar recording victories by Mesha king of Moab in the ninth century B.C., describes his taking of Nebo from Israel in identical terms: 'I took it and slew all: seven thousand men, boys, women, and (girls) and female slaves, for I had consecrated it to Ashtar-Chemosh.' To *put...under ban* means to consecrate to the deity by destruction. The horrifying detail in the narrative here reminds us that ruthless warfare was part of the life of the ancient world. But again, while not condoning an evil practice, we must understand why the story was told, and see its theological point in announcing the total repudiation of all that is opposed to God's will. The Amalekites are here symbols of the enemies of God.

4. *Telaim:* an unknown place, presumably in the south. The numbers suggest that the narrator sees this as a battle between

the enemy and all Israel, and not just *the levy* (literally 'the people').

5. Saul comes to the Amalekite capital, unnamed and unidentifiable. He appears to have laid an ambush in the gorge, for that is what the word rendered *halted* probably means.

6. *The Kenites* had close association with Israel. According to one tradition, Moses' father-in-law, Hobab, was a Kenite (cp. Judg. 1: 16). The story of the victory over Sisera shows Jael the Kenite as friendly to Israel (Judg. 5: 24). They are warned to desert their Amalekite associates and escape the massacre; as friends of God's people, and hence of God, they are to live. The concluding couplet of the Song of Deborah provides a fitting comment:

'So perish all thine enemies, O LORD;
 but let all who love thee be like the sun rising in strength'
                                                    (Judg. 5: 31).

7. The places named must be well to the south-west.

8f. *Saul and his army* disobey the divine command. *Agag the king* is taken prisoner; he too becomes a symbol of all that is opposed to God, for the book of Esther, belonging to a very late period, perhaps as late as the second century B.C., tells of the great enemy of the Jewish people then as Haman the Agagite (Esther 3: 1). The disobedience consists in destroying only the valueless spoil; since what is put to the ban is consecrated to God, this is tantamount to offering to him only the poorest sacrifice instead of what he commands. The statements pave the way for Samuel's denunciation of disobedience (verses 22 f.). ✶

THE REJECTION OF SAUL

Then the word of the LORD came to Samuel: 'I repent of 10, 11 having made Saul king, for he has turned his back on me and has not obeyed my commands.' Samuel was angry;

12 all night he cried aloud to the LORD. Early next morning
he went to meet Saul, but was told that he had gone to
Carmel; Saul had set up a monument for himself there,
13 and had turned and gone down to Gilgal. There Samuel
found him, and Saul greeted him with the words, 'The
LORD's blessing upon you! I have obeyed the LORD's
14 commands.' But Samuel said, 'What then is this bleating
of sheep in my ears? Why do I hear the lowing of cattle?'
15 Saul answered, 'The people have taken them from the
Amalekites. These are what they spared, the best of the
sheep and cattle, to sacrifice to the LORD your God. The
16 rest we completely destroyed.' Samuel said to Saul, 'Let
be, and I will tell you what the LORD said to me last night.'
17 'Tell me', said Saul. So Samuel went on, 'Time was when
you thought little of yourself, but now you are head of
the tribes of Israel, and the LORD has anointed you king
18 over Israel. The LORD sent you with strict instructions to
destroy that wicked nation, the Amalekites; you were to
19 fight against them until you had wiped them out. Why
then did you not obey the LORD? Why did you pounce
upon the spoil and do what was wrong in the eyes of the
20 LORD?' Saul answered Samuel, 'But I did obey the LORD;
I went where the LORD sent me, and I have brought back
Agag king of the Amalekites. The rest of them I destroyed.
21 Out of the spoil the people took sheep and oxen, the
choicest of the animals laid under ban, to sacrifice to the
22 LORD your God at Gilgal.' Samuel then said:

> Does the LORD desire offerings and sacrifices
>   as he desires obedience?
> Obedience is better than sacrifice,
>   and to listen to him than the fat of rams.

> Defiance of him is sinful as witchcraft,   23
>   yielding to men[a] as evil as[b] idolatry.[c]
> Because you have rejected the word of the LORD,
>   the LORD has rejected you as king.

* 11. Disobedience brings judgement. But to Samuel this is a
source of deep distress, and in anger he confronts God with an
appeal to him to relent. So Moses stood between God and his
people, willing to bear the whole weight of divine judgement
(Exod. 32: 30ff.), and Amos pleaded for the northern kingdom
(Amos 7: 2, 5). The prophet is often the intercessor.

12. The geographical setting is not clear, except that Gilgal,
the place of kingship (11: 14f.), is to be the place of rejection.
Carmel (cp. 25: 2) is clearly in the south (see map, p. 169) and
not to be confused with mount Carmel in the north-west.
a monument: we may suppose this to be a victory pillar, perhaps
inscribed with an account of the victory like the Moabite
Stone (see on verse 3), and presumably still to be seen in the
narrator's time and pointed out as 'Saul's monument'. No
such pillars have so far been discovered marking the victories
of Israel's rulers.

13. Does Saul already know what is to come? His greeting
of Samuel and his confident affirmation of obedience form a
striking contrast to the coming judgement. *The people have
taken them:* Saul is not shifting the responsibility, for he is king
and leader of his people.

15. Saul's reply is devious, for he must know that to
destroy the poorest alone and keep the best, even to offer a
sacrifice, is a denial of the command (see on verses 8f.).

16–19. Samuel gives no direct reply, but recounts first the
exaltation of Saul from his original humble station (see 9: 21)
to be *head of the tribes of Israel, king over Israel.* Now Saul has
failed in the test.

[a] yielding to men: *or* arrogance *or* obstinacy.
[b] as evil as: *prob. rdg.; Heb.* evil and...
[c] *Or* household gods; *Heb.* teraphim.

20f. Saul's argument is specious. The command was to destroy, not to offer sacrifice.

22f. It is from this grim story of destruction and the ban that the important principle is drawn out: obedience to the command of God is the primary duty; sacrifices, religious observances, do not stand first. The point is one that appears in the words of the great prophets, as, for example, in Hos. 6: 6:

'loyalty is my desire, not sacrifice,
        not whole-offerings but the knowledge of God'
and the theme is picked up in the New Testament when we find Jesus approving the wisdom of a scribe who could thus expound the meaning of love to God and love to neighbour (Mark 12: 28-34). The use of this story as a vehicle for such teaching is an indication of how little interest there is in the actual happening and how much in the divine will. The misplaced religious zeal of the ban could become a thing of the past, repudiated by those who learnt better ways and better understanding of God's nature; but the principle of obedience remains. Samuel's pronouncement has poetic form, having something of prophetic and something of proverbial style. The first half of verse 23 states the case in extreme form; dis-obedience is as bad as *witchcraft*, such a rejection of God as was to be resorted to by Saul (28: 3 ff.); to fall in with human desires is as bad as *idolatry*. The precise meaning of this phrase is not clear; see N.E.B. footnote for alternative meanings. The word used for idolatry is *teraphim*, a term for household gods (see on 19: 13).

With an effective play upon words, the poetic saying ends in the rejection of Saul. ✳

THE KINGDOM LOST

24 Saul said to Samuel, 'I have sinned. I have ignored the LORD's command and your orders: I was afraid of the
25 people and deferred to them. But now forgive my sin,

I implore you, and come back with me, and I will make
my submission before the LORD.' Samuel answered, 'I will 26
not come back with you; you have rejected the word of
the LORD and therefore the LORD has rejected you as king
over Israel.' He turned to go, but Saul caught the edge of 27
his cloak and it tore. And Samuel said to him, 'The LORD 28
has torn the kingdom of Israel from your hand today and
will give it to another, a better man than you. God who is 29
the Splendour of Israel does not deceive or change his
mind; he is not a man that he should change his mind.'
Saul said, 'I have sinned; but honour me this once before 30
the elders of my people and before Israel and come back
with me, and I will make my submission to the LORD
your God.' So Samuel went back with Saul, and Saul 31
made his submission to the LORD. Then Samuel said, 32
'Bring Agag king of the Amalekites.' So Agag came to
him with faltering step*a* and said, 'Surely the bitterness of
death has passed.' Samuel said, 'Your sword has made 33
women childless, and your mother of all women shall be
childless too.' Then Samuel hewed Agag in pieces before
the LORD at Gilgal.

Saul went to his own home at Gibeah, and Samuel went 34
to Ramah; and he never saw Saul again to his dying day, 35
but he mourned for him, because the LORD had repented
of having made him king over Israel.

* 24.   Saul's acknowledgement of his error is combined with
the excuse that he *deferred to* the people. As anointed king, his
function was to lead and to make known God's will, not to
give way to pressure.

   [a] with faltering step: *prob. rdg., cp. Sept.; Heb.* delicately.

26. The impossibility of a further chance is expressed in a restatement of the twofold rejection theme of verse 23. Saul, by his rejection of *the word of the LORD*, has produced a situation in which his unfitness to be king is expressed in God's rejection of him.

There is here a theological problem which is not worked out. We may ask why forgiveness should not be possible, and the answer is no doubt in part to be found in the recognition that the story as now presented is offering an interpretation of what has already happened in the past. The kingship of Saul did come to nothing; his family did not endure whereas that of David did. We might give a political explanation of this. The writer of this narrative is, however, concerned only with the ways in which the relationship between God and man may be discerned. From his profound conviction that obedience is an absolute demand (so verse 22), he interprets what has taken place. This oversimplifies the problem; it is bound to suggest that success means divine blessing and failure divine judgement. Such a view underlies the discussions in the book of Job. But alongside this, there is in the Old Testament a deepening understanding that God is at work in all aspects of human experience. Even the disasters do not mean the absence of a divine purpose. This has already been clear in the story of the Ark in chapters 4–6. In the dark years of exile, and in persecution and suffering in the second century B.C., the community was to learn more fully to read the will of God in the bitterness of apparent failure.

27f. What looks like an accident is interpreted as the revealing of the divine will. But it is better to translate the text to mean that Samuel deliberately tore Saul's cloak; this makes the meaning of verse 28 clearer. The tearing of the cloak is a symbolic action, expressive of God's purpose. A similar symbol is described in 1 Kings 11: 29–32, and the narrative here may well depend upon that fuller story. Such symbolic actions, often described as carried out by the prophets, are really extensions of the divine word; in the action, as in the word, God declares and brings into operation what he has decreed. Ezekiel's portrayal of Jerusalem on a tile (Ezek. 4), as a sign of judgement, is a clear example of such actions performed and interpreted (see also on 11: 7). *a better man:* i.e. David, because he is obedient and because the promise of God is given to him.

29. *Splendour of Israel:* the word used is rare in this sense, but offers another way of speaking of 'glory' (cp. 4: 21f.). See also the list of attributes in 1 Chron. 29: 11: 'greatness, power, glory, splendour, majesty'. The underlying basis of Samuel's words is the unchanging purpose of God: *he is not a man that he should change his mind.* The same expression is used in the Balaam story in Num. 23: 19, where it emphasizes the divine promise. Again there is the awareness that it is difficult for men to understand the ways of God; they are consistent with his nature and purpose, but are sometimes described in the Old Testament as resulting in an apparent inconsistency. Thus verse 11 describes God as repenting of his choice of Saul, and in the visions of Amos, God is described as withdrawing his threat when the prophet appeals on behalf of Israel's weakness (Amos 7: 1–6).

30f. It seems probable that this passage is designed to meet the problem that though Saul is rejected, he is still king for the remainder of the narratives of this book. The judgement is not yet to take full effect.

32f. Samuel himself fulfils what Saul should have done in completion of the ban (see on verse 3 for this). *with faltering step:* a very obscure word. We might prefer an emendation giving the sense 'in fetters'. Agag's words are not easy to understand. It is probable that they represent an acceptance of inevitable death; his capture could only lead to this, and now that the moment of death comes, he knows himself to be in effect dead already. Less likely is the supposition that he is making a last appeal for mercy. The judgement of Agag by Samuel is a poetic saying, like that in verses 22f. On Agag, see also the note on verses 8f.

34. *his own home at Gibeah:* archaeological work at the probable site of Gibeah has revealed an important though not large building which may be this 'fortress'. It seems not unlikely that it was a Philistine building, subsequently occupied by Saul.

35. *to his dying day:* an ambiguous expression. It could mean that Saul never saw Samuel again (but see 19: 18–24). Or it could mean that they met only on the day of Saul's death when the witch of En-dor called up Samuel's spirit to pronounce doom on Saul (28: 7–20).

The end of this chapter marks a division in the narrative. The reign of Saul continues, but what have been only hints of his successor are now made explicit in the story of David's anointing. *

Saul and David

THE ANOINTING OF DAVID

16 THE LORD SAID to Samuel, 'How long will you mourn for Saul because I have rejected him as king over Israel? Fill your horn with oil and take it with you; I am sending you to Jesse of Bethlehem; for I have 2 chosen myself a king among his sons.' Samuel answered, 'How can I go? Saul will hear of it and kill me.' 'Take a heifer with you,' said the LORD; 'say you have come to 3 offer a sacrifice to the LORD, and invite Jesse to*[a]* the sacrifice; then I will let you know what you must do. You 4 shall anoint for me the man whom I show you.' Samuel did as the LORD had told him, and went to Bethlehem. The elders of the city came in haste to meet him, saying, 5 'Why have you come? Is all well?' 'All is well,' said

[a] *So Sept.; Heb.* with.

Samuel; 'I have come to sacrifice to the LORD. Hallow
yourselves and come with me to[a] the sacrifice.' He himself
hallowed Jesse and his sons and invited them to the
sacrifice also. They came, and when Samuel saw Eliab he 6
thought, 'Here, before the LORD, is his anointed king.'
But the LORD said to him, 'Take no account of it if he is 7
handsome and tall; I reject him. The LORD does not see as
man sees;[b] men judge by appearances but the LORD judges
by the heart.' Then Jesse called Abinadab and made him 8
pass before Samuel, but he said, 'No, the LORD has not
chosen this one.' Then he presented Shammah, and 9
Samuel said, 'Nor has the LORD chosen him.' Seven of his 10
sons Jesse presented to Samuel, but he said, 'The LORD has
not chosen any of these.' Then Samuel asked, 'Are these 11
all?' Jesse answered, 'There is still the youngest, but he is
looking after the sheep.' Samuel said to Jesse, 'Send and
fetch him; we will not sit down until he comes.' So he 12
sent and fetched him. He was handsome, with ruddy
cheeks and bright eyes.[c] The LORD said, 'Rise and anoint
him: this is the man.' Samuel took the horn of oil and 13
anointed him in the presence of his brothers. Then the
spirit of the LORD came upon David and was with him
from that day onwards. And Samuel set out on his way
back to Ramah.

* This story is immediately linked to what precedes it in
chapter 15. The anointing is described as taking place in the
family of Jesse, and presumably therefore in private. There is,
however, no allusion to it in the narratives that follow, and

[a] So *Vulg.*; *Heb.* with.
[b] The LORD...sees: *so Sept.*; *Heb.* For not what a man sees.
[c] and bright eyes: *prob. rdg.*; *Heb. obscure.*

when David did become king, he is said to have been anointed at Hebron (2 Sam. 2: 4). The Chronicler has no mention of it. It is probable that it is a fairly late element, utilizing ancient tradition and motifs, but designed to draw a sharp contrast with the rejection of Saul, and providing a foil to the popular tale of Saul's anointing in 9: 1–10: 16. It thus provides an introduction to the David story which imposes a new interpretation on the various narratives which run to the end of the book.

1. The words *mourn* and *rejected* provide immediate verbal links to chapter 15. That Samuel should anoint the new king is in the spirit of those narratives which give him a position of primary importance in Israel. The family of *Jesse of Bethlehem* (see map, p. 48) is introduced without any explanation or comment. David was a Judaean, unlike Saul who came from Benjamin. The book of Ruth, also based on a popular tale, provides a story later told about David's ancestry. The choice of Bethlehem was to be picked up by Micah (5: 2) and thence to influence the narratives concerning the birth of Jesus in Luke and Matthew.

2. The sacrifice provides a parallel to the Saul narrative of 9: 1–10: 16.

4. *came in haste*: better 'came anxiously' or 'came in reverence', suggesting that Samuel inspired awe, as did later prophets whose words brought doom. So the king of Israel (Ahab) feared Micaiah for his harsh prophecies (1 Kings 22: 8).

5. Samuel himself *hallowed Jesse and his sons*, carrying out the appropriate rituals of purification before the sacrifice. Thus the story puts Samuel in a position in which he is shown each of Jesse's sons in turn and can hear the will of God regarding them.

6. A slight change would give: 'Yahweh's prince, his anointed', the term 'prince' being the one used in earlier narratives (see note on 9: 16).

7. The *handsome and tall* appearance of the eldest son not unnaturally suggests his suitability. External appearance is a

sign of divine favour; compare the picture of Saul in 9: 2; 10: 23 and of David in verse 12. But the comment which shows that he is not the chosen one stresses the contrast between divine and human assessment.

10. *Seven of his sons:* the number is a favourite in biblical and other stories; compare the dreams of Pharaoh in Gen. 41.

11. The absence of David is at first overlooked, and thus the hearer's sense of suspense is heightened. Can it be that there is no suitable candidate? But *the youngest* remains to be thought of, and here again we see a motif common to the stories of many lands. In popular stories the youngest is often given the preference, and so too when the mystery of divine choice is considered. We find this in the Jacob/Esau tradition (Gen. 27) and with Joseph's sons (Gen. 48: 8-22). *looking after the sheep:* literally 'shepherding the flock'. For the king as shepherd, see the note on 12: 2. *sit down:* or perhaps 'go around', i.e. in the sacrificial procession.

12. The text is somewhat confused here, perhaps because something is missing. David's good appearance was evidently an ancient element in the tradition; we find that his son Absalom in particular inherited it (2 Sam. 14: 25-7).

13. The anointing of David, like that of Saul, is associated with the power of *the spirit of the LORD* 'rushing upon him'— the same word as is used in 10: 6. The manifestation of this spirit will be in his heroism and military prowess, and in the establishment of kingship and the assurance of divine blessing. The name *David* appears to be connected with a word meaning 'beloved' (used in the vineyard love-song of Isa. 5: 1-7), an appropriate name for the chosen one of God.

By setting this story at the head of the narratives which concern David and Saul, the compiler has made clear his understanding of what follows. Explanations are given of the relationship between David and Saul and to account for Saul's failure. But these are subordinated to the recognition of God's will. At the same time, this story offers a meaning for all that follows concerning David's rise to power. Political scheming, the fortunes of war, the death of Saul and his family—all these eventually made possible his kingship; but to the interpreter, all this stands within the purpose of God whose choice alone counts. ✻

DAVID SOOTHES THE SPIRIT OF SAUL

14 The spirit of the LORD had forsaken Saul, and at times an
15 evil spirit from the LORD would seize him suddenly. His servants said to him, 'You see, sir, how an evil spirit from
16 God seizes you; why do you not command your servants here to go and find some man who can play the harp?— then, when an evil spirit from God comes on you, he can
17 play and you will recover.' Saul said to his servants, 'Find me a man who can play well and bring him to me.'
18 One of his attendants said, 'I have seen a son of Jesse of Bethlehem who can play; he is a brave man and a good fighter, wise in speech and handsome, and the LORD is
19 with him.' Saul therefore sent messengers to Jesse and asked him to send him his son David, who was with the
20 sheep. Jesse took a homer of bread, a skin of wine, and a
21 kid, and sent them to Saul by his son David. David came to Saul and entered his service; and Saul loved him dearly,
22 and he became his armour-bearer. So Saul sent word to Jesse: 'Let David stay in my service, for I am pleased with
23 him.' And whenever a spirit from God came upon Saul, David would take his harp and play on it, so that Saul found relief; he recovered and the evil spirit left him alone.

✻ 14. The divine power which enabled Saul to win victories is now said to be withdrawn; the leader without such power is like Samson, shorn of his hair and deprived of his strength (Judg. 16). Thus the failure of Saul rests in the withdrawal of divine favour. *an evil spirit from the LORD:* what comes to a man, good or ill, is seen as from God. We might describe what happened as due to fits of extreme depression; subsequently Saul appears to suffer from a kind of persecution mania. To the Hebrew, this could be described as due to an *evil spirit*, and since favour or disfavour lies with God, it must be from him. This raises difficult questions about the nature of God, questions which appear acutely in the story of Micaiah in 1 Kings 22, for there one of the heavenly beings is described as deliberately misleading the prophets to bring doom on Ahab (verses 20–3). These passages are not precise definitions but descriptions of human experience in terms of the will of God, attempts at setting out an understanding of what happens to men as being under God's ultimate control. *seize:* a different word for the power of the spirit, suggesting terror and dismay.

16. *harp:* better 'lyre', the small hand-instrument in the form of a flat-sounding box, with two wooden arms joined by a cross-piece. The strings, usually four in number, were stretched from the box to the cross-piece. Music was believed to have power. Elisha called for a musician to play and the hand of God came upon him so that he prophesied (2 Kings 3: 15). Here the power of music is to assuage Saul's depression and to remove from him the effects of what was seen as the withdrawal of God.

18. The introduction of David is without reference to the preceding narrative, and the David who appears is in most respects quite different, a warrior, evidently of experience, a man skilled in the use of words to persuade and to have good effect (the gift that Moses disclaimed, Exod. 4: 10), as well as being *handsome* or perhaps better 'a man of presence' (a different expression from those used in the previous narrative). This is neither the David of the previous passage, nor the David of chapter 17. As with the Samuel narratives, different parts of the material present different pictures. *the LORD is with him:* the courtier says more than he is aware, for this is to be the mark of David, the true king.

19. *who was with the sheep:* an awkwardly added phrase, designed to harmonize the stories.

20. *a homer of bread:* the text is uncertain, the word rendered *homer* being actually one meaning 'ass' (*ḥamōr*). A *homer* would be about 11 bushels (400 litres), a substantial quantity but perhaps a fit offering for the king. A smaller measure, with a similar sounding name, is an 'omer', about 1 gallon (4 litres), but perhaps this is too small. We might have expected a number indicating how many loaves of bread, or we might emend to 'Jesse took an ass and loaded it with bread'.

21. David *entered* Saul's *service,* like other valiant men whom Saul chose (14: 52). The affection Saul felt was to be in tension with the jealousy that overcame him. As *armour-bearer* David would be a close associate of the king, standing by his side in battle. When Saul died, his armour-bearer was with him and killed himself rather than survive his master (31: 4–6).

23. David's skilful playing and the relief it brought appear again in the narratives that follow.

Here we have David introduced to Saul and brought into close association with him. Saul's affection binds them together, as does the position David occupies in his entourage. In this a certain irony appears; the ruler unwittingly takes into his closest service the one who is to supplant and succeed him. David's musicianship is an important element in the tradition and ultimately to be of great significance, for it is the first element in the growth of the picture of David as 'the singer of Israel's psalms' (2 Sam. 23: 1). ✳

THE PHILISTINE CHAMPION

17 The Philistines collected their forces for war and massed at Socoh in Judah; they camped between Socoh and Azekah
2 at Ephes-dammim. Saul and the Israelites also massed, and camped in the Vale of Elah. They drew up their lines
3 facing the Philistines, the Philistines occupying a position

on one hill and the Israelites on another, with a valley
between them. A champion came out from the Philistine 4
camp, a man named Goliath, from Gath; he was over
nine feet[a] in height. He had a bronze helmet on his head, 5
and he wore plate-armour of bronze, weighing five
thousand shekels. On his legs were bronze greaves, and 6
one of his weapons was a dagger of bronze. The shaft of 7
his spear was like a weaver's beam, and its head, which was
of iron, weighed six hundred shekels; and his shield-bearer
marched ahead of him. The champion stood and shouted 8
to the ranks of Israel, 'Why do you come out to do battle,
you slaves of Saul? I am the Philistine champion; choose
your man to meet me. If he can kill me in fair fight, we 9
will become your slaves; but if I prove too strong for him
and kill him, you shall be our slaves and serve us. Here 10
and now I defy the ranks of Israel. Give me a man,' said
the Philistine, 'and we will fight it out.' When Saul and 11
the Israelites heard what the Philistine said, they were
shaken and dismayed.

* The story contained in the whole of this chapter is a complex
one, in which different elements of the David tradition have
been brought together.

1 f. *the Vale of Elah* ('of the terebinth') runs westwards from
the hill country of Judah, roughly in the latitude of Bethlehem
(see map, p. 48). It was an obvious route of advance for the
Philistines from their cities in the coastal plain. Like the stories
in chapters 13 and 14, this is to be understood as a localized
incident in the intermittent warfare, an incident subsequently
retold as one of total war between the two people.

3. The armies face one another across a narrow *valley*, a
ravine.

[a] over nine feet: *lit.* six cubits and a span.

4. *A champion:* stories in which a single combat replaces battle between two armies are known in many communities, ancient and more modern. A similar practice appears in 2 Sam. 2: 12–16, when twelve young men from each side are engaged. From the second millennium B.C., we know the story of an Egyptian, Sinuhe, who was forced into such combat with a warrior 'who had no equal; he had conquered all the land... he thought that he would despoil me and rob me of my beasts'. But after skilful evasion of the champion's arrows, Sinuhe killed him in hand to hand fighting: 'My arrow pierced his neck. He cried out and fell on his nose; I felled him with his own battle-axe and uttered my battle cry over his back.' Single combat is found also in Greek story, as between Achilles and Hector in book VII of the *Iliad*, and much later in the sad Persian tale of Rustem and Sohrab.

5. *Goliath, from Gath:* in 2 Sam. 21: 19 he is said to have been killed by 'Elhanan son of Jair of Bethlehem'. This raises various problems which affect the interpretation of that verse. But not improbably, the story here originally had no name for the giant, who is most often simply referred to as 'the Philistine'. Later the well-known name of Goliath was added.

4–7. The detailed and picturesque description accentuates the terror inspired by this colossal warrior. *a weaver's beam:* or 'leash rod', the piece of wood which separates the threads of the warp so that the shuttle can be passed between them. The beam would be supplied with loops which enabled the alternate threads to be lifted and lowered. The weight of the armour would amount to about 125 lbs (56 kg), that of the spear head to about 16 lbs (7 kg). The use of iron for the latter and the clearly superior quality of the Philistine equipment recall 13: 19–22; it is probably to be compared with equipment known in the Greek world.

8. Terror is produced by the champion's words.

10. *defy:* a word often used of defiance against God, a theme developed later in the story. The uttering of curses and threats is itself part of the contest (see on 14: 6).

11. The terror of the king and army is to be answered by words of encouragement from David (see on verse 32).

The scene is set, but before the challenge can be taken up a new story element is introduced, bringing David into the picture. ✳

DAVID COMES TO THE BATTLE-LINE

David was the son of an Ephrathite[a] called Jesse, who had 12
eight sons. By Saul's time he had become a feeble old 13
man, and his three eldest sons had followed Saul to the
war. The eldest was called Eliab, the next Abinadab, and
the third Shammah; David was the youngest. The three 14
eldest followed Saul, while David used to go to Saul's 15
camp and back to Bethlehem to mind his father's flocks.

Morning and evening for forty days the Philistine came 16
forward and took up his position. Then one day Jesse said 17
to his son David, 'Take your brothers an ephah of this
parched grain and these ten loaves of bread, and run with
them to the camp. These ten cream-cheeses are for you to 18
take to the commanding officer. See if your brothers are
well and bring back some token from them.' Saul and the 19
brothers and all the Israelites were in the Vale of Elah,
fighting the Philistines. Early next morning David left 20
someone in charge of the sheep, set out on his errand and
went as Jesse had told him. He reached the lines just as the
army was going out to take up position and was raising
the war-cry. The Israelites and the Philistines drew up 21
their ranks opposite each other. David left his things in 22
charge of the quartermaster, ran to the line and went up
to his brothers to greet them. While he was talking to 23
them the Philistine champion, Goliath, came out from the

[a] *Prob. rdg.; Heb. adds* Is this the man from Bethlehem in Judah?

Philistine ranks and issued his challenge in the same words
24 as before; and David heard him. When the Israelites saw
25 the man they ran from him in fear. 'Look at this man who
comes out day after day to defy Israel', they said. 'The
king is to give a rich reward to the man who kills him; he
will give him his daughter in marriage too and will
26 exempt his family from service due in Israel.' Then David
turned to his neighbours and said, 'What is to be done for
the man who kills this Philistine and wipes out our
disgrace? And who is he, an uncircumcised Philistine, to
27 defy the army of the living God?' The people told him
how the matter stood and what was to be done for the
28 man who killed him. His elder brother Eliab overheard
David talking with the men and grew angry. 'What are
you doing here?' he asked. 'And who have you left to
look after those few sheep in the wilderness? I know you,
you impudent young rascal; you have only come to see
29 the fighting.' David answered, 'What have I done now?
30 I only asked a question.' And he turned away from him to
someone else and repeated his question, but everybody
gave him the same answer.

31   What David had said was overheard and reported to
Saul, who sent for him.

✴ 12. *David* is introduced as if he had not been mentioned
previously. *Ephrathite*: a clan name from the Judaean area,
associated with Bethlehem (cp. Mic. 5: 2). The phrase omitted
in N.E.B. (see footnote) makes the link clear, probably
to co-ordinate this story with chapter 16.

13. The picture of Jesse as *a feeble old man* does not really
accord with 16: 1–13. The meaning of the text is not, in fact,
quite clear. A small change would give: 'he was too old to go
with the soldiers, but his three eldest sons...'.

13–15. The text is very repetitive, possibly as a result of endeavours to harmonize the different stories. Did this story originally know only four sons of Jesse (see verse 28)? Verse 15 may be intended to suggest that David—already at court according to 16: 21–3—spent part of his time there and part at home.

16. A link appears with the previous section, providing a picture of the continuing threat and anxiety.

17f. *parched grain*: or 'roasted grain', a delicacy prepared by roasting the ears in an iron pan (cp. Ruth 2: 14 for its use). The army would be dependent on supplies from their home villages, and it would be well also to gain the favour of the section commander. *some token*: some item which would give an assurance of their well-being.

19. Another linking and harmonizing verse.

20. Each morning the army advances to the battle from the camp and raises the *war-cry* to alarm the enemy; but all to no avail. The term for *lines* seems to indicate not the battle-lines but a camp surrounded by a rough rampart or possibly the area occupied by the supply wagons. *the quartermaster*: the officer left in charge of the baggage (cp. 30: 24).

24f. The fear of the Israelite army is now elaborated in David's hearing. A new element is introduced with the popular motif of the offer of wealth, the king's daughter, and freedom from service for the hero's family. It here points forward to David's eventual royal position.

26. David's questions develop the theme further and make plain that defiance of Israel is defiance of God (see on verse 10). *the living God*: a common expression, significantly stressing the reality and power of Yahweh. This is the theme of the Elijah story in 1 Kings 17–18. *uncircumcised Philistine*: a term of ridicule, as in 14: 6.

28f. The unjust attitude of the eldest brother reminds us of the story of Joseph (Gen. 37f.) and of many popular tales in which the youngest son is the hero, much to the disgust of elder brothers and sisters. *I only asked a question*: the terse expression might mean: 'Is it not a matter of importance?'

31 provides a link to the resumption of the previous narrative by bringing David into Saul's entourage. David's words contained an implied challenge to the champion.

The compiler has made use here of a popular tale; it does not exactly tally with other parts of the story, but it serves to bring together the various statements about David and it paves the way for his successful fight with the Philistine. Underlying the narrative is discernible the story-teller's sense of the hand of God leading David to that moment of victory. ✶

THE VICTORY OF FAITH

32 David said to him, 'Do not lose heart, sir.[a] I will go and
33 fight this Philistine.' Saul answered, 'You cannot go and fight with this Philistine; you are only a lad, and he has
34 been a fighting man all his life.' David said to Saul, 'Sir, I am my father's shepherd; when a lion or bear comes and
35 carries off a sheep from the flock, I go after it and attack it and rescue the victim from its jaws. Then if it turns on me,
36 I seize it by the beard and batter it to death. Lions I have killed and bears, and this uncircumcised Philistine will fare no better than they; he has defied the army of the living
37 God. The LORD who saved me from the lion and the bear will save me from this Philistine.' 'Go then,' said Saul;
38 'and the LORD will be with you.' He put his own tunic on David, placed a bronze helmet on his head and gave him a
39 coat of mail to wear; he then fastened his sword on David[b] over his tunic. But David hesitated, because he had not tried them, and said to Saul, 'I cannot go with these, because I have not tried them.' So he took them off.
40 Then he picked up his stick, chose five smooth stones from

[a] Do not...sir: *so Sept.; Heb.* Let no one lose heart.
[b] he then...on David: *so Sept.; Heb.* David fastened on his sword.

the brook and put them in a shepherd's bag which served
as his pouch.[a] He walked out to meet the Philistine with
his sling in his hand.

The Philistine came on towards David, with his shield- 41
bearer marching ahead; and he looked David up and down 42
and had nothing but contempt for this handsome lad with
his ruddy cheeks and bright eyes.[b] He said to David, 'Am 43
I a dog that you come out against me with sticks?' And he
swore at him in the name of his god. 'Come on,' he said, 44
'and I will give your flesh to the birds and the beasts.'
David answered, 'You have come against me with sword 45
and spear and dagger, but I have come against you in the
name of the LORD of Hosts, the God of the army of Israel
which you have defied. The LORD will put you into my 46
power this day; I will kill you and cut your head off and
leave your carcass and the carcasses of the Philistines[c] to the
birds and the wild beasts; all the world shall know that
there is a God in Israel. All those who are gathered here 47
shall see that the LORD saves neither by sword nor spear;
the battle is the LORD's, and he will put you all into our
power.'

When the Philistine began moving towards him again, 48
David ran quickly to engage him. He put his hand into his 49
bag, took out a stone, slung it, and struck the Philistine on
the forehead. The stone sank into his forehead, and he fell
flat on his face on the ground. So David proved the victor 50
with his sling and stone; he struck Goliath down and gave
him a mortal wound, though he had no sword. Then he 51

[a] which...pouch: *so Sept.; Heb.* which was his and in the pouch.
[b] handsome...bright eyes: *prob. rdg.; Heb. obscure.*
[c] leave...Philistines: *so Sept.; Heb.* leave the carcass of the Philistines.

ran to the Philistine and stood over him, and grasping his sword, he drew it out of the scabbard, dispatched him and cut off his head. The Philistines, when they saw that their
52 hero was dead, turned and ran. The men of Israel and Judah at once raised the war-cry and hotly pursued them all the way to Gath[a] and even to the gates of Ekron. The road that runs to Shaaraim, Gath, and Ekron was strewn
53 with their dead. On their return from the pursuit of the
54 Philistines, the Israelites plundered their camp. David took Goliath's head and carried it to Jerusalem, leaving his weapons in his tent.

✯ This vivid story portrays the conviction of faith that God is himself the deliverer; human power cannot withstand him, nor can human power alone be victorious.

32. The narrative, picking up here from verse 11, refers to David, already armour-bearer of Saul, who declares his assurance to the king.

33. David is the young lad, newly called to the court, inexperienced (16: 18 has anticipated his later prowess), and a total contrast to the professional warrior who threatens Israel.

34–7. The one who can rescue the shepherd from *lions* and *bears*—in ancient times common enough in the wilder parts of Palestine—can certainly deliver from a man who sets himself against *the army of the living God*. Another such hero was Benaiah, one of David's chosen band (2 Sam. 23: 20f.). David's faith meets with a like response in Saul: *the LORD will be with you*.

38. *he...fastened his sword on David*: the Hebrew makes David put on his own sword (see on verse 51).

39. David's unwillingness to wear Saul's garments and armour may be seen as natural enough. But the story is probably intended to suggest that though one day David is to wear the royal apparel, his hour has not yet come.

[a] *So Sept.; Heb.* a valley.

40. *his pouch*: the obscurity of the Hebrew (see N.E.B. footnote) may be due to the words *shepherd's bag* being added to explain the rare word for *pouch*. *his sling in his hand*: slingers were a regular part of the army and may be seen portrayed on Assyrian monuments. The accurate throwing of the stone was a highly skilled operation.

42. *with his ruddy cheeks and bright eyes*: possibly added from 16:12 and including the textual confusion already present there.

43 f. The Philistine mocks David, despising his youth (verse 42) and calling down curses upon him. The exposure of a corpse, depriving it of proper burial, was a terrible thing to ancient Israel (see 31: 8-13, and Jeremiah's judgement on his countrymen, e.g. Jer. 7: 33; 8: 1-2).

45-7. David's reply is equally in the form of a taunt, mocking the one who trusts in human strength and who supposes that he can stand against the reality and power of Israel's God whom he has defied. The theme of Jonathan's confidence (see on 14: 6) is here reiterated. On *LORD of hosts*, see 1: 3. Expressed in these verses is the basic confidence of Israel; victory is God's and he will prevail. The human contest is subordinated to the theological statement. This has meaning for Israel—*all those who are gathered here*, the technical term for the religious assembly of Israel rather than the army—but it is also for *all the world*. So Ezekiel sees the significance of God's saving action; it will make his nature plain to the nations that witness it (Ezek. 39: 23).

49. As the fight is engaged, David wins a surprise success by the skill of his slinging; for the description, compare the story of Sinuhe quoted at verse 4.

50. Here is a comment on the implications of the contest. Against such odds, David could have been victorious only with God's help.

51. The text does not in fact make it clear whether it was the Philistine's sword—not mentioned in the list of his equipment —or David's (see on verse 38). There are some slight discrepancies within the tale. The death of their champion,

according to the challenge (verse 9), should have involved Philistine submission. Here a different picture is given, that of an army routed in fear, its confidence lost when the *hero* is dead.

52 f. The Philistines are now an easy prey for the pursuing army of Israel. The mention of *Israel and Judah* here presupposes the divided kingdom after Solomon. *Shaaraim* is an unidentified place in the region of Azekah; possibly we should read 'from Shaaraim to Gath'.

54. *Jerusalem* was still a Jebusite city and did not come into David's possession until later (cp. 2 Sam. 5). The reference here is an anachronism, but possibly points to the existence of a legend that Goliath's skull could be seen at Jerusalem. Goliath's *weapons* were perhaps taken not to *his* (David's) *tent*, but to 'his (Yahweh's) tent-sanctuary'; in 21: 9 the 'sword of Goliath' is in the sanctuary at Nob. ✷

DAVID THE HERO

55 Saul had said to Abner his commander-in-chief, when he saw David going out against the Philistine, 'That boy there, Abner, whose son is he?' 'By your life, your
56 majesty,' said Abner, 'I do not know.' The king said to
57 Abner, 'Go and find out whose son the lad is.' When David came back after killing the Philistine, Abner took him and presented him to Saul with the Philistine's head
58 still in his hand. Saul asked him, 'Whose son are you, young man?', and David answered, 'I am the son of your servant Jesse of Bethlehem.'

18 1–2   That same day, when Saul had finished talking with David, he kept him and would not let him return any more to his father's house, for he saw that Jonathan had given his heart to David and had grown to love him as
3 himself. So Jonathan and David made a solemn compact
4 because each loved the other as dearly as himself. And

Jonathan stripped off the cloak he was wearing and his
tunic, and gave them to David, together with his sword,
his bow, and his belt. David succeeded so well in every 5
venture on which Saul sent him that he was given a command in the army, and his promotion pleased the ordinary
people, and even pleased Saul's officers.

* 55. *Abner:* see on 14: 50. It is quite clear that this little
narrative is unconnected with those of chapter 16, and indeed
it does not fit well with what immediately precedes. It would
seem to be part of a story in which David went out to meet the
Philistine challenge without any conversation with Saul; it
could thus be linked with verses 12–30. It was as a result of his
exploit—so this story tells—that David came to be at the
court of Saul, for on his return (18: 1 f.) Saul made the decision
to keep David there.

18: 1–4. The close bond—in the form of *a solemn compact*
or 'covenant' (the word used for the relationship between God
and his people and for other such relationships)—between
David and Jonathan has become proverbial. Its fullest expression is to be found in David's lament at the death of Saul and
his sons (2 Sam. 1: 19–27, esp. verses 25 f.). The significance
of this lies in its relation to the point already made in chapter
14. Jonathan, the hero of that story, is surely the fit successor to
Saul; but Saul's house is not to endure. So in the bond between
David and Jonathan, the royalty which should belong to
Jonathan passes to David. The presentation of *cloak* and *tunic*,
together with military equipment, expresses the closeness of
the bond; but it is understood as a recognition by Jonathan
that David is to be king. This is not as yet expressed in words,
but in the narrative of chapter 20 it becomes explicit (see esp.
20: 15 f.). As so often, what is to come is foreshadowed in the
unconscious action of the characters.

5. David's success *in every venture* leads to *promotion*, one
that pleased everyone, including already established royal

officers. This too is a foreshadowing of David's eventual recognition.

The compiler skilfully prepares for the contrasting attitude of Saul which is to follow immediately. The succeeding chapters relate the two sides of Saul's involvement with David—the deep affection which drew him to David and the bitter hatred which turned against him.

17: 12–31 and 17: 55–18: 5 are missing from the Septuagint manuscript Codex Vaticanus. It also lacks 17: 41 and 50 (which contains an obviously later comment) and some further verses in chapter 18. The evidence is important, for it shows that different forms of a text, longer and shorter, existed. The relationship between such texts and their history is not easy to disentangle. In this instance, a further point may be made, for the two main passages not found in this important manuscript clearly belong to a separate tradition. This helps to explain a problem often observed in the Old Testament. We often find two accounts of the same event lying side by side (so the two creation accounts of Gen. 1: 1–2: 4a and 2: 4b–25). Or we find two narratives, which can be reasonably clearly separated, interwoven the one with the other (so the flood narratives in Gen. 6–8). The texts we have represent particular stages in the formation of the books; and in some cases, as in 1 Sam. 17, we can see different stages which have been reached in the use of the same material. Originally separate accounts of the same incident are placed side by side, or interwoven, and gradually, by further additions or small modifications, brought more closely into one. The compilers were concerned to preserve all that they saw to be of value: they tried to put the different parts into some sort of order. But in the end, they were more concerned with what the stories meant than with merely smoothing out unevenness. It is to this fact that we owe the richness of the material we have, even though we have to accept that we cannot reconstruct what happened or necessarily say with confidence what is historical and what is legendary. *

SAUL TURNS AGAINST DAVID

At the home-coming of the army when David returned 6
from the slaughter of the Philistines, the women came out
from all the cities of Israel to look on, and the dancers[a]
came out to meet King Saul with tambourines, singing,
and dancing. The women as they made merry sang to one 7
another:

> Saul made havoc among thousands
> but David among tens of thousands.

Saul was furious, and the words rankled. He said, 'They 8
have given David tens of thousands and me only thousands; what more can they do but make him king?' From 9
that day forward Saul kept a jealous eye on David.

   Next day an evil spirit from God seized upon Saul; he 10
fell into a frenzy[b] in the house, and David played the harp
to him as he had before. Saul had his spear in his hand, and 11
he hurled it at David, meaning to pin him to the wall; but
twice David swerved aside. After this Saul was afraid of 12
David, because he saw that the LORD had forsaken him
and was with David. He therefore removed David from 13
his household and appointed him to the command of a
thousand men. David led his men into action, and 14
succeeded in everything that he undertook, because the
LORD was with him. When Saul saw how successful he 15
was, he was more afraid of him than ever; all Israel and 16
Judah loved him because he took the field at their head.

✶ In this passage, two themes which recur in the following
narratives are interwoven. In reality they offer alternative
explanations of Saul's hostility to David. First we are told that

[a] *So Sept.; Heb.* and the dances.   [b] *Or* fell into prophetic rapture.

it was his military prowess which provoked Saul's jealousy
and hatred. Second, the affliction which came over Saul is
shown so to have affected his mind that he saw David as his
enemy.

6. *the Philistines*: actually singular, 'the Philistine', possibly
used in a collective sense for the people, but probably indicating that this verse is to be linked to the killing of Goliath in
chapter 17. The processional welcome given by *the women*,
with singers and *dancers*, is characteristic of occasions of
victory. Jephthah's daughter greeted her father thus (Judg.
11: 34), and the crossing of the Sea, as a great victory for God,
was hailed by Miriam and 'all the women' (Exod. 15: 20).
dancing: or 'three-stringed instruments' or something
similar.

7. The words of a brief refrain are given—quoted again in
21: 11 and 29: 5—perhaps part of a longer act of praise.
(In Exod. 15: 21 a similar refrain is quoted; in Exod. 15: 1–18
there is a long psalm, based on the same theme.) Clearly the
words here envisage many campaigns by David (cp. verse 5);
the victory over Goliath has been drawn into a larger understanding of his heroism. This paves the way for the story in
verses 17–29.

8. The acclaim of David is such as would be given to a king;
the women are in a sense already acknowledging him. Such a
sentiment is put into Saul's words here, and is expressed again
in verse 12.

10f. These verses are possibly an addition to the text here
from 19: 9f., designed to bring together the theme of Saul's
rejection by God and that of his hostility to David. The *evil
spirit* was explained in 16: 14–23; now it is shown to direct
Saul against David. *he fell into a frenzy*: the term used (see
N.E.B. footnote) is that appropriate to prophetic ecstasy and
speech. The idea is found more fully developed in 19: 18–24.
We may note that the external effect of possession is the same
whether the *spirit* is thought to be good or *evil*.

12. *because he saw that...with David*: no words appear for

he saw that, and the whole phrase is better put in parenthesis as a comment by the compiler.

13–16 repeat the theme of verse 5 which appears again in verse 30. But by putting it here, the compiler suggests that Saul promoted David only in order to cause his death; in so prominent a place, he would be in greater danger. We may compare David's successful device for getting rid of Uriah (2 Sam. 11: 14ff.). Saul's plan fails; David's success and popularity become all the greater.

The passage begins the fuller underlining of the tragedy of Saul. What should be the marks of triumph become forebodings of ultimate disaster. What is designed to remove a threat to his kingship works in the opposite direction. What counts is the presence and power of God, as the comment in verse 12*b* makes plain. ✶

DAVID AND THE ROYAL FAMILY

Saul said to David, 'Here is my elder daughter Merab; I 17 will give her to you in marriage, but in return you must serve me valiantly and fight the LORD's battles.' For Saul meant David to meet his end at the hands of the Philistines and not himself. David answered Saul, 'Who am I and 18 what are my father's people, my kinsfolk, in Israel, that I should become the king's son-in-law?' However, when 19 the time came for Saul's daughter Merab to be married to David, she had already been given to Adriel of Meholah. But Michal, Saul's other daughter, fell in love with David, 20 and when Saul was told of this, he saw that it suited his plans. He said to himself, 'I will give her to him; let her be 21 the bait that lures him to his death at the hands of the Philistines.' So Saul proposed a second time to make David his son-in-law, and ordered his courtiers to say to David 22

privately, 'The king is well disposed to you and you are
dear to us all; now is the time for you to marry into the
23 king's family.' When Saul's people spoke in this way to
David, he said to them, 'Do you think that marrying the
king's daughter is a matter of so little consequence that a
poor man of no consequence, like myself, can do it?'
24,25 Saul's courtiers reported what David had said, and he
replied, 'Tell David this: all the king wants as the bride-
price is the foreskins of a hundred Philistines, by way of
vengeance on his enemies.' Saul was counting on David's
26 death at the hands of the Philistines. The courtiers told
David what Saul had said, and marriage with the king's
daughter on these terms pleased him well. Before the
27 appointed time, David went out with his men and slew
two hundred Philistines; he brought their foreskins and
counted them out to the king in order to be accepted as his
son-in-law. So Saul married his daughter Michal to
28 David. He saw clearly that the LORD was with David, and
knew that Michal his daughter had fallen in love with
29 him; and so he grew more and more afraid of David and
was his enemy for the rest of his life.

30   The Philistine officers used to come out to offer single
combat; and whenever they did, David had more success
against them than all the rest of Saul's men, and he won a
great name for himself.

✳ 17-19. It would be natural to suppose that Saul's offer of
his *elder daughter* to David is the sequel to the royal promise
mentioned by the people in 17: 25, though no reference back
is made. The absence of these verses from Codex Vaticanus
(as also 17: 12-31; see note on p.148) may indicate that they
are part of the same source. But the theme is now used to point

to Saul's evil intentions; in battle against the Philistines, David will *meet his end* and Saul will have no direct responsibility. We may again compare David's device for getting rid of Uriah (2 Sam. 11).

18. David's disclaimer: *Who am I . . . ?* is characteristic of stories which tell of the giving of honour. Gideon (Judg. 6: 15) and Saul (9: 21) similarly speak humbly of their position. Such disclaimers may be seen as part of the normal practice in polite eastern conversation; they also serve in many Old Testament passages to emphasize the primary authority of the divine will (see Jer. 1: 6ff.).

19. The marriage of Merab to another man represents a common story motif: that of the king (or other person) who promises the hero his daughter only to refuse on some trumped up excuse. We may compare Laban's behaviour to Jacob in regard to marriage with Rachel (Gen. 29: 15ff.) and one of the incidents in the stories of Samson (Judg. 14: 1–15: 2).

20f. The second story of a marriage planned for David develops much more fully the same theme as the first. Again the stress rests on the way Saul plans to bring about David's downfall. It also, by stressing the love that Michal has for David, shows the closeness of David's bond with the family. Saul was deeply attached to him (16: 21); so too was Jonathan (18: 2ff.), and now Michal. The family is shown to look favourably on the successor to the throne.

21. N.E.B. paraphrases and simplifies the text. Actually it says: 'Saul said to David: Today you will become my son-in-law for the second time', as if David had already married Merab. Possibly the word for *a second time* is designed to harmonize the stories; perhaps it contains an error (see on verse 26).

22. The *courtiers'* words and David's reply (verse 23) suggest that there has been no previous proposal of a marriage. David's favourable position at court (as in verse 5) invites ambition.

23. David again utters a disclaimer. This not only represents

courtesy, but also suggests that David has no resources to pay a
bride-price and no royal ambitions. He is content to let the
divine purpose take effect. A *bride-price* does not represent the
purchase of a wife, but probably compensation to her family;
it may in some instances have provided a dowry.

25. The evil intention of Saul is now exposed in his impos-
ing an ordeal instead of asking a normal bride-price. Such an
ordeal is again a common story motif; here it also serves to
pour scorn on the alien uncircumcised Philistines (see note on
14: 6).

26. *Before the appointed time:* no such time has been
mentioned, though some scholars have suggested that the
word rendered 'a second time' in verse 21 could be emended
to read 'within two years'.

27. David's heroism enables him to double the required
bride-price and win Michal.

28f. The commentator here explains Saul's action. How
can he resist what is obviously the work of God to bring
David to success? The mention of Michal's love as an added
reason for Saul's behaviour appears repetitive after verse 20,
and we may prefer an alternative reading: 'and that all Israel
loved him'. The divine intention, as in verse 5, is expressed in
what is to be the total adherence of the people to the coming
king.

30. An additional note. If N.E.B.'s interpretation is correct
—the text does not mention *single combat*—then David's
heroism in chapter 17 is regarded as only one of many such
fights. Alternatively the text may simply mean that David was
continuously successful in all the Philistine wars. *The Philistine
officers...combat:* this could, with only a slight change, be
rendered: 'they went into Philistine territory'.

No matter what Saul attempts against him, David's evident
enjoyment of divine favour and protection leads to an opposite
result. Marriage with Saul's daughter will also strengthen his
eventual claim to be Saul's legitimate successor and to rule all
Israel (see 2 Sam. 3: 13ff.). ✷

THREAT AND ESCAPE

Saul spoke to Jonathan his son and all his household about **19** killing David. But Jonathan was devoted to David and 2 told him that his father Saul was looking for an opportunity to kill him. 'Be on your guard tomorrow morning,' he said; 'conceal yourself, and remain in hiding. Then I 3 will come out and join my father in the open country where you are and speak to him about you, and if I discover anything I will tell you.' Jonathan spoke up for 4 David to his father Saul and said to him, 'Sir, do not wrong your servant David; he has not wronged you; his conduct towards you has been beyond reproach. Did he 5 not take his life in his hands when he killed the Philistine, and the LORD won a great victory for Israel? You saw it, you shared in the rejoicing; why should you wrong an innocent man and put David to death without cause?' Saul listened to Jonathan and swore solemnly by the LORD 6 that David should not be put to death. So Jonathan called 7 David and told him all this; then he brought him to Saul, and he was in attendance on the king as before.

War broke out again, and David attacked the Phili- 8 stines and dealt them such a blow that they ran before him.

An evil spirit from the LORD came upon Saul as he was 9 sitting in the house with his spear in his hand; and David was playing the harp. Saul tried to pin David to the wall 10 with the spear, but he avoided the king's thrust so that Saul drove the spear into the wall. David escaped and got safely away. That night Saul sent servants to keep watch 11 on David's house, intending to kill him in the morning, but David's wife Michal warned him to get away that

night, 'or tomorrow', she said, 'you will be a dead man.'
12 She let David down through a window and he slipped
13 away and escaped. Michal took their household gods[a] and
put them on the bed; at its head she laid a goat's-hair rug
14 and covered it all with a cloak. When the men arrived to
15 arrest David she told them he was ill. Saul sent them back
to see David for themselves. 'Bring him to me, bed and
16 all,' he said, 'and I will kill him.' When they came, there
were the household gods on the bed and the goat's-hair
17 rug at its head. Then Saul said to Michal, 'Why have you
played this trick on me and let my enemy get safe away?'
And Michal answered, 'He said to me, "Help me to
escape or I will kill you."'

* Three distinct stories (verses 1–7, 9–10 and 11–17) are here
joined, with a link verse (8).

1. The text expresses more than a discussion of Saul's plan:
it implies a definite threat, almost perhaps an order to *Jonathan*
and *all his household.* Jonathan's love for David is mentioned as
if it had not been spoken of in 18: 2–4.

2f. The plan contrived by Jonathan is not fully developed.
It looks like an alternative version of the longer and fuller
story in chapter 20. The implication is that David will be
hidden within earshot, while Jonathan persuades his father to
relent.

4f. The theme of David's innocence in his dealings with
Saul is more fully worked out in two narratives in chapters 24
and 26, when David finds Saul in his power. Jonathan's appeal
is to David's heroism and to Saul's recognition that in this *a
great victory* was given to Israel by God. The valour of God's
chosen ones is the expression of his own saving purpose.

6f. Saul's withdrawal of his threat is solemnly sworn. But
David's restoration to a close relationship is only temporary.

[a] *Heb.* teraphim.

8. A link verse, with an allusion to a further victory of David over *the Philistines*. The compiler thus skilfully introduces the idea of Saul's jealousy, without actually mentioning it.

9f. These verses—see also 18: 10f.—are really a second story, now used to introduce the third. The hostility of Saul is attributed to the withdrawal of divine favour which results in possession by what is described as *an evil spirit from the LORD*. *escaped and got safely away:* this implies more than a return home, but it has now been linked to a different story of Saul's hostility. *That night:* actually part of verse 10, but better to be seen as the beginning of the third story. It provides a clear chronological link, but perhaps it originally referred to David's and Michal's wedding night. That would be the natural moment for Saul's hatred to become evident.

11f. *Michal* in this story plays the same part as was played by Jonathan in verses 1–7 (see note on 18: 20f.). The story leaves much unsaid. How, if Saul's servants were watching David's house, did he succeed in getting away *through a window*? We are not told that the house was by the city wall, as in the story of Rahab and the spies (Josh. 2: 15). If he had escaped, what was the purpose of pretending that he was ill in bed? Was it to give him more time, or should we suppose another version in which he eluded the servants of Saul while they returned to the king? It looks as though there are reminiscences of two stories here, alternative versions of the stratagem devised by Michal.

13. What Michal did is also not really clear. *household gods* (N.E.B. footnote gives the Hebrew word 'teraphim'): such evidence as we have suggests that these were small objects. Rachel stole her father's teraphim—they could clearly be easily carried—and hid them in the camel-bag and sat on them (Gen. 31: 34). Teraphim may be a term covering more than one type of religious object. The Jacob narrative strongly suggests a connection with the headship of the clan, and this

may be paralleled in the texts from Nuzi in northern Mesopotamia. A tablet from there, dating from about 1500 to 1400 B.C., says that an adopted son may share in the inheritance, but the natural son inherits the household gods. In Judg. 17: 5, teraphim appear in a household shrine. The present story may suggest a connection with healing, or with the interpretation of dreams and omens which would be of value to a sick man. The N.E.B. rendering suggests a full-size figure which could look like a person lying in bed. But it is more probable that Michal put the *goat's-hair rug* at the bed head to look like David's hair, and suggested her husband's figure by arranging the bedding. The *household gods* she placed 'beside' the bed— the Hebrew can be so translated. The figurines would thus have a protective function; a sick man would naturally want them near him, just as many religious people, Christians and others, like to have emblems of holy men, or icons. They are not worshipped, but can be seen as symbols of divine power and care.

14–16. We should perhaps suppose that the men looked through the door and saw the 'household gods' and what appeared to be a figure on the bed. It would appear to them improper to come near and interfere with the sick man. Only when they are specially commanded do they pick up the bed, and *when they came*, that is, into Saul's presence, the subterfuge is discovered.

17. Saul's hostility to Michal is to be paralleled by his anger at Jonathan's behaviour in 20: 30f.

The compiler has his theological purpose in mind; all the time we move on towards David's kingship. But meantime, he tells a good story, and one in which the laugh is against Saul. *

DAVID ESCAPES AGAIN

18 Meanwhile David made good his escape and came to Samuel at Ramah, and told him how Saul had treated him. Then he and Samuel went to Naioth and stayed

there. Saul was told that David was there, and he sent a 19,20
party of men to seize him. When they saw the company
of prophets in rapture, with Samuel standing at their
head, the spirit of God came upon them and they fell into
prophetic rapture. When this was reported to Saul he 21
sent another party. These also fell into a rapture, and when
he sent more men a third time, they did the same. Saul 22
himself then set out for Ramah and came to the great
cistern in Secu. He asked where Samuel and David were
and was told that they were at Naioth in Ramah. On his 23
way there the spirit of God came upon him too and he
went on, in a rapture as he went, till he came to Naioth in
Ramah. There he too stripped off his clothes and like the 24
rest fell into a rapture before Samuel and lay down naked
all that day and all that night. That is why men say, 'Is
Saul also among the prophets?'

* 18. The reappearance of *Samuel* at this point comes as
somewhat of a surprise, especially in view of 15: 34f. He has
not appeared since 16: 1-13, and in the intervening chapters
there is no place for him in the events. His mention would seem
to be due partly to the existence of this piece of tradition and
partly to a compiler's desire to suggest that behind the events,
as it were watching over them, is the figure of the prophet, the
king-maker. The fortunes of David are his concern, for he is
the spokesman of God. *Naioth:* a proper name, or a word
meaning 'pastures' or 'dwellings', at *Ramah* or nearby,
perhaps a prophetic settlement, like the one mentioned in
2 Kings 6: 1.

19-21. Saul's threefold attempt at arresting David provides
a link to the preceding narrative; it is reminiscent also of the
attempts at arresting Elijah in 2 Kings 1: 9ff., though the latter
is grim where this is almost comic. *prophetic rapture:* for this as

contagious, see note on 10: 5 and also Num. 11: 24–30. *Samuel*, remarkably, appears as the leader of this prophetic company; we have seen that this may be inferred in chapter 10 (see note on p. 85).

22. When the messengers fail, Saul goes himself. A note is made of an otherwise unknown landmark on the way, *the great cistern* or well in *Secu*, presumably a great artificial water store. The place is otherwise unknown; Sept. has 'at the threshing-floor on the height'.

23. The prophetic power comes upon Saul *on his way*, an example of contagion at a distance as also in Num. 11: 25 f., where 'prophetic ecstasy' falls on a large group and also on two members of the group elsewhere.

24. In this state, *he too stripped off his clothes*, apparently like all the other members of the band—did this include Samuel and David?—and the messengers. Examples of such endurance are known from religious practice in many parts of the world. In such a state, men do not show awareness of the normal experiences; daytime might be very hot and night-time very cold. *Is Saul also among the prophets?*—the proverb already explained at 10: 10–12; see the note there. The double explanation inevitably leaves us in doubt which, if either, is correct.

It is a curious story, but one which by implication brings out the divine protection of David. Here, through Samuel and his company, the divine will reaches out to frustrate Saul's repeated attacks. ✳

DAVID AND JONATHAN IN COVENANT

20 Then David made his escape from Naioth in Ramah and came to Jonathan. 'What have I done?' he asked. 'What is my offence? What does your father think I have done 2 wrong, that he seeks my life?' Jonathan answered him, 'God forbid! There is no thought of putting you to death. I am sure my father will not do anything whatever with-

out telling me. Why should my father hide such a thing
from me? I cannot believe it!' David said, 'I am ready to ₃
swear to it: your father has said to himself, "Jonathan
must not know this or he will resent it", because he
knows that you have a high regard for me. As the LORD
lives, your life upon it, there is only a step between me
and death.' Jonathan said to David, 'What do you want ₄
me to do for you?' David answered, 'It is new moon ₅
tomorrow, and I ought to dine with the king. Let me go
and lie hidden in the fields until the third evening. If your ₆
father happens to miss me, then say, "David asked me for
leave to pay a rapid visit to his home in Bethlehem, for it
is the annual sacrifice there for the whole family." If he ₇
says, "Well and good", that will be a good sign for me;
but if he flies into a rage, you will know that he is set on
doing me wrong. My lord, keep faith with me; for you ₈
and I have entered into a solemn compact before the LORD.
Kill me yourself if I am guilty. Why let me fall into your
father's hands?' 'God forbid!' cried Jonathan. 'If I find ₉
my father set on doing you wrong I will tell you.' David ₁₀
answered Jonathan, 'How will you let me know if he
answers harshly?' Jonathan said, 'Come with me into the ₁₁
fields.' So they went together into the fields, and Jonathan ₁₂
said to David, 'I promise you, David, in the sight of the
LORD*a* the God of Israel, this time tomorrow I will sound
my father for the third time and, if he is well disposed to
you, I will send and let you know. If my father means ₁₃
mischief, the LORD do the same to me and more, if I do
not let you know and get you safely away. The LORD be
with you as he has been with my father! I know that as ₁₄

[a] David, 'I promise...of the LORD: *so Pesh.; Heb.* David, the LORD...

long as I live you will show me faithful friendship, as the
15 LORD requires; and if I should die, you will continue loyal
to my family for ever. When the LORD rids the earth of all
16 David's enemies, may the LORD call him*a* to account if he
17 and his house are no longer my friends.'*b* Jonathan pledged
himself afresh to David*c* because of his love for him, for he
18 loved him as himself. Then he said to him, 'Tomorrow is
the new moon, and you will be missed when your place
19 is empty. So go down at nightfall for the third time to the
place where you hid on the evening of the feast and stay
20 by the mound there.*d* Then I will shoot three arrows
21 towards it, as though I were aiming at a mark. Then I will
send my boy to find the arrows. If I say to him, "Look,
the arrows are on this side of you, pick them up", then
you can come out of hiding. You will be quite safe, I
22 swear it; for there will be nothing amiss. But if I say to the
lad, "Look, the arrows are on the other side of you,
23 further on", then the LORD has said that you must go; the
LORD stand witness between us for ever to the pledges we
have exchanged.'

✻ Chapter 20 offers a new story, in some respects resembling
that in 19: 1–7. It is again evident that different forms of the
same tradition have been combined. At one point the warning
is to be given by a previously arranged sign, at another point
the warning is given directly. The text of the chapter is
particularly difficult and uncertain, as the N.E.B. footnotes in
part reveal; but the main points are clear enough.
    1. The opening clause links the new story to the one in

[a] *So Luc. Sept.; Heb.* David's enemies.
[b] he and...friends: *so Sept.; Heb. obscure.*
[c] pledged...to David: *so Sept.; Heb.* made David swear.
[d] *Prob. rdg., cp. Sept.; Heb.* by the Azel stone.

19: 18–24, set at *Ramah*. David's perplexity at Saul's hostility and Jonathan's confidence that no such hostile intention exists are both surprising after the preceding narratives. We must simply accept that the compiler has woven together different traditions.

2. *I cannot believe it*: a free paraphrase of words which mean simply: 'not this'.

3. The friendship of Jonathan is presented by David as the motive for Saul's concealment of his plans; the hostile intentions of Saul are only too plain to him. *only a step*: a vivid metaphor for the expression of danger.

5–7. David has a plan to test Saul's intentions, a method by which a word will be spoken either of good omen or of ill. Saul's reaction here can be given a rational explanation—if he is content at David's absence, all is well; if he is angry, then he may be assumed to suspect David's intentions. This latter point is brought out in verses 26ff. Yet it is through his response that the will of God for David is expressed, for so God will show his protection. *new moon*: a special day of religious celebration, mentioned a number of times in the Old Testament alongside the Sabbath; thus in 2 Kings 4: 23 it is regarded as specially suitable for consulting a prophet. Here it appears to be the occasion of an *annual sacrifice*, presumably therefore a great occasion. The celebration appears to be for three days, but the note may be designed to harmonize this part of the narrative with the sequel.

8. The *compact* between Jonathan and David is here noted again; cp. 18: 3. It is described as a 'covenant of the LORD', which suggests one which is ratified before God, perhaps in a shrine. The appeal to Jonathan to kill him if he is guilty suggests that David sees that the only point at which such a guilt could be incurred is if he has broken faith with the family of Saul.

11. It is not at all clear why, at this point, David and Jonathan go into the open country; possibly there is here an element of a separate tradition which laid stress on the

secrecy of the covenant between the two and which appears to have envisaged a consultation between them during the period of the feast.

12. *for the third time*: probably a harmonizing phrase.

13. Jonathan's words are in the form of a solemn oath, invoking disaster upon himself if he does not warn David.

14. *faithful friendship, as the LORD requires*: literally 'loyalty of the LORD', that expression of a bond between man and man which corresponds to the bond which exists between God and Israel. The word *ḥesed* used here is a central term in Old Testament thinking about the relationship between God and man, and between man and man; it means 'loyalty, faithfulness' and often 'love, lovingkindness, grace'.

15. The covenant is to be a perpetual one, between David and the whole family of Jonathan. This is picked up subsequently, after the defeat of David's enemies (noted in 2 Sam. 7: 1 and described in 2 Sam. 8), in the story of David's protection and favour to a lame son of Jonathan named Mephibosheth (2 Sam. 9).

17 is possibly explanatory, linking this story of the covenant with the earlier statements in 18: 3.

18. An alternative story of the feast begins here. Now it is Jonathan who raises the question of David's absence and sees it as an opportunity for discovering Saul's intentions.

19. *for the third time*: another harmonizing addition. The text of this verse is very confused and obscure. *the mound*: or 'stone-heap', probably a well-known landmark, pointed out in later times as the site of the story. In the comparable phrase in verse 41, there is a different textual corruption.

20–2. The sign to be given to David is described. Clearly it envisages David in hiding (cp. 19: 2f.), and the *boy* with Jonathan as unaware of his presence. What Jonathan does and says has a double meaning, thus conveying warning or hope to David without the boy being able to know what has taken place. Jonathan's precautions seem designed to provide a

witness who can assure Saul that he did not meet David while
out shooting.

23. The solemn bond is again stated. *witness between us:* God
himself ensures the covenant. We may compare the covenant
description in Gen. 15 in which very ancient ideas of covenant
ritual are preserved. ✻

DAVID WARNED TO ESCAPE

So David hid in the fields. The new moon came, the 24
dinner was prepared, and the king sat down to eat. Saul 25
took his customary seat by the wall, and Abner sat beside
him; Jonathan too was present, but David's place was
empty. That day Saul said nothing, for he thought that 26
David was absent by some chance, perhaps because he was
ritually unclean. But on the second day,[a] the day after the
new moon, David's place was still empty, and Saul said to 27
his son Jonathan, 'Why has not the son of Jesse come to
the feast, either yesterday or today?' Jonathan answered 28
Saul, 'David asked permission to go to Bethlehem. He 29
asked my leave and said, "Our family is holding a sacrifice
in the town and my brother himself has ordered me to be
there. Now, if you have any regard for me, let me slip
away to see my brothers." That is why he has not come to
dine with the king.' Saul was angry with Jonathan, 'You 30
son of a crooked and unfaithful mother! You have made
friends with[b] the son of Jesse only to bring shame on
yourself and dishonour on your mother; I see how it will
be. As long as Jesse's son remains alive on earth, neither 31
you nor your crown will be safe. Send at once and fetch
him; he deserves to die.' Jonathan answered his father, 32

[a] on the second day: *so Sept.; Heb.* the second.
[b] *So Sept.; Heb.* You are choosing.

33 'Deserves to die! Why? What has he done?' At that, Saul picked up his spear and threatened to kill him; and he
34 knew that his father was bent on David's death. Jonathan left the table in a rage and ate nothing on the second day of the festival; for he was indignant on David's behalf because his father had humiliated him.

35 Next morning, Jonathan went out into the fields to meet David at the appointed time, taking a young boy
36 with him. He said to the boy, 'Run and find the arrows; I am going to shoot.' The boy ran on, and he shot the
37 arrows over his head. When the boy reached the place where Jonathan's arrows had fallen, Jonathan called out
38 after him, 'Look, the arrows are beyond you. Hurry! No time to lose! Make haste!' The boy gathered up the
39 arrows and brought them to his master; but only Jonathan and David knew what this meant; the boy knew nothing.
40 Jonathan handed his weapons to the boy and told him to
41 take them back to the city. When the boy had gone, David got up from behind the mound*a* and bowed humbly three times. Then they kissed one another and shed tears together, until David's grief was even greater than
42 Jonathan's. Jonathan said to David, 'Go in safety; we have pledged each other in the name of the LORD who is witness for ever between you and me and between your descendants and mine.'

*b*David went off at once, while Jonathan returned to the city.

✻ 24. *the dinner was prepared:* the text is not clear; probably we should read *the king sat down* 'at the table'. The same phrase

[a] *Prob. rdg., cp. Sept.; Heb.* the Negeb.　　[b] *21: 1 in Heb.*

appears in verse 29 where 'to dine with the king' is literally 'to the king's table'.

25. The king sits with his back to the wall, a position of safety and no doubt of honour, with his army commander *Abner* at his side. *Jonathan too was present:* we might follow Sept.: 'Jonathan was in front of him', which is implied by verse 33.

26. The feast is a religious occasion, and ritual impurity could prevent David's attendance. He might, for example, have come in contact with a dead body, or be otherwise temporarily unfit to be present (cp. the regulations in Deut. 23: 10; Lev. 15: 16).

28 f. Jonathan repeats David's excuse, in a form somewhat more elaborate than in verse 6, emphasizing the family obligation.

30. Saul's curse on Jonathan imputes the cause of his folly to his mother, with the implication that he is no true son. Actually, the phrase translated *crooked and unfaithful mother* is far from clear. Jonathan's folly is further said to bring *shame on yourself and dishonour on your mother*, for it will, as verse 31 makes plain, lose him the kingdom. *You have made friends with:* the implication here may be that as David is loyal to his family so Jonathan should be to his. N.E.B. footnote shows that the Heb. has 'you are choosing'. The words differ only in the order of the letters. This suggests the idea that Jonathan is in a sense 'choosing' David whom God has chosen. Did a copyist make the alteration because he saw this possible meaning in the text?

34. Friendship for David explains Jonathan's *rage*; David has been humiliated by Saul's words of doom. But underlying this, the story-teller sees the acceptance by Jonathan that the crown is David's not his. The humiliating of David is in a sense due to Saul's refusal to acknowledge this. Saul refuses to give him the honour due to him, and the humiliated chosen king must go into exile.

35-9 relate the sign with the arrows. All that is left now is for David to escape while Jonathan and the boy return to the city.

40. Unexpectedly, however, Jonathan dismisses the boy and the two men meet.

41. *bowed humbly three times:* an appropriate gesture to the king's son, though perhaps here also an acknowledgement of God's will in the events. *until David's grief was even greater...:* an obscure phrase. It seems not unlikely that something is missing. Sept. has 'to a great climax'.

42. The covenant is yet again repeated; it is between the two families of David and Jonathan. The second half of the verse provides a link to the next story, being regarded in the Hebrew text as the beginning of the new section.

The narrative is involved, but the main point is clear. Jonathan's covenant with David is fundamental to him; thereby he accepts the coming kingship of David. Such an acceptance of David counters any suggestion that he was a usurper on the throne. With this goes the assurance that David will not, like some kings of new lines (cp. the Jehu story in 2 Kings 9–10), wipe out the survivors of the preceding royal house. In fact, we are shown David angered at the death of Ishbosheth (2 Sam. 4) and benevolent to Jonathan's son (2 Sam. 9). The emphasis on David's coming kingship provides the introduction to stories which tell largely of David as a hunted fugitive, a humiliated king. ✳

DAVID AND AHIMELECH

21[a] David made his way to the priest Ahimelech at Nob, who hurried out to meet him and said, 'Why have you 2 come alone and no one with you?' David answered Ahimelech, 'I am under orders from the king: I was to let no one know about the mission on which he was sending me or what these orders were. When I took leave of my men I told them to meet me in such and such a place.

[a] 21: 2 in Heb.

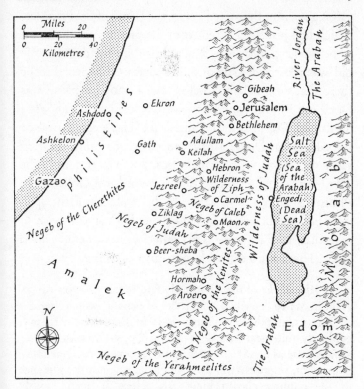

3. The southern area (mainly 1 Samuel 20–30)

Now, what have you got by you? Let me have five 3
loaves, or as many as you can find.' The priest answered 4
David, 'I have no ordinary bread available. There is only
the sacred bread; but have the young men kept themselves
from women?' David answered the priest, 'Women have 5
been denied us hitherto, when I have been on campaign,
even an ordinary campaign, and the young men's bodies
have remained holy; and how much more will they be
holy today?' So, as there was no other bread there, the 6

priest gave him the sacred bread, the Bread of the Presence, which had just been taken from the presence of the LORD to be replaced by freshly baked bread on the day that the
7 old was removed. One of Saul's servants happened to be there that day, detained before the LORD; his name was Doeg the Edomite, and he was the strongest of all Saul's
8 herdsmen. David said to Ahimelech, 'Have you a spear or sword here at hand? I have no sword or other weapon
9 with me, because the king's business was urgent.' The priest answered, 'There is the sword of Goliath the Philistine whom you slew in the Vale of Elah; it is wrapped up in a cloak behind the ephod. If you wish to take that, take it; there is no other weapon here.' David said, 'There is no sword like it; give it to me.'

✶ 1. *Ahimelech:* of the Eli priestly family (see note on 14: 3). *Nob:* in 22: 19 described as 'the city of priests', which suggests an important religious centre. It is in Benjamite territory, evidently quite near Jerusalem (see map, p. 48). *hurried out:* the same phrase as in 16: 4; better 'came in reverence', since this, here again, suggests awe, the awe of the priest at the presence of the coming chosen king. Ahimelech is unconsciously offering homage to David.

2. David conceals that he is a fugitive. *I told them to meet me:* an alternative rendering has been proposed: 'I said farewell to the young men...' This would picture David as now continuing alone, as indeed the next narrative (verses 10–15) suggests, though the stories are not to be regarded as in chronological order.

4. *sacred bread:* more fully explained in verse 6. In view of the size of the settlement (see 22: 18 f.), the lack of *ordinary bread* is inexplicable. The point of the story must be that David is to receive the holy food as befits a king. The priest's inquiry is designed to ensure that David and his company are in a

ritually fit state to touch the sacred food, for otherwise they would be in danger from its holiness. Ritual purity involved abstinence from sexual intercourse (cp. Exod. 19: 15).

5. The precise meaning of this verse is not clear. For an *ordinary campaign* such abstinence is proper; for a sacred undertaking, the demand for holiness is all the greater. 2 Sam. 11: 6–13 shows Uriah, the husband of Bathsheba, respecting these campaign customs even though he is at home.

6. *the sacred bread, the Bread of the Presence:* or 'shrewbread' as N.E.B. footnote at Exod. 25: 30. These were the loaves, twelve in number according to Lev. 24: 5, which were placed regularly in the shrine before the deity, and removed at intervals (Lev. 24: 8 indicates that this was done each Sabbath) to be replaced by *freshly baked bread*, literally 'hot' bread. According to Lev. 24, only the priests could eat it (cp. Mark 2: 23–8), but at an earlier time, as appears here, the only requirement was strict ritual cleanness. We may, however, detect here that this sacred bread is appropriate for the chosen king. A similar token is given to Saul after his anointing (10: 4). Jesus' use of this passage may suggest that he was not only arguing on the basis of a precedent, but that he was also pointing to himself as the new David, the new chosen king.

7. This verse points forward to the disaster at Nob described in 22: 9–23. *Doeg the Edomite* was evidently a notable warrior. His Edomite ancestry is stated without comment (Sept. has 'Aramaean'); yet it was perhaps felt fitting that this man should belong to that hated people. *detained:* the word suggests that he was in some way under constraint by the divine will. The term is used of Jeremiah, unable to go to the temple (Jer. 36: 5), and of a prophet Shemaiah in Neh. 6: 10. Was Doeg perhaps a religious official, a herdsman of temple flocks and herds, held at Nob by religious constraint and strangely used by God to bring disaster? The context offers no explanation, but see also the note on 22: 22.

9. David's request for a weapon leads to his receiving *the sword of Goliath*. The narrative of chapter 17 leaves some

uncertainty about what happened to Goliath's weapons, but, as we saw at 17: 54, the words possibly suggest that they were placed in a 'tent-shrine'. Again, the implication is that the coming king is to be armed with a sword of unparalleled quality. *the ephod* here appears to be a solid object.

The story, like so many Old Testament narratives, is to be read at two levels. At one, it is a straightforward story of the fugitive David, skilfully getting food and a weapon for himself from the innocent priest. At the other, it shows how the priest of Saul himself acknowledges the coming king, offering protection and help, and it points the way into another event, the slaughter at Nob, which shows how unsuited Saul is for the royal position. ✴

DAVID AT GATH—I

10 That day, David went on his way, eluding Saul, and came
11 to Achish king of Gath. The servants of Achish said to him, 'Surely this is David, the king of his country, the man of whom they sang as they danced:

> Saul made havoc among thousands
> but David among tens of thousands.'

12 These words were not lost on David, and he became very
13 much afraid of Achish king of Gath. So he altered his behaviour in public and acted like a lunatic in front of them all, scrabbling on the double doors of the city gate and
14 dribbling down his beard. Achish said to his servants, 'The
15 man is mad! Why bring him to me? Am I short of madmen that you bring this one to plague me? Must I have this fellow in my house?'

✴ An alternative account of David's contact with Achish is found in 27: 1–6, with a sequel in chapter 29. There is a curious contrast between David, the wielder of Goliath's sword (verse 9), and David, the fugitive.

10. 27: 1 pictures David as only then deciding that real escape is impossible except in alien, Philistine, territory. Here he comes without explanation, presumably supposing that as an enemy of Saul he may be acceptable in Gath. *Achish:* a Philistine name, perhaps an equivalent of the name Anchises used in Homer and Virgil for the father of Aeneas. *king:* the normal Hebrew word, as also in chapter 27, not the word used for the Philistine lords in 5: 8 (see note).

11. *David, the king of his country:* actually 'of the land'. Is this an anachronism, or are we to see that the Philistines too are among those who already perceive David's kingship? A very slight emendation would give 'the one who smites the land', a reminiscence of his attacks on the Philistines. The men of Gath repeat in awe the refrain by which David was hailed (18: 7).

13. *he altered his behaviour:* or 'his behaviour was altered', the text perhaps meaning that God changed him and thereby enabled him to escape the danger. The story would then provide a counterpart to 19: 18–24, and the next verses suggest this too. *in front of them all:* actually, 'in their hands'. This phrase, together with the word 'bring' in verse 15, suggests an actual arrest of David by Achish's servants. The sudden change in his demeanour would then even more appropriately be described as due to divine intervention.

14. Madness and prophetic inspiration are not necessarily distinguishable. The prophet who was sent by Elisha to anoint Jehu is described as 'this crazy fellow' (2 Kings 9: 11), but he has brought the divine command; the possibility of confusion is pointed out in Hos. 9: 7: 'the prophet shall be made a fool and the inspired seer a madman'. The ravings of the mad are thought to be due to the activity of a divine spirit and may contain divine revelation.

The tale is not without its humour, reminiscent of the tricks played by Samson; but basically it too is concerned with men's recognition of David and God's protection of him. *

173

DAVID THE OUTLAW

22 David made his escape and went from there to the cave of Adullam. When his brothers and all his family heard that
2 he was there, they joined him. Men in any kind of distress or in debt or with a grievance gathered round him, about
3 four hundred in number, and he became their chief. From there David went to Mizpeh in Moab and said to the king of Moab, 'Let my father and mother come and take shelter
4 with you until I know what God will do for me.' So he left them at the court of the king of Moab, and they stayed there as long as David was in his stronghold.

5 The prophet Gad said to David, 'You must not stay in your stronghold; go at once into Judah.' So David went
6 as far as the forest of Hareth. News that David and his men had been seen reached Saul while he was in Gibeah, sitting under the tamarisk-tree on the hill-top with his spear in his hand and all his retainers standing about him.
7 He said to them, 'Listen to me, you Benjamites: do you expect the son of Jesse to give you all fields and vineyards, or make you all officers over units of a thousand and a
8 hundred? Is that why you have all conspired against me? Not one of you told me when my son made a compact with the son of Jesse; none of you spared a thought for me or told me that my son had set my own servant against me, who is lying in wait for me now.'

* 1. *cave of Adullam*: Adullam is a city in the hill country to the south-west of Jerusalem (see map, p.169). But whether the cave is nearby is not known. One might have expected the refuge to be in the wild country east of Bethlehem, nearer to Moab. In verses 4f., there is reference, however, to a 'strong-

hold', a word very similar to the word for *cave*. Perhaps we should read 'stronghold' here and suppose that David occupied the city of Adullam, as subsequently we find him at Keilah (23: 1 ff.) in the same area. In the narratives of these chapters, various pictures are given of David's activities and they do not exactly fit together. He is a fugitive, hiding in remote places; he is a powerful military leader, defeating the Philistines; he is the leader of a band offering protection to the Judaean communities. All these are now woven together to portray a divinely-decreed progress to final triumph. That David's family joined him is a natural procedure, for Saul might be expected to aim an attack at them. The risk to those who are connected with David becomes plain in verses 9 ff.

2. David as outlaw is joined by a band of malcontents, just as was the hero Jephthah (Judg. 11: 3). The story-teller does not comment adversely on these *men...with a grievance*, any more than the 'idle men' (better perhaps 'propertyless men') with Jephthah are viewed with disapproval.

3. *Mizpeh* (the same word as 'Mizpah', see on 7: 5): a common place name, meaning 'watchtower'. David found shelter among the Philistine enemies of Saul (cp. 21: 10ff., 27); so too *the king of Moab* would protect one who was the opponent of a neighbouring ruler. The book of Ruth, telling the story of a Moabite woman who accepted Israel's God and became a full member of the community, links her with the family of David. The story may have become attached to the Davidic tradition because of this reference to David's friendly contacts with the Moabite royal house. 2 Sam. 8: 2, however, records David's later brutal defeat and suppression of Moab. *what God will do for me*: underlying all David's actions, there is a deep religious sense, almost a religious fatalism; if God wills it, he will be king, but if God decrees otherwise, then who can withstand him? He shows this attitude very plainly at the time of his son Absalom's rebellion (2 Sam. 15: 24–6).

4. *his stronghold*: cp. the note on verse 1. The Syriac translation, here and in the next verse, has 'Mizpeh', suggesting that

David himself was for a time a refugee in Moab. This accords better with the content of verse 5.

5. *The prophet Gad* is introduced without explanation and appears again similarly as prophetic adviser in 2 Sam. 24. Later tradition (1 Chron. 29: 30) ascribes to Gad, and to Samuel and Nathan, the other prophets closely associated with David, the recording of the events of the period of David. David must return to Judah, for it is there that his destiny will be fulfilled. Cp. Luke 13: 33: 'it is unthinkable for a prophet to meet his death anywhere but in Jerusalem'. *Hareth:* or 'Hereth', an unknown place in Judah, perhaps a dialect spelling of the name Horesh (23: 15).

6. Saul at *Gibeah* holds a war-council, sitting under a notable tree (see note on 10: 3), perhaps in the shrine, since for *hill-top* we might read 'high-place'. For *had been seen* the alternative 'had joined together' has been proposed.

7. Here there appears to be a clear echo of 8: 12, 14. Saul's retainers are reminded of the advantages of serving him; as Benjamites they could expect no favours from a Judaean king. The implication may be that David's kingship will be quite different.

8. Saul interprets the actions of Jonathan as deliberate incitement of David to rebellion. Curiously enough, Jonathan now disappears from the story, apart from a repetition of his covenant with David in 23: 16ff. and his death with Saul at Mount Gilboa (31: 2). *lying in wait:* Sept. has 'as an enemy', reading a very similar word (cp. on verse 13).

The story is told from David's point of view, pointing forward all the time. To Saul, the outlaw and his band must have seemed a serious threat. ✳

THE MASSACRE OF THE PRIESTS

Then Doeg the Edomite, who was standing with the servants of Saul, spoke: 'I saw the son of Jesse coming to
10 Nob, to Ahimelech son of Ahitub. Ahimelech consulted

the LORD on his behalf, then gave him food and handed over to him the sword of Goliath the Philistine.' The 11 king sent for Ahimelech the priest and his family, who were priests at Nob, and they all came into his presence. Saul said, 'Now listen, you son of Ahitub', and the man 12 answered, 'Yes, my lord?' Then Saul said to him, 'Why 13 have you and the son of Jesse plotted against me? You gave him food and the sword too, and consulted God on his behalf; and now he has risen against me and is at this moment lying in wait for me.' 'And who among all your 14 servants', answered Ahimelech, 'is like David, a man to be trusted, the king's son-in-law, appointed to your staff and holding an honourable place in your household? Have I on this occasion done something profane in 15 consulting God on his behalf? God forbid! I trust that my lord the king will not accuse me or my family; for I know nothing whatever about it.' But the king said, 'Ahimelech, 16 you must die, you and all your family.' He then turned 17 to the bodyguard attending him and said, 'Go and kill the priests of the LORD; for they are in league with David, and, though they knew that he was a fugitive, they did not tell me.' The king's men, however, were unwilling to raise a hand against the priests of the LORD. The king therefore 18 said to Doeg the Edomite, 'You, Doeg, go and fall upon the priests'; so Doeg went and fell upon the priests, killing that day with his own hand eighty-five men who could carry the ephod.[a] He put to the sword every living thing 19 in Nob, the city of priests: men and women, children and babes in arms, oxen, asses, and sheep. One son of Ahime- 20 lech named Abiathar made his escape and joined David.

[a] *So Sept.; Heb.* the linen ephod.

21 He told David how Saul had killed the priests of the LORD.
22 Then David said to him, 'When Doeg the Edomite was there that day, I knew that he would inform Saul. I have
23 gambled with the lives of all your father's family. Stay here with me, have no fear; he who seeks your life seeks mine, and you will be safe with me.'

✻ 9. The section begins as a sequel to verses 6–8, but the phrase *who was standing with the servants of Saul* could very easily be a harmonizing addition to bring the passages together; originally this story may have followed more directly on 21: 1–9.

10. *consulted the LORD:* this is not stated in 21: 1–9. Now, set with the giving of *food* and *the sword of Goliath*, it emphasizes that unwittingly (so verse 15) Ahimelech has declared himself for David.

12. *you son of Ahitub* is not to be regarded as a scornful form of address. He is his father's son, holder of his father's office, a priest of high status.

13. *and now he has risen...for me:* possibly to be rendered: 'to rise against me as one who lies in wait' (or as Sept. 'as an enemy', cp. verse 8), thus describing Ahimelech himself as a rebel by reason of his support for David.

14. Ahimelech's reply is unconsciously ironic; he acknowledges his adherence to the true successor. *appointed to your staff:* possibly to be rendered 'officer over your staff (bodyguard)'.

15. Again here we see how the story is to be read at two levels. Ahimelech did not know what was going on, and disclaims any involvement; but he has done what he must, acting in accordance with a higher purpose, and by his acknowledgement of David has set himself inevitably against Saul.

17. Saul, it is now shown, is so impious as to turn against the whole priestly house which has set itself on David's side. Josephus (*Antiquities* VI, 12.7; 14.9) attributes his downfall to this and the failure described in chapter 15. The adherents of

the true ruler meet thus with opposition and death. The
compiler may have had in mind other occasions when faithfulness meant disaster. Faithful prophets were to die at
Jezebel's hand (1 Kings 18: 4), and much later, those who
resisted the commands of Antiochus Epiphanes were to face
martyrdom (1 Macc. 1: 41–64 and the stories in 2 Macc. 6 and
7). Saul has become one with the aliens who set themselves
against God. Even *the king's men* refuse to carry out such a
terrible order.

18 f. So it is the alien *Doeg the Edomite* who carries out the
slaughter—the whole priestly house and the whole population
of Nob. It is as if the city had been put to the ban, a terrible
reversal of that holy war which is waged against the opponents
of God (cp. note on 7: 9f.).

20. *Abiathar*, the *one son* who escapes, is to be priest and
close associate of David. The theme of divine blessing continuing through such a survivor is found in other stories, as in
that of Athaliah's massacre of the royal house of Judah from
which Joash alone was rescued to bring about her downfall
(2 Kings 11). A different version of Abiathar's escape appears
at 23: 6.

22. David's acknowledgement that he *knew that* Doeg
would inform Saul raises the question why he did not do anything to protect the priestly family. The story-teller is not
concerned with this, but only with showing how Saul's action,
designed to undermine David's position, in fact works God's
will by making his future kingship even clearer. Such a man as
Saul cannot endure. A further point may be implied in the
phrase *I have gambled*. The meaning is uncertain; many scholars
emend to 'I am guilty'. But a similar expression in 1 Kings
12: 15 describes how God himself has brought about a mis-
fortune, in this case the division of the kingdom. David
perhaps sees himself as the instrument of God's judgement on
the house of Eli, pronounced in 2: 27–36 and now completely
fulfilled.

23. The fortunes of David and Abiathar are to be inextric-

ably linked. Royal and priestly houses stand together. And
with Gad as his prophet (verse 5), David is fully authorized.

Saul has been rejected by Samuel (chapters 13 and 15); now
he has cast off entirely the priestly family which supported him
(cp. 14: 3, 36f.). *

DAVID AT KEILAH

23 The Philistines were fighting against Keilah and plunder-
2 ing the threshing-floors; and when David heard this, he
consulted the LORD and asked whether he should go and
attack the Philistines. The LORD answered, 'Go, attack
3 them, and relieve Keilah.' But David's men said to him,
'As we are now, we have enough to fear from Judah. How
much worse if we challenge the Philistine forces at
4 Keilah!' David consulted the LORD once again and the
LORD answered him, 'Go to Keilah; I will give the
5 Philistines into your hands.' So David and his men went
to Keilah and fought the Philistines; they carried off their
cattle, inflicted a heavy defeat on them and relieved the
6 inhabitants. Abiathar son of Ahimelech made good his
escape and joined David at Keilah, bringing the ephod
7 with him. Saul was told that David had entered Keilah,
and he said, 'God has put him into my hands; for he has
walked into a trap by entering a walled town with gates
8 and bars.' He called out the levy to march on Keilah and
9 besiege David and his men. When David learnt how Saul
planned his undoing, he told Abiathar the priest to bring
10 the ephod, and then he prayed, 'O LORD God of Israel, I
thy servant have heard news that Saul intends to come to
11 Keilah and destroy the city because of me. Will the
citizens of Keilah surrender me to him? Will Saul come
as I have heard? O LORD God of Israel, I pray thee, tell

thy servant.' The LORD answered, 'He will come.' Then 12
David asked, 'Will the citizens of Keilah surrender me
and my men to Saul?', and the LORD answered, 'They
will.' Then David left Keilah at once with his men, who 13
numbered about six hundred, and moved about from
place to place. When the news reached Saul that David
had escaped from Keilah, he made no further move.

✻ 1. *Keilah:* in the hill country not far from Adullam (see
map, p. 169) amid corn-growing valleys. The season of
threshing was a natural one for raids of this kind, as in the
story of Gideon (Judg. 6: 11). David is in a position to inflict
a defeat on the Philistines—scornfully described as 'these
Philistines' in verse 2 (N.E.B. renders simply 'the Philistines'),
for they are the uncircumcised enemies of God (see on 14: 6).
This will put him in favour with the Judaeans, while at the
same time he gains a stronger position for himself.

2f. David's consultation of the oracle—the precise means is
not named—indicates immediate action, but his men need
further conviction. *relieve Keilah:* the word means 'save' and
is often used of the Judges (e.g. Judg. 2: 16). David is a true
deliverer.

4. The second consultation brings an even firmer assurance
of victory. *Go to Keilah:* strictly 'go down', that is, from the
higher Judaean hills.

6. This verse explains how David is able to consult God
making use of *the ephod* carried by the proper priest (see note
on 2: 28f.). Since we are not told in 22: 20 where David was
when Abiathar joined him, the two statements can be
harmonized; but it is more natural to suppose that we have
here a relic of a different story of how the descendant of Eli
came to be on David's side.

7. *God has put him into my hands:* the Hebrew word suggests
rejection by God, but probably an emended text suggested by
Sept. should be read with the sense of 'deliver' or 'sell'. *he has*

walked into a trap: literally 'he has delivered himself up', the word used of the citizens of Keilah in verses 11f.

10. The inquiry is prefaced by a brief prayer form (cp.1:11).

11. The first question is here premature, having been accidentally copied from verse 12, and should be omitted. The reply here is to the second question only. The correct text, with the two questions and answers in clear sequence, is preserved in a Qumran fragment.

12f. *The citizens of Keilah* have just been delivered from the Philistine attacks by David. Gratitude might suggest that they should protect him, but the possibility of total disaster, such as fell on Nob, indicates prudence. By handing him over, they could hope for clemency. Compare the story of Sheba at Abel-beth-maacah in 2 Sam. 20: 14–22; such might have been David's fate had he not been divinely warned to escape.

David is now both fugitive and deliverer. Having saved Keilah, he does not put its people at risk nor let them incur guilt by laying their hands on him. ✳

DAVID AMONG THE ZIPHITES

14 While David was living in the fastnesses of the wilderness of Ziph, in the hill-country, Saul searched for him day
15 after day, but God did not put him into his power. David well knew that Saul had come out to seek his life; and
16 while he was at Horesh in the wilderness of Ziph, Saul's son Jonathan came to him there and gave him fresh
17 courage in God's name: 'Do not be afraid,' he said; 'my father's hand shall not touch you. You will become king of Israel and I shall hold rank after you; and my father
18 knows it.' The two of them made a solemn compact before the LORD; then David remained in Horesh and
19 Jonathan went home. While Saul was at Gibeah the Ziphites brought him this news: 'David, we hear, is in

hiding among us in the fastnesses of Horesh on the hill of
Hachilah, south of Jeshimon. Come down, your majesty, 20
come whenever you will, and we are able to surrender
him to you.' Saul said, 'The LORD has indeed blessed you; 21
you have saved me a world of trouble. Go now and make 22
further inquiry, and find out exactly where he is and who
saw him there. They tell me that he by himself is crafty
enough to outwit me. Find out which of his hiding-places 23
he is using; then come back to me at such and such a place,
and I will go along with you. So long as he stays in this
country, I will hunt him down, if I have to go through all
the clans of Judah one by one.' They set out for Ziph 24
without delay, ahead of Saul; David and his men were in
the wilderness of Maon in the Arabah to the south of
Jeshimon. Saul set off with his men to look for him; but 25
David got wind of it and went down to a refuge in the
rocks, and there he stayed in the wilderness of Maon.
Hearing of this, Saul went into the wilderness after him;
he was on one side of the hill, David and his men on the 26
other. While David and his men were trying desperately
to get away and Saul and his followers were closing in for
the capture, a runner brought a message to Saul: 'Come 27
at once! the Philistines are harrying the land.' So Saul 28
called off the pursuit and turned back to face the Philistines. This is why that place is called the Dividing Rock.
David went up from there and lived in the fastnesses of 29[a]
En-gedi.

* 14. *wilderness of Ziph*: further south, beyond Hebron (see
map, p.169). The verse is rather overloaded with topographical
detail. God's protection of David is made plain. *

[a] *24: 1 in Heb.*

15. *David well knew:* or 'was afraid', which provides a clearer background to the sequel in verses 16 ff. *Horesh:* see on 22: 5.

16–18. The reappearance of Jonathan is surprising, but it is clear that this re-statement of the covenant between him and David is designed to stress God's protection. The most explicit statement yet is made of David's coming kingship, with Jonathan seeing himself as occupying the second place in the new kingdom. Even Saul is said to be aware of the realities.

19. Like the people of Keilah, *the Ziphites* see a means to advantage. *Hachilah* is mentioned again in 26: 1; its precise position is unknown. 26: 1–3 is in fact a duplicate of this narrative, and both of these stories of David's difficulties serve to introduce incidents in which David has Saul in his power (chapter 24 and 26: 4–25). *Jeshimon:* probably not a proper name, but a word used for barren desert (e.g. in Deut. 32: 10).

22. *and who saw him there:* an ungrammatical phrase which possibly conceals an adjective giving the meaning 'find out exactly where his fleeting foot rests' or an adverb meaning 'speedily'.

23. *at such and such a place:* or possibly 'assuredly'. The implication of the second sentence is that David will either be caught or be driven out of Judah.

24. *Maon in the Arabah:* probably further south and east. *The Arabah* is the name given to the rift valley of which the Dead Sea forms a part. David is pressed further into the extreme part of Judah.

26 f. The pursuit becomes more and more tense, and David is surely to be caught when, providentially, a Philistine raid necessitates Saul's return.

28. The *rocks* mentioned in verse 25 are now identified; no doubt they were a landmark whose name was linked with the story. The name more probably means 'slippery'.

29. This verse is a link verse, joined in the Hebrew to chapter 24. *En-gedi* lies at the edge of the Dead Sea, built by one of the fresh water springs which make settlement possible

(see map, p. 169). David takes refuge in the rough country to which fugitives in other periods were to go—the Jewish nationalists of the war of A.D. 66–73 and the adherents of Bar-cocheba in A.D. 132–5, remains of whose stay have been found in the caves of the area and at Masada just south of En-gedi.

The two narratives of this chapter make it clear that Saul was still powerful, able to exert considerable control over Judah. We may see how the story has gradually been overlaid with the emphasis on David's superior position and his enjoyment of God's protection. ✶

SAUL AT THE MERCY OF DAVID—I

When Saul returned from the pursuit of the Philistines, he **24** learnt that David was in the wilderness of En-gedi. So he 2 took three thousand men picked from the whole of Israel and went in search of David and his men to the east of the Rocks of the Wild Goats. There beside the road were 3 some sheepfolds, and near by was a cave, at the far end of which David and his men were sitting concealed. Saul came to the cave and went in to relieve himself. His 4–7[a] men said to David, 'The day has come: the LORD has put your enemy into your hands, as he promised he would, and you may do what you please with him.' David said to his men, 'God forbid that I should harm my master, the LORD's anointed, or lift a finger against him; he is the LORD's anointed.' So David reproved his men severely and would not let them attack Saul. He himself got up stealthily and cut off a piece of Saul's cloak; but when he had cut it off, his conscience[b] smote him. Saul rose, left the cave and went on his way; whereupon David also 8

[a] *Verses 4–7 are re-arranged thus:* 4*a*, 6, 7*a*, 4*b*, 5, 7*b*. [b] *Lit.* heart.

came out of the cave and called after Saul, 'My lord the king!' When Saul looked round, David prostrated him-
9 self in obeisance and said to him, 'Why do you listen
10 when they say that David is out to do you harm? Today you can see for yourself that the LORD put you into my power in the cave; I had a mind to kill you, but no, I spared your life and said, "I cannot lift a finger against
11 my master, for he is the LORD's anointed." Look, my dear lord, look at this piece of your cloak in my hand. I cut it off, but I did not kill you; this will show you that I have no thought of violence or treachery against you, and that I have done you no wrong; yet you are resolved to take
12 my life. May the LORD judge between us! but though he may take vengeance on you for my sake, I will never lift
13 my hand against you; "One wrong begets another", as the old saying goes, yet I will never lift my hand against
14 you. Who has the king of Israel come out against? What
15 are you pursuing? A dead dog, a mere flea. The LORD will be judge and decide between us; let him look into my cause, he will plead for me and will acquit me.'

16 When David had finished speaking, Saul said, 'Is that
17 you, David my son?', and he wept. Then he said, 'The right is on your side, not mine; you have treated me so
18 well, I have treated you so badly. Your goodness to me this day has passed all bounds: the LORD put me at your
19 mercy but you did not kill me. Not often does a man find his enemy and let him go safely on his way; so may the LORD reward you well for what you have done for me
20 today! I know now for certain that you will become king, and that the kingdom of Israel will flourish under your
21 rule. Swear to me by the LORD then that you will not

exterminate my descendants and blot out my name from
my father's house.' David swore an oath to Saul; and Saul 22
went back to his home, while David and his men went up
to their fastness.

* This chapter contains the first of two narratives relating
how David, having Saul in his power, refuses to take advantage of the position. The second is in chapter 26. In both, the
climax is reached in Saul's acknowledgement of David's
coming kingship.

1. *wilderness of En-gedi*: this provides a link to the end of
chapter 23.

2. *three thousand*: the story-teller emphasizes the odds in
favour of Saul. David's band is here small enough to hide in a
cave (verse 3). A neat contrast is thus made between the
powerful Saul and the fugitive David into whose hands he
falls. *Rocks of the Wild Goats*: En-gedi means 'spring of the
goat-kid' (the word may also be used of a young sheep); it is
possible that this story has been attached at this point because
of the association in the two names. The name of the rocks
here suggests inaccessible crags.

3. *sheepfolds* and *a cave*: the closer identifying of the precise
place suggests that later generations pointed out this as the
very spot where the story happened.

4–7. The rearrangement undertaken in N.E.B. is indicated
in the footnote. It is not really very complicated. Verses 4*b*–5
(*He himself got up . . . his conscience smote him*) stand in the Hebrew
text after verse 4*a*, after the words *do what you please with him*.
On this view, verses 4*b*–5 have simply been inserted in the text
at the wrong point, perhaps because a scribe accidentally
omitted them, added them later in the margin (examples of
such additions can be seen in the Qumran manuscripts), and
the next copyist wrote them into the text at the wrong point.
It is, however, possible that two alternative stories have been
combined in this passage. In one, David is urged by his men to

kill Saul; he refuses, because Saul is the anointed king, and when Saul leaves the cave, David follows him and speaks, disclaiming all evil intentions and calling on God to judge between them (verses 4a, 6–10, 15); in the other, David cuts off a piece of Saul's cloak and subsequently regrets his action (on this, see the note below); he reveals that he has done it, and, as in the first story, disclaims evil intentions and calls on God (verses 4b–5, 11–14). This second story is closely akin to that of chapter 26.

4a. *your enemy:* or 'your enemies', suggesting that an earlier divine promise to David is being quoted.

6. David's reproof of his men is based on his view that Saul is *the LORD's anointed* (so too in verse 10), the chosen king, whose life is sacrosanct. In 2 Sam. 1: 1–16 David executes the Amalekite because he had 'killed the LORD's anointed'. It is not generosity that checks David but respect for the divine will expressed in Saul's position.

4b–5. *his conscience smote him:* the removal of the piece of the cloak has some resemblance to a story told in 2 Sam. 10 of the treatment of David's envoys to Ammon; the action may be designed to embarrass the wearer by exposing his body. It could simply be to provide evidence that David had Saul in his power (see verse 11). But perhaps we should see in it a symbolic action like the tearing of the cloak at Saul's rejection in 15: 27.

11. *my dear lord:* literally 'and my father', probably to be taken as the conclusion of verse 10. Saul is to David both king and protector.

12. God is invoked to decide (as also in verse 15). *though he may take vengeance on you for my sake:* this offers an interpretation of the final disaster to Saul as a divine act of retribution for Saul's conduct to David. The story in chapter 31 does not suggest this, and chapter 28 offers another explanation of the disaster.

13. The *old saying* quoted is a poetic fragment, literally 'out of the wrong ones comes something wrong', not unlike the riddle propounded by Samson:

'out of the eater came something to eat;
out of the strong came something sweet'   (Judg. 14:14).

It is described as a 'proverb'—the word used in 10: 12—
'of the ancient ones'. Proverbial literature is often described as
handed down from ancient times. Thus Bildad the Shuhite in
his first address to Job summons such proverbial wisdom to his
support, 'the experience of their fathers' (Job 8: 8), and quotes
a long string of proverbs (8: 11–19).

14. *A dead dog, a mere flea:* David uses a characteristic oriental
style of speech. The words may be part of a proverbial
expression, for it is found a number of times in the Old
Testament and elsewhere in the ancient east. Hazael, told that
he is to be king of Aram, says to Elisha: 'But I am a dog, a
mere nobody' (2 Kings 8: 13).

16. *and he wept:* the text speaks of Saul weeping loudly.
Such vehement expression of emotion was natural to an
Israelite. It could also be the appropriate accompaniment of an
act of penitential worship (see note on 1: 9–10).

19 f. Saul invokes blessing on David, and follows this by a
confession of David's coming kingship. This was anticipated
in 23: 17 and it is virtually an alternative to Jonathan's acknowledgement of David. Saul himself knows that the kingdom is David's and prophesies future good for *the kingdom of
Israel*.

21. Like Jonathan (20: 14 ff.), Saul asks a solemn oath from
David that his family will be spared. The outcome of this
may be seen expressed in David's lament in 2 Sam. 1: 19–27
and also in his protection of Mephibosheth, the surviving son
of Jonathan (2 Sam. 9). But another, blacker, side of David's
conduct to the house of Saul is shown in the grim tale in
2 Sam. 21.

22. The departure of Saul and David implies a period of
peace, but David remains in the remoter regions, and chapter
26 returns to the theme of pursuit and reconciliation.

The theme of the story is mercy and conciliation. It points

to the close bond between David and the person of Saul
(cp. 18: 1f.); it stresses again that David's kingship is no
usurpation, but the proper and recognized succession to his
predecessor. *

THE DEATH OF SAMUEL

25 Samuel died, and all Israel came together to mourn for
him, and he was buried in his house in Ramah.

* This brief note is quite unconnected with the surrounding
narratives. No indication is given as to why it is placed here,
and it is repeated at 28: 3 a as an introduction to the appearance
of Samuel's 'ghostly form' to pronounce doom on Saul.
Perhaps here it comments on the acceptance of David's
kingship by Saul; there is no further need for Samuel to be in
the background, watching over the events until David
becomes ruler of all Israel.

The prominence given to Samuel is an important element
in the compiler's interpretation of the period. In this great
personage, around whom so much tradition has gathered, he
has summed up his conviction of the overruling purpose of
God; in Samuel the word of God is made known. This
prophetic aspect of Samuel's function is given a central place.
Samuel is the one through whom God speaks; this is most
clearly affirmed in 3: 19f. He is associated with the prophetic
movement of his time. As prophet, he anoints and deposes
kings and intercedes for his people. He is also a priest, the
successor to Eli. Yet this, evident as it is in some narratives
(e.g. chapters 13 and 15), plays a lesser part, and alongside
Samuel we see other priests of Eli's line, particularly Abiathar
who plays a fuller part in the reign of David. Samuel is also a
judge—one who adjudicates in the affairs of Israel, travelling
on circuit (7: 15ff.), and one who delivers Israel from her
enemies, though this appears only in the late tradition of 7:2–14.

Thus the book's main themes are centred upon Samuel. The
move from tribal organization to kingship, the development

of priesthood, the appearance of the prophetic line, are all
associated with him. The historical figure of Samuel is
difficult to discern; the portraits are too rich to allow a simple
reconstruction. But we may see how the compiler's understanding of the working out of God's purposes in this period
has been focused on this one man and on the traditions which
have gathered around him. *

DAVID AND ABIGAIL

Afterwards David went down to the wilderness of Paran.   I *b*

There was a man at Carmel in Maon, who had great   2
influence and owned three thousand sheep and a thousand
goats; and he was shearing his flocks in Carmel. His name   3
was Nabal and his wife's name Abigail; she was a beautiful
and intelligent woman, but her husband, a Calebite, was
surly and mean. David heard in the wilderness that Nabal   4
was shearing his flocks, and sent ten of his men, saying to   5
them, 'Go up to Carmel, find Nabal and give him my
greetings. You are to say, "All good wishes for the year   6
ahead! Prosperity to yourself, your household, and all
that is yours! I hear that you are shearing. Your shepherds   7
have been with us lately and we did not molest them;
nothing of theirs was missing all the time they were in
Carmel. Ask your own people and they will tell you.   8
Receive my men kindly, for this is an auspicious day with
us, and give what you can to David your son and your
servant."' David's servants came and delivered this mes-   9
sage to Nabal in David's name. When they paused, Nabal   10
answered, 'Who is David? Who is this son of Jesse? In
these days every slave who breaks away from his master
sets himself up as a chief.*a* Am I to take my food and my   11

[a] *Or* In these days there are many slaves who break away from their
master.

wine[a] and the meat I have provided for my shearers and give it to men who come from I know not where?'

12 David's men turned and made their way back to him and
13 told him all this. He said to his men, 'Buckle on your swords, all of you.' So they buckled on their swords and followed David, four hundred of them, while two hundred stayed behind with the baggage.

14   One of the young men said to Abigail, Nabal's wife, 'David sent messengers from the wilderness to ask our master politely for a present, and he flew out[b] at them.
15 The men have been very good to us and have not molested us, nor did we miss anything all the time we
16 were going about with them in the open country. They were as good as a wall round us, night and day, while we
17 were minding the flocks. Think carefully what you had better do, for it is certain ruin for our master and his whole family; he is such a good-for-nothing[c] that it is no
18 good talking to him.' So Abigail hastily collected two hundred loaves and two skins of wine, five sheep ready dressed, five measures[d] of parched grain, a hundred bunches of raisins, and two hundred cakes of dried figs,
19 and loaded them on asses, but told her husband nothing about it. Then she said to her servants, 'Go on ahead, I will
20 follow you.' As she made her way on her ass, hidden by the hill, there were David and his men coming down
21 towards her, and she met them. David had said, 'It was a waste of time to protect this fellow's property in the wilderness so well that nothing of his was missing. He has

[a] *So Sept.; Heb.* water.
[b] flew out: *or* screamed.   [c] *Lit.* such a son of Belial.
[d] *Heb.* seahs.

repaid me evil for good.' David swore a great oath: 'God   22
do the same to me*a* and more if I leave him a single
mother's son alive by morning!'

   When Abigail saw David she dismounted in haste and   23
prostrated herself before him, bowing low to the ground   24
at his feet, and said, 'Let me take the blame, my lord, but
allow me, your humble servant, to speak out and let my
lord give me a hearing. How can you take any notice of   25
this good-for-nothing? He is just what his name Nabal
means: "Churl" is his name, and churlish his behaviour.
I did not myself, sir, see the men you sent. And now, sir,   26
the LORD has restrained you from bloodshed and from
giving vent to your anger. As the LORD lives, your life
upon it, your enemies and all who want to see you ruined
will be like Nabal. Here is the present which I, your   27
humble servant, have brought; give it to the young men
under your command. Forgive me, my lord, if I am   28
presuming; for the LORD will establish your family for
ever, because you have fought his wars. No calamity shall
overtake you as long as you live. If any man sets out to   29
pursue you and take your life, the LORD your God will
wrap your life up and put it with his own treasure, but
the lives of your enemies he will hurl away like stones
from a sling. When the LORD has made good all his   30
promises to you, and has made you ruler of Israel, there   31
will be no reason why you should stumble or your
courage falter because you have shed*b* innocent blood or
given way to your anger.*c* Then when the LORD makes all

[a] *So Sept.; Heb.* David's enemies.
[b] because...shed: *so some MSS.; others* or you should shed.
[c] or given...anger: *so Sept.; Heb.* or deliver yourself.

you do prosper, you will remember me, your servant.'
32 David said to Abigail, 'Blessed is the LORD the God of
33 Israel who has sent you today to meet me. A blessing on
your good sense, a blessing on you because you have saved
me today from the guilt of bloodshed and from giving
34 way to my anger. For I swear by the life of the LORD the
God of Israel who has kept me from doing you wrong: if
you had not come at once to meet me, not a man of
Nabal's household, not a single mother's son, would have
35 been left alive by morning.' Then David took from her
what she had brought him and said, 'Go home in peace, I
have listened to you and I grant your request.'

36 On her return she found Nabal holding a banquet in his
house, a banquet fit for a king. He grew merry and became
very drunk, so drunk that his wife said nothing to him,
37 trivial or serious, till daybreak. In the morning, when the
wine had worn off, she told him everything, and he had a
38 seizure and lay there like a stone. Ten days later the LORD
39 struck him again and he died. When David heard that
Nabal was dead he said, 'Blessed be the LORD, who has
himself punished Nabal for his insult, and has kept me
his servant from doing wrong. The LORD has made
Nabal's wrongdoing recoil on his own head.' David then
sent to make proposals that Abigail should become his
40 wife. And his servants came to Abigail at Carmel and said
41 to her, 'David has sent us to fetch you to be his wife.' She
rose and prostrated herself with her face to the ground,
and said, 'I am his slave to command, I would wash the
42 feet of my lord's servants.' So Abigail made her prepara-
tions with all speed and, with her five maids in attendance, accompanied by David's messengers, rode away

on an ass; and she became David's wife. David had also 43
married Ahinoam of Jezreel; both these women became
his wives. Saul meanwhile had given his daughter Michal, 44
David's wife, to Palti son of Laish from Gallim.

* A vivid and romantic story tells how David came to marry
the beautiful Abigail, formerly wife of Nabal 'the churl'. On
the face of it, what David is doing would today be called
'running a protection racket'. Those who respond to his
demand for 'gifts' are protected; those who do not are
doomed. There is a softening implication in the hint that the
protection has in fact been real (verses 15 f., 21; see also chapters
27 and 30). The story is at the same time romantic. The husband
is 'surly and mean', the wife 'beautiful and intelligent'. Is she
a schemer? She certainly plays her cards well and wins David
as her husband. It is not a moral tale, but it makes a good story.

We can, however, detect something more. Nabal is a
Calebite, a member of an important tribe of the south,
closely associated with Judah; alliance by marriage with such
a group could be vital for David's eventual position. He was
to be made king at Hebron, the main town of the Calebite
area (Judg. 1: 20). And Abigail herself expresses the confidence that it is David who will reign supreme. So this story
too is linked with the progress of David towards the throne
over all Israel.

1*b*. *Afterwards:* not in the text. This new story has no direct
link to verse 1*a* or to chapter 24. *wilderness of Paran:* elsewhere
(e.g. Num. 13: 26), this is indicated as near Kadesh, the centre
of Israel's wilderness period. This is much too far south.
Either another area is meant, or we should accept the alternative 'wilderness of Maon' found in Sept. (see verse 2).

2. *Carmel in Maon:* see note on 15: 12 and map, p. 169.
Carmel means 'orchard' or 'garden land'. The description of
the wealthy Nabal is something like that of Job (Job 1: 2f.).
great influence: or simply (like Job) 'a very great man'. Sheep

shearing marked a notable moment in the year, appropriate for feasting (see verse 36); Absalom held such a feast (2 Sam. 13: 23, 28).

3. This descriptive verse is in parenthesis, for strictly we should render the end of verse 2 and the beginning of verse 4 together: 'Now while he (Nabal) was shearing his flocks in Carmel, David heard...' Nabal's name is explained in verse 25; here only a description of his character is given. The contrast of husband and wife is skilfully introduced to anticipate events and to whet the appetite of the hearer for what is to come. *Calebite*: see the general comment above on the tribe. The word could mean 'like his heart', i.e. 'his nature' (cp. verse 25). Possibly the writer intended a pun.

7. The implication (cp. verse 16) is that not only did David and his men touch none of Nabal's flocks, but they also protected them from all alien attacks, whether of raiders (cp. Job 1: 14f., 17 for examples of such a danger) or of wild beasts (cp. David's account of the shepherd's life in 17: 34f.).

8. Nabal does not ask his servants; it is they who will advise Abigail (verse 14). *an auspicious day*: possibly a religious festival for which Nabal's gifts would be appropriate.

10. *Who is David...?*: contemptuous questions. Nabal, unlike Abigail, is unable to see who David really is and will be. He regards David as an upstart leader, a runaway slave.

11. *my wine*: N.E.B. footnote 'my water', a scribe's absent-minded slip.

13. *two hundred stayed behind with the baggage*: evidently normal procedure. In chapter 30, this will be the theme of a legal decision by David. David makes now an immediate decision to bring doom on Nabal. This may be read at two levels: it is part of the story by which David will win Abigail, but it is also an act of judgement decreed on one who does not acknowledge David.

15f. The protection given by David to Nabal's shepherds is here made explicit.

17. The inevitable consequences are clear to Nabal's

servants. *good-for-nothing:* not really strong enough; 'curmudgeon' would be a good word. N.E.B. footnote has 'son of Belial', see note on 1: 16.

18. Abigail proposes to offer a gift; it is in effect her tribute to the coming king (see on 10: 4; 21: 6), made plain in verses 28 ff. *measures:* literally 'seahs', a seah being one third of an ephah (about three gallons dry measure or 13 litres).

21. The story-teller skilfully postpones until now the precise statement of David's intentions, having only hinted at them in verse 13. At the very moment when he meets with Abigail, we are told of the terrible oath which David had sworn.

22. *David swore:* the text has 'May God do to the enemies of David the same and more...'. The word for 'enemies' has been added to soften the meaning and avoid the implication that David, the great king, had been forsworn. A similar correction appears in the text at 2 Sam. 12: 14 to avoid the suggestion that David had shown contempt for God. Such corrections were made by the scribes for reasons of piety. *single mother's son:* the Hebrew expression is a good deal more coarse, 'everyone who pees against the wall', i.e. 'every male' (so too in verse 34).

24. *blame:* or 'guilt' or 'sin'. Abigail invites David to effect his oath on her instead of on Nabal and all his family and possessions. By such a gesture, David's anger may be turned aside. Abigail throughout her speech uses polite expressions to suggest her humility and David's magnanimity. So we should address a superior, particularly a ruler.

25. *Nabal:* the word means 'fool' in the sense of one who does not have any appreciation of what is right and proper. So *churl* is a good equivalent here. The same word in Ps. 14: 1 (= 53: 1) is rendered 'impious fool'; this is the man who has not the sense to recognize the reality of God's activity. Abigail in her reply plays on the name and its meaning. *his behaviour:* or 'his nature'.

26. *from giving vent to your anger:* the same phrase appears in verses 31 and 33. An idiomatic expression, more literally 'from

letting your own power save you'. David would have incurred guilt by acting himself, instead of leaving the appropriate judgement to God. We may compare the warning in Rom. 12: 19 that retribution is to be God's. The remainder of the verse elaborates this, and makes it plain that Abigail is pronouncing doom upon her husband: *your enemies and all who want to see you ruined will be like Nabal.*

27. *present:* literally 'a blessing' because it expresses good will.

28. Now Abigail begins to pronounce a blessing in words upon David. His *family,* i.e. his dynasty, will endure; the phrase, literally 'a firmly established house', is elaborated in 2 Sam. 7, especially verse 16. David is champion of God, fighting *his wars* against all God's enemies.

29. Protection for David is like being 'wrapped up in the wrapping of the living'; the picture is perhaps of a bundle in which silver or other precious objects may be tied together for safety—Hag. 1: 6 refers to such 'a purse with a hole in it'; or it may be that there is reference to a bag holding pebbles, used by the shepherd to check the number of sheep and goats in a flock. This latter makes a good contrast with the picture of the enemies of David being thrown out like sling-stones.

30. The promise of the kingdom is made explicit. *ruler:* the term used of Saul in 9: 16 (see note) and of David in 13: 14.

31. Abigail sees it as essential that no blood guilt should fall on the future king, for such guilt brings inevitable retribution. In the later story of David, the diasaster of Absalom's rebellion is seen as due either to the blood guilt brought about by the death of Uriah the Hittite (2 Sam. 12: 10f.; 16: 21f.), or to that incurred by his actions against the family of Saul (2 Sam. 16: 5–8). Abigail asks to be remembered in the day of David's coming to full success; neatly the story-teller points forward to Nabal's death and her marriage to David.

32–4. David's reply begins with an act of praise to God who has brought about this avoidance of guilt. He repeats his oath as a reminder of what terrible vengeance he would have exacted.

35. The acceptance of the gift is the outward sign of the reconciliation expressed in David's words. *I grant your request:* literally 'I have lifted up your face', i.e. shown you favour. The phrase is used in the priestly blessing in Num. 6: 26.

36. The story of Nabal is picked up again at the sheep-shearing feast; but while he is *merry* and *very drunk*, Abigail says nothing.

37. She chooses her moment. The effect of the wine has *worn off* and no doubt the hangover leaves Nabal in a state in which the thought of the disaster he has so narrowly escaped brings on *a seizure*, a stroke which leaves him paralyzed.

39. David sees Nabal's death as an act of God; so David has been saved from blood guilt, but Nabal has not escaped the consequence of his behaviour. We may detect a contrast with the story of David and Bathsheba; then, to get the woman he wants, David stops at nothing and retribution comes on him (2 Sam. 11-12). Nabal's death offers him the chance to marry Abigail, and his proposal of marriage is speedily accepted (verse 41).

43-4. The story has a brief appendix on David's marriages. We are told of his marriage to *Ahinoam of Jezreel*, also a southern place (see map, p. 169), and probably this too represents the establishing of links with the southern clans. Some further details of David's marriages are given at 2 Sam. 3: 2-5. An added note explains what has become of Michal. She has played her part in saving David (19: 11-17); later she will be restored to him as part of a political bargain (2 Sam. 3: 13-16) and will be again involved in David's affairs (2 Sam. 6). But in the meantime, she has been given to another husband, as was Merab (18: 19). It would seem that David is regarded as having forfeited his rights. The location of *Gallim* is uncertain.

For the larger theme of David's rise to power, the speech of Abigail is of prime importance. Here in verses 28-31 are the expressions of confidence in the sureness of his dynasty, of his

protection by God, and of the fulfilment of divine promise.
Here too is the conviction that the king is himself the protector
of his people from wrong and calamity. ✳

SAUL AT THE MERCY OF DAVID—II

26 The Ziphites came to Saul at Gibeah to report that David
was in hiding on the hill of Hachilah overlooking
2 Jeshimon. Saul went down at once to the wilderness of
Ziph, taking with him three thousand picked men, to
3 search for David there. He encamped beside the road on
the hill of Hachilah overlooking Jeshimon, while David
was still in the wilderness. As soon as David knew that
4 Saul had come to the wilderness in pursuit of him, he sent
out scouts and found that Saul had reached such and such
5 a place. Without delay, he went to the place where Saul
had pitched his camp and observed where Saul and Abner
son of Ner, the commander-in-chief, were lying. Saul
lay within the lines with his troops encamped in a circle
6 round him. David turned to Ahimelech the Hittite and
Abishai son of Zeruiah, Joab's brother, and said, 'Who
will venture with me into the camp, to go to Saul?'
7 Abishai answered, 'I will.' David and Abishai entered the
camp at night and found Saul lying asleep within the
lines with his spear thrust into the ground by his head.
8 Abner and the army were lying all round him. Abishai
said to David, 'God has put your enemy into your power
today; let me strike him and pin him to the ground with
one thrust of the spear; I shall not have to strike twice.'
9 David said to him, 'Do him no harm; who has ever
lifted a finger against the LORD's anointed and gone
10 unpunished? As the LORD lives,' went on David, 'the

LORD will strike him down; either his time will come and
he will die, or he will go down to battle and meet his end.
God forbid that I should lift a finger against the LORD's 11
anointed! But now let us take the spear which is by his
head, and the water-jar, and go.' So David took the spear 12
and the water-jar from beside Saul's head and they went.
The whole camp was asleep; no one saw him, no one
knew anything, no one even woke up. A heavy sleep sent
by the LORD had fallen on them.

Then David crossed over to the other side and stood on 13
the top of a hill a long way off; there was no little distance
between them. David shouted across to the army and 14
hailed Abner, 'Answer me, Abner!' He answered, 'Who
are you to shout to the king?' David said to Abner, 'Do 15
you call yourself a man? Is there anyone like you in
Israel? Why, then, did you not keep watch over your lord
the king, when someone came to harm your lord the
king? This was not well done. As the LORD lives, you 16
deserve to die, all of you, because you have not kept watch
over your master the LORD's anointed. Look! Where are
the king's spear and the water-jar that were by his head?'

Saul recognized David's voice and said, 'Is that you, 17
David my son?' 'Yes, sir, it is', said David. 'Why must 18
your majesty pursue me? What have I done? What mischief am I plotting? Listen, my lord, to what I have to 19
say. If it is the LORD who has set you against me, may an
offering be acceptable to him; but if it is men, a curse on
them in the LORD's name; for they have ousted me today
from my share in the LORD's inheritance and have banished
me to serve other gods! Do not let my blood be shed on 20
foreign soil, far from the presence of the LORD, just

because the king of Israel came out to look for a flea, as one
21 might hunt a partridge over the hills.' Saul answered, 'I
have done wrong; come back, David my son. You have
held my life precious this day, and I will never harm you
again. I have been a fool, I have been sadly in the wrong.'
22 David answered, 'Here is the king's spear; let one of your
23 men come across and fetch it. The LORD who rewards
uprightness and loyalty will reward the man into whose
power he put you today, when I refused to lift a finger
24 against the LORD's anointed. As I held your life precious
today, so may the LORD hold mine precious and deliver
25 me from every distress.' Then Saul said to David, 'A
blessing is on you, David my son. You will do great things
and be victorious.' So David went on his way and Saul
returned home.

* This story is clearly an alternative to that found in chapter
24.

  1. This verse is virtually identical with 23: 19. See notes on
23: 14 ff. for the place names, and particularly Jeshimon, which
here too should probably be treated as a general name for 'the
wilderness'.

  2. *three thousand:* as in 24: 2.

  4. *such and such a place:* see on 23: 23 where the same expression is used. Possibly render: 'that Saul really had come'.

  5. From the hill above the road, David and his men can see
the camp below them, with Saul in the most secure spot.

  6. *Ahimelech the Hittite:* not elsewhere mentioned. The
appellative 'Hittite' appears with Uriah (2 Sam. 11), also a
notable warrior; perhaps both these men were foreign
mercenaries in David's service. *Abishai* and *Joab* both play
important roles in the story of David, and there is a third
brother, Asahel; their mother Zeruiah was David's sister,
according to 1 Chron. 2: 16.

7. *the camp:* the text has 'the people', probably a scribal error.

8. Abishai tempts David here as his followers do in 24: 4ff.

9. David's respect is for *the LORD's anointed.* God will not let a sacrilegious action go *unpunished.*

10. As in 24: 12 and 25: 26, the point is made that vengeance belongs to God. More clearly than in chapter 24, the words of David here anticipate Saul's death in battle at Mount Gilboa (chapter 31). *meet his end:* literally 'be swept away'.

11. *the water-jar:* a small round jar with two handles for cords so that it may be slung round the neck. Such a jar was carried by a traveller or by a soldier on campaign for his personal use. It is not mentioned in verse 22; possibly this indicates that there were two alternative versions of this story, one concerning the spear and the other the water-jar. (Cp. the indications of variants within chapter 24.)

12. *A heavy sleep sent by the LORD:* Saul and his men were not just asleep, they were prevented by divine action from waking while David carried out his exploit. The whole event lies under God's control. The word for *heavy sleep* is that used of the first man at the creation of woman (Gen. 2: 21), where N.E.B. renders 'the LORD God put the man into a trance'; so too for Abraham at the making of the covenant (Gen. 15: 12).

13. We may assume a time-lapse; the next stage of the story takes place, we may naturally suppose, at dawn.

14. *shout to the king:* Abner is in effect the king's representative.

16. *you deserve to die:* literally 'you are sons of death', a phrase suggesting that they already belong to the realm of the dead at least in the sense that death would be an appropriate penalty for their neglect of the king. David uses this phrase in 2 Sam. 12: 5 when, without knowing it, he passes judgement upon himself for his sin against Uriah.

19. If God has incited Saul against David, then his anger

may be appeased by the appropriate sacrificial procedure; but if it is men, then they are to be cursed and thereby brought to disaster. David's sense of injustice is here very sharply expressed. He has been put outside the community to which he belongs and forced into an area in which he must *serve other gods*. The sense of the closeness of the bond between God and the people was felt so strongly that anywhere outside *the LORD's inheritance*—a favourite expression for the promised land—could be thought to be totally alien territory. The religion of a community is bound up with its whole life and cannot be thought of readily as practised elsewhere, for there would be no suitable shrine available.

20. If David dies a violent death *on foreign soil*, his blood will not be avenged. *to look for a flea*: possibly this has been added here from 24: 14, since the image of hunting *a partridge* is very different.

23 f. David indirectly pronounces the blessing upon himself, and this is confirmed by Saul in verse 25. *As I held your life precious today*: not the same idiom as in verse 21. Here the word *precious* suggests something important, of great moment.

25. As in 24: 22, the reconciliation leads to nothing. David goes back to his outlaw life and Saul to Gibeah. ✳

DAVID AT GATH—II

27 David thought, 'One of these days I shall be killed by Saul. The best thing for me to do will be to escape into Philistine territory; then Saul will lose all further hope of finding me anywhere in Israel, search as he may, and I 2 shall escape his clutches.' So David and his six hundred men crossed the frontier forthwith to Achish son of 3 Maoch king of Gath. David settled in Gath with Achish, taking with him his men and their families and his two wives, Ahinoam of Jezreel and Abigail of Carmel, 4 Nabal's widow. Saul was told that David had escaped to

Gath, and he gave up the search. David said to Achish, 5
'If I stand well in your opinion, grant me a place in one
of your country towns where I may settle. Why should
I remain in the royal city with your majesty?' Achish 6
granted him Ziklag on that day: that is why Ziklag still
belongs to the kings of Judah.

David spent a year and four months in Philistine country. 7
He and his men would sally out and raid the Geshurites, 8
the Gizrites, and the Amalekites, for it was they who
inhabited the country from Telaim*a* all the way to Shur
and Egypt. When David raided the country he left no one 9
alive, man or woman; he took flocks and herds, asses
and camels, and clothes too, and then came back again
to Achish. When Achish asked, 'Where was your raid to- 10
day?', David would answer, 'The Negeb of Judah' or
'The Negeb of the Jerahmeelites' or 'The Negeb of the
Kenites'. Neither man nor woman did David bring back 11
alive to Gath, for fear that they should denounce him and
his men for what they had done. This was his practice as
long as he remained with the Philistines. Achish trusted 12
David, thinking that he had won such a bad name among
his own people the Israelites that he would remain his
subject all his life.

* 1. *I shall be killed*: literally 'swept away' (cp. 26: 10).
David the fugitive is weak and unprotected, able to find safety
only in an alien land. There is no suggestion that David had
done this before, and we should see this passage as containing
an account quite separate from that of 21: 10–15 (see also on
29: 5).

2. *Achish*: cp. note on 21: 10. *son of Maoch*: the name appears

[a] from Telaim: *prob. rdg.; Heb.* from of old.

as Maacah in 1 Kings 2: 39, but this may represent the assimilating of the Philistine name to a form familiar in the Old Testament. *Maoch*, like Achish, is likely to represent a native Philistine name, and a comparison has been made with Machas or Macha, also from Asia Minor.

5. David asks a favour of Achish, the grant of a town, where he may settle and which may be a base of operations for him. The implication is that he and his men are too great a burden on Gath; clearly the move is to give David more freedom to act as he plans. In fact, verse 11 seems to envisage that he will operate from Gath, but in chapter 30, Ziklag is clearly the centre of his activity. *the royal city*: the city of royal residence, as contrasted with the *country towns*—towns situated out in the open country which belonged to the territory of the king of Gath.

6. *Ziklag*: the location is not certain (see map, p. 169), but it is evidently in the Judaean area, probably at the edge of the territory controlled by Gath and likely to provide convenient entry into the 'Negeb' (see on verse 10). The verse contains an important historical note about the particular position of Ziklag. It was a crown property, belonging personally to *the kings of Judah*; the tradition, rightly or wrongly, attributed this special position to the gift made by Achish.

7. *a year and four months*: the text is not entirely clear; a similar phrase appears in 29: 3.

8 f. The various peoples are enemies of Judah, and David's strategy was to leave no survivor after his raids. This enabled him to pretend that he was attacking Judah and its allies, while he was in fact protecting the southern tribes from their opponents. *Geshurites*: the name is used here of a people occupying the coastal area to the south-west (so Josh. 13: 2 f.). *Gizrites*: or 'Girzites'. It can hardly be 'the people of Gezer' which is too far north, but must refer to a people in this same area. It could be an error for Girgashites, a name used of ancient inhabitants of the land. *Amalekites*: cp. on 15: 2. *Telaim*: cp. 15: 4; the Hebrew text has 'from of old', but a

northern limit is needed to match the southern one. *Shur:* an area to the east of the Nile delta.

10. *Negeb:* this is the term regularly used for the southern part of Judah. The word comes to mean simply 'south', though its original meaning is likely to have been the 'dry country'. The three areas mentioned must be particular districts, associated with tribes closely linked with Judah. *Jerahmeelites* (or Yerahmeelites): a clan associated with David's policy of building up contacts in the south (30: 29), and later fully integrated into Judah. *Kenites:* see on 15: 6. In 30: 14 we have mention of two further districts, 'the Negeb of the Kerethites' (or Cherethites) and 'the Negeb of Caleb' (see map, p. 169 for possible locations). Thus we appear to have a geographical description of the southern area, over which David was in due course to claim sovereignty. The full settlement of this area came only in the centuries after David; at this stage it was still in the hands of groups which moved about from one pasturage to another.

11. There may be something missing in this verse. It could be rendered: 'for, he said, they might denounce us saying... (the actual words are not there). Thus David acted, and thus was his practice...'

12. *he had won such a bad name:* or 'he had acted so shamefully'. Achish not unreasonably thought that there was no going back for David. By becoming a subject of a Philistine ruler, he would forfeit the allegiance and affection of his own people. By raiding their territory, as Achish believed he was doing, he was building up even more enmity. David's position was certainly a delicate one and liable to be misunderstood. But the story has a neat irony: while Achish counts on David as an enemy of his own people, David himself is steadily preparing the way for his rule.

The picture of David is not congenial to a modern reader. But we must see that to the compiler it had attraction as an example of successful guile and significance as pointing to David's progress to the throne. In some respects, the story of

David among the Philistines, continued in 28: 1–2; 29; 30, is like that of the Ark of God in chapters 4–6. David appears to be in the hands of the enemy, even to be fighting on their side; but it is to mock them that he is there, and his true power, that is, God's power in him, will soon be declared (cp. the comment at the end of chapter 6). *

Saul and his sons killed

WAR WITH THE PHILISTINES

28 IN THOSE DAYS the Philistines mustered their army for an attack on Israel. Achish said to David, 'You know that you and your men must take the field with me.' 2 David answered Achish, 'Good, you will learn what your servant can do.' And Achish said to David, 'I will make you my bodyguard for life.'

* These verses really form part of the story just related in chapter 27, and they provide the introduction to the narrative found in chapter 29.

1. The Philistine move against Israel is to culminate in the death of Saul and his sons; the story proceeds relentlessly and tragically to that end.

2. David's somewhat ambiguous assurance of heroic action is answered by Achish showing him favour. *bodyguard*: literally 'the keeper of my head'; it is to David that Achish entrusts his personal safety. *

SAUL AT EN-DOR

3 By this time Samuel was dead, and all Israel had mourned for him and buried him in Ramah, his own city; and Saul had banished from the land all who trafficked with ghosts

and spirits. The Philistines mustered and encamped at 4
Shunem, and Saul gathered all the Israelites and encamped on Gilboa; and when Saul saw the Philistine force, 5
fear struck him to the heart. He inquired of the LORD, but 6
the LORD did not answer him, whether by dreams or by
Urim or by prophets. So he said to his servants, 'Find me 7
a woman who has a familiar spirit, and I will go and
inquire through her.' His servants told him that there was
such a woman at En-dor. Saul put on different clothes 8
and went in disguise with two of his men. He came to the
woman by night and said, 'Tell me my fortunes by consulting the dead, and call up the man I name to you.' But 9
the woman answered, 'Surely you know what Saul has
done, how he has made away with those who call up
ghosts and spirits; why do you press me to do what will
lead to my death?' Saul swore her an oath: 'As the LORD 10
lives, no harm shall come to you for this.' The woman 11
asked whom she should call up, and Saul answered,
'Samuel.' When the woman saw Samuel appear, she 12
shrieked and said to Saul, 'Why have you deceived me?
You are Saul!' The king said to her, 'Do not be afraid. 13
What do you see?' The woman answered, 'I see a ghostly
form coming up from the earth.' 'What is it like?' he 14
asked; she answered, 'Like an old man coming up,
wrapped in a cloak.' Then Saul knew it was Samuel, and
he bowed low with his face to the ground, and prostrated
himself. Samuel said to Saul, 'Why have you disturbed 15
me and brought me up?' Saul answered, 'I am in great
trouble; the Philistines are pressing me and God has
turned away; he no longer answers me through prophets
or through dreams, and I have summoned you to tell me

16 what I should do.' Samuel said, 'Why do you ask me, now
   that the LORD has turned from you and become your
17 adversary? He has done what he foretold through me.
   He has torn the kingdom from your hand and given it to
18 another man, to David. You have not obeyed the LORD,
   or executed the judgement of his fury against the Amale-
19 kites; that is why he has done this to you today. For the
   same reason the LORD will let your people Israel fall into
   the hands of the Philistines and, what is more, tomorrow
   you and your sons shall be with me. Yes, indeed, the
   LORD will give the Israelite army into the hands of the
20 Philistines.' Saul was overcome and fell his full length to
   the ground, terrified by Samuel's words. He had no
   strength left, for he had eaten nothing all day and all
   night.

21   The woman went to Saul and saw that he was much
   disturbed, and she said to him, 'I listened to what you said
22 and I risked my life to obey you. Now listen to me: let me
   set before you a little food to give you strength for your
23 journey.' But he refused to eat anything. When his
   servants joined the woman in pressing[a] him, he yielded,
24 rose from the ground and sat on the couch. The woman
   had a fatted calf at home, which she quickly slaughtered.
   She took some meal, kneaded it and baked unleavened
25 cakes, which she set before Saul and his servants. They ate
   the food and departed that same night.

* Saul's consulting a witch to know his future interrupts the
narrative of the Philistine warlike advance. But the compiler
has seen the value of showing Saul's frame of mind at this
point, just as subsequently he offers an account of how David

[a] *Prob. rdg., cp. Sept.; Heb.* in breaking out on...

was acting during the war (chapter 30). Here the Philistines already confront Saul who is at Gilboa (verse 4); in 28: 1 they are still on the way to the battlefield and only advance into the Jezreel area in 29: 11 (see map, p. 212).

3 *a. his own city:* possibly a slip for 'in his own grave'. The death of Samuel has already been noted at 25: 1 in almost identical words. At this point, it introduces the appearance of Samuel from the dead (verses 12, 14).

3 *b.* This should be treated as a new sentence beginning: 'Now Saul had banished...'; the sentence is explanatory, paving the way for the story. But it is of great interest, for it shows Saul, the faithful adherent of Yahweh, taking action against necromancy and other forms of religious malpractice. Such practices were contrary to the absolute claim of God to give guidance to men; the law as set out in Deut. 18: 11 lists a whole variety of practitioners. But witchcraft and astrology and necromancy and the like always hold a certain fascination for those who have no secure faith. Isa. 8: 19 provides a vivid comment on such futility:

> But men will say to you,
> 'Seek guidance of ghosts and familiar spirits
>   who squeak and gibber;
> a nation may surely seek guidance of its gods,
> of the dead on behalf of the living,
>   for an oracle or a message?'

ghosts and spirits: the precise meaning of the terms is not clear. The first appears in verse 7 as 'familiar spirit' (a modern term would be 'control'); the second seems to mean 'beings that know', i.e. the future, or 'intimate ones', i.e. also 'familiar spirits'. There may well be some overlap.

4. *Shunem:* a place associated with a story concerning Elisha (2 Kings 4); *Gilboa:* the name of a mountain area on the southern side of the plain of Jezreel (see map, p. 212). The Philistines are encamped to the north, on a slope facing Saul.

5 f. In terror at the sight of the enemy, perhaps with a clear

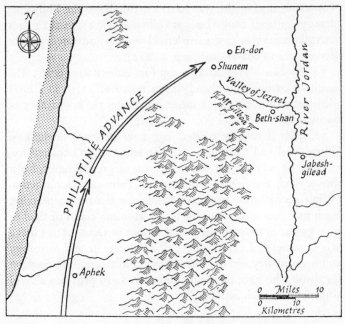

4. The last battle (1 Samuel 28, 29, 31)

presentiment of doom, Saul tries to get guidance and a sign of
favour from God. But there is no answer (see note on 14: 37).
Three media of revelation are mentioned. God may speak to
men through *dreams*; such dreams are described and interpreted
by men of wisdom in the stories of Joseph and Daniel. The
word may also be virtually the equivalent of 'vision'. *Urim*:
see on 14: 18, the priestly oracular mechanism. *prophets*: by
whom the divine word should be given. We may note that
Jer. 18: 18 (so too Ezek. 7: 26) speaks of three such types of
revelation: the prophet's word, the priest's oracle, and the
wise man's counsel.

7. It is one thing to prohibit a popular religious practice and
quite another to abolish it. Josiah of Judah also attempted such
an abolition (2 Kings 23: 24), but the practices did not end

there (see Isa. 66: 17). Apparently without difficulty Saul's *servants* can get information about a suitable woman, who, by means of *a familiar spirit*, will answer Saul's inquiries. *En-dor* (see map, p. 212): further north than the Philistine position. Saul's disguise (verse 8) would serve the double purpose of getting him and his two companions past the Philistine out-posts and—so he supposed—of concealing his identity from the woman.

8. *by night:* not simply for concealment but no doubt also because this would be the suitable moment for such illicit consultation. The method requested is that commonly associated with spiritualist mediums: a dead person is evoked to give a message. This may be given directly or through some other agent. It is assumed that the dead can know the future; the witches in Macbeth call up the dead Banquo to point to future kings (Act IV, Scene I). The Old Testament gives no completely consistent picture of the fate of the dead; they are most often thought to be existing only as shadows in a land of darkness, called Sheol or simply 'the underworld' (see on verse 13). This place is thought to be remote from God. Sometimes, as here, the dead are thought to have special powers. Many of the psalms reveal the variety of belief, for example, Ps. 88.

9. Does the woman suspect a trap? The phrase *why do you press me?* could be rendered: 'why do you lay a trap for me?'

11. Saul's request that Samuel should be summoned is a reminder that it is he who is seen as the guiding spirit in Israel throughout this period. Though he is dead, his influence and his mediation of God's will continue.

12. A puzzling verse, capable of more than one interpreta-tion. We may note that a small number of Greek manuscripts have 'Saul' instead of *Samuel*. If this was the original reading, then we are to assume that when Saul asked for Samuel, the woman realized who he was. In spite of his disguise, he could be recognized, just as the wife of the king Jeroboam could be recognized, though in disguise, by the blind prophet Ahijah

(1 Kings 14: 1–6). The woman realized with dismay that she had indeed fallen into a trap.

If the text as we have it is correct, as seems most probable, then two explanations of the woman's behaviour seem to be available. (1) By some process not made clear, the appearance of Samuel brought about the realization that it was Saul who was present, and this brought an understandable terror. (2) The woman's terror could have been produced not by her discovery of Saul's presence, but by the appearance of the 'ghostly form' of Samuel. Has she suddenly found herself confronted by something which has gone beyond her control? This possibility raises questions about the narrator's intentions and beliefs. Did he believe that the woman really could call up Samuel? This is quite possible, for the Old Testament is not averse from seeing the will of God declared even through mechanisms which it regarded as alien (see note on 6: 2). God's purpose is stronger than man's limited contrivances. Or did the narrator perhaps just relate an old story, not troubling about whether or not it could have happened? It seems at least possible that he was telling the story with a touch of irony. Here was Saul, consulting a medium to get guidance; but such practices were forbidden by Israel's religious law, so it could not be supposed that she could really do what he asked. But Samuel did appear. The woman is dumbfounded. It could only have been God himself who made this possible, and it was a shock to the woman to realize that she was in the grip of something much more powerful than she had supposed. We cannot be sure of the precise interpretation to be given.

13f. The description of what the woman sees—it is not visible to Saul—suggests the appearance of the prophet. The *cloak* (cp. 15: 27) is perhaps a prophetic garment (cp. Elijah's cloak in 2 Kings 2, though a different word is used there). *ghostly form:* the word is '*elohim*', a word most often used for God. It is a plural form, but here, as in Isa. 8: 19 (see p. 211), it is used for the unearthly spirit of a dead man. *coming up from the earth:* or better 'from the underworld'; the word for 'earth' is often used in that sense.

15. The dead are thought to be at peace—see the description of death as a haven for the troubled in Job 3: 13–15, 17–19— they are reluctant to be *disturbed*. In his distress Saul knows of only one who can intercede for him or reveal to him the purposes of God.

16. The rejection of Saul makes his questioning idle. *and become your adversary:* the word used is strange, perhaps erroneous. A very simple change would give: 'and gone over to be with your companion (associate)' (i.e. David), the same word as is translated 'another man' in verse 17.

17. *He has done:* the text adds an idiomatic 'for himself'. If the alternative suggestion for verse 16 is correct, then we may render 'for him' (David); the following sentence then expands this statement.

18. The allusion is to the rejection story in chapter 15. There are several links between that passage and the narrative here, e.g. the comment on witchcraft in 15: 23 and the 'tearing away of the kingdom' in verse 17 and 15: 28. It is possible that the story in this chapter has been expanded, e.g. by the addition of verses 17–19 *a*, to emphasize the theological point and the relationship to chapter 15. If this is so, the overloading and repetition in verse 19 would be the result of this expansion.

19. Saul's failure brings judgement on all Israel, not just on the royal house, for king and people belong together. Judgements in the books of Kings are upon the whole people for the failure of their rulers.

20. *Saul was overcome:* the Hebrew word here means 'to be hurried', and probably is an error for a not too dissimilar word which is used in verse 21, meaning 'disturbed'. Fear brings loss of strength, and this is aggravated by fasting, undertaken possibly as part of the attempt at making an approach to God.

21 f. Even in this dark moment, Saul inspires pity and loyalty, as again at his death. The woman appeals to him on

the strength of her own response to his request; he should eat and be strong. (N.E.B. omits an imperative 'eat' after *a little food*.)

23. Only when his two companions urge him does he agree. *pressing him*: the word so rendered is almost identical with the one in the text, rendered 'breaking out' in N.E.B. footnote.

24f. *a fatted calf*: it is difficult not to suppose that this is here intended to suggest that a special meal was offered to Saul. He was, after all, still the king. Josephus (*Antiquities* VI, 14. 3–4) elaborates the picture of the woman's generosity, and follows this with an exhortation to his readers to take her as an example of kindly behaviour to those in need.

The final word of judgement has been spoken against Saul; nothing can now avert the tragedy of his defeat and death. If the narrator wished to suggest that Saul had committed a final act of apostasy in consulting the medium, he does not stress the point; and in fact no such stress was needed, for Saul is already rejected. The Chronicler attributes the final disaster to this consultation of 'ghosts' (1 Chron. 10: 13). But even in this black moment, the words of Samuel point forward once more to what is to come. Disaster will come upon Israel; but David is the chosen king. *

DAVID DISMISSED BY THE PHILISTINES

29 The Philistines mustered all their troops at Aphek, while
2 the Israelites encamped at En-harod[a] in Jezreel. The Philistine princes were advancing with their troops in units of a hundred and a thousand; David and his men
3 were in the rear of the column with Achish. The Philistine commanders asked, 'Why are those Hebrews there?' Achish answered, 'This is David, the servant of Saul king of Israel who has been with me now for a year or more.

[a] *Prob. rdg.; Heb.* at the spring.

I have had no fault to find in him ever since he came over
to me.' The Philistine commanders were indignant and 4
said to Achish, 'Send the man back to the town which
you allotted to him. He shall not fight side by side with
us, or he may turn traitor in the battle. What better way
to buy his master's favour, than at the price of our lives?
This is that David of whom they sang, as they danced: 5

> Saul made havoc among thousands
> but David among tens of thousands.'

Achish summoned David and said to him, 'As the 6
LORD lives, you are an upright man and your service with
my troops has well satisfied me. I have had no fault to
find with you ever since you joined me, but the other
princes are not willing to accept you. Now go home in 7
peace, and you will then be doing nothing that they can
regard as wrong.' David protested, 'What have I done, or 8
what fault have you found in me from the day I first
entered your service till now, that I should not come and
fight against the enemies of my lord the king?' Achish 9
answered David, 'I agree that you have been as true to me
as an angel of God, but the Philistine commanders insist
that you shall not fight alongside them. Now rise early in 10
the morning with those of your lord's subjects who have
followed you, and go to the town which I allotted to you;
harbour no evil thoughts, for I am well satisfied with you.[a]
Rise early and start as soon as it is light.' So David and his 11
men rose early to start that morning on their way back to
the land of the Philistines, while the Philistines went
on to Jezreel.

[a] and go...with you: *so Sept.; Heb. om.*

✻ This chapter forms the sequel to 27: 1–28: 2.

1. *Aphek:* cp. 4: 1 (see map, p. 212). The reference here is to an important Philistine military post, used as a rallying point for the various contingents of the army as they march northwards along the coastal plain to the plain of Jezreel. Each Philistine prince, Achish included, brings his own section. All are passed in review and sent forward, but at the end of the column come David and his men with Achish, and then questions are asked. *En-harod:* some Greek texts suggest En-dor (see 28: 7), perhaps influenced by the previous chapter and implying that Israel's defeat follows from that event. *En-harod* means 'spring of fright' (see N.E.B. footnote to Judg. 7: 1), an appropriate name for the place where the dismayed Saul awaits his end. *Jezreel* denotes here the whole plain.

2. *princes:* here and in verses 6 and 7 the technical Philistine word is used (see note on 5: 8), whereas in verses 3, 4 and 9 the normal Hebrew word for 'commanders' appears, presumably for subordinate officers, though the distinction has not been made quite strictly.

3. Achish is confident, from the experience he has had (see chapter 27), that David is loyal; he is quite unaware of David's skilful duplicity. *a year or more:* see note on 27: 7. *came over to me:* more precisely 'deserted to me', a rendering which brings out better the contrast with the description of David as *the servant of Saul king of Israel.* Achish is not mincing his words.

4. A man who has once deserted can hardly be trusted not to do so again. A judicious change of sides in the middle of the battle could well turn the scales (see on 14: 21), and would restore David to favour with Saul. *traitor:* the word is *satan,* used here in its simple sense of 'adversary, opposer'. It is used for a member of the heavenly court who opposes or challenges the ways of men (Job 1–2; Zech. 3: 1), and later as a name for the evil power.

5. The poetic saying is here quoted against David, as also in the alternative tradition in 21: 10–15. It appears in the welcome to David in 18: 7.

6. *your service:* literally 'your going out and your coming

in', a phrase often used to suggest a man's whole way of life (so in Ps. 121: 8 where we might paraphrase: 'the LORD will guard your whole life').

8. David's protest is again ambiguous (cp. chapter 27). There has been no fault to find with his activities; but Achish knows only part of the truth. There is no indication in the story that David was intending to sabotage the Philistine campaign as verse 4 envisages, though it is possible to see in the phrase *the enemies of my lord the king* a veiled reference to Saul as still David's true overlord.

9. *as an angel of God:* a recognition of the blessing and success which come through such a man as David. The same phrase is used of him again in 2 Sam. 14: 17, 20 and 19: 27 in reference to his skill as a judge of right and wrong.

10. The Hebrew, as N.E.B. footnote indicates, has an accidental omission of a substantial phrase. It is possible that there is some further confusion in that the opening and closing phrases are largely duplicates. *no evil thoughts:* the Greek probably corresponds to the Hebrew word *beli'al* which (see note on 1: 16) suggests anything associated with the evil power.

David is spared the embarrassment of fighting against Israel; the Philistines advance against Saul without him. We might be inclined to ask whether David, had he been engaged in the battle on Israel's side, could not have swung the balance in Saul's favour. But the question is not relevant to the understanding of the events as they are seen by the compiler. For him, Saul is doomed. It is right that David will not be there, and by way of counterpoise, he again interrupts the course of events to tell of David's heroism in the south. While Saul awaits his inevitable end, David continues his progress towards the throne as the deliverer of the oppressed. *

DAVID RESCUES THE CAPTIVES

On the third day David and his men reached Ziklag. Now **30** the Amalekites had made a raid into the Negeb, attacked

2 Ziklag and set fire to it; they had carried off all the women, high and low, without putting one of them to death. These they drove with them and continued their march.

3 When David and his men approached the town, they found it destroyed by fire, and their wives, their sons, and

4 their daughters carried off. David and the people with him

5 wept aloud until they could weep no more. David's two wives, Ahinoam of Jezreel and Abigail widow of Nabal

6 of Carmel, were among the captives. David was in a desperate position because the people, embittered by the loss of their sons and daughters, threatened to stone him.

7 So David sought strength in the LORD his God. He told Abiathar the priest, son of Ahimelech, to bring the ephod.

8 When Abiathar had brought the ephod, David inquired of the LORD, 'Shall I pursue these raiders? and shall I overtake them?' The answer came, 'Pursue them: you will over-

9 take them and rescue everyone.' So David and his six hundred men set out and reached the ravine of Besor.[a]

10 Two hundred of them who were too weary to cross the ravine stayed behind, and David with four hundred pressed on in pursuit.

11 In the open country they came across an Egyptian and took him to David. They gave him food to eat and water

12 to drink, also a lump of dried figs and two bunches of raisins. When he had eaten these he revived; for he had had nothing to eat or drink for three days and nights.

13 David asked him, 'Whose slave are you? and where have you come from?' 'I am an Egyptian boy,' he answered, 'the slave of an Amalekite, but my master left me behind

14 because I fell ill three days ago. We had raided the Negeb

[a] *Prob. rdg.; Heb. adds* those who were left over remained.

of the Kerethites, part of Judah, and the Negeb of Caleb;
we also set fire to Ziklag.' David asked, 'Can you guide 15
me to this band?' 'Swear to me by God', he answered,
'that you will not put me to death or hand me back to my
master, and I will guide you to them.' So he led him 16
down, and there they were scattered everywhere, eating
and drinking and celebrating the capture of the great mass
of spoil taken from Philistine and Judaean territory.

David attacked from dawn till dusk and continued till 17
next day; only four hundred young men mounted on
camels made good their escape. David rescued all those 18
whom the Amalekites had taken, including his two wives.
No one was missing, high or low, sons or daughters, and 19
none of the spoil, nor anything they had taken for themselves: David recovered everything. They took all the 20
flocks and herds, drove the cattle before him[a] and said,
'This is David's spoil.'

✻ 1. *The Negeb*: the whole southern area, though in verse 14
specific districts are mentioned, as similarly in 27: 10 (see note
on this). This verse and the next briefly describe a characteristic raid by the tribesmen who live on the fringe of the settled
land. For *the Amalekites*, see on 15: 2.

2. The captive *women* alone are mentioned, but verse 3
makes it clear that the children too were taken. It is difficult to
believe that the city had been left entirely without men during
David's campaign, but perhaps we should relate this to David's
supreme faith as it is revealed at the end of verse 6. It would
be better here to follow Sept. and read 'carried off the women
and all who were in it' (N.E.B. has introduced the word *all*
without accepting this alternative).

[a] They took...before him: *prob. rdg.; Heb.* David took all the flocks
and herds; they drove before that cattle.

4. A great lamentation of a ritual kind is engaged in (see on 1: 9f.).

5. The mention of *David's two wives* has been prepared for by 25: 42f.

6. It is a critical moment; while *the people* are embittered and hostile, lacking in faith, David turns to God. *the LORD his God:* the specially close relationship between king and deity is often expressed in such a phrase as this.

7f. For the use of *the ephod*, cp. 23: 2f. and see note on 14: 37f.

9. *the ravine of Besor* (strictly 'the Besor'): not identifiable, but presumably not far from Ziklag. The name may have been thought to mean 'the good news', an appropriately good omen. N.E.B. footnote indicates that the Hebrew text contains an additional phrase; this may offer a variant reading to part of verse 10, or possibly the phrases of the two verses are out of order.

10. The leaving behind of *two hundred* provides a link with the similar point made in the planned attack on Nabal (25: 13). Here it serves two purposes. It paves the way for the legal enactment of verses 21–5, and it emphasizes that victory is won even by small numbers over great armies (cp. on 13: 15).

13. *Egyptian boy:* clearly the finding of this half-dead slave is not to be seen as accidental; it is part of God's ordering of the events.

14. On the Negeb areas, see note on 27: 10. *Kerethites:* probably a Philistine area (cp. note on 4: 1*b*). *part of Judah:* possibly we should understand this to mean 'the Negeb which belongs to Judah', i.e. 'the Negeb of Judah' as in 27: 10.

15. A slave turned informer would be at the mercy both of his captor and his former master.

16. *celebrating:* the term is that used for religious festivals, and indeed such a victory would naturally be expressed in an act of worship, including feasting and no doubt excessive drinking.

17. The attack is made at *dawn*, when the enemy is sleeping

off the effects of the carousing. *continued till next day*: a very
abbreviated expression. A simple emendation would give
'to put them to the ban' (see note on 15: 3). The acceptance of
this emendation would have the advantage of providing yet
another contrast between Saul and David. Saul, ordered to
put the Amalekites to the ban, failed to do so and was rejected;
David, given the opportunity, puts the matter right and thereby reveals himself as fit for kingship. It is true that verses 26–31
indicate a great deal of booty in addition to the recovery of
what had been taken from Ziklag and other places raided; but
possibly these verses are in reality part of an independent
tradition (see note on p. 225). The escape of the camel troops,
the most rapidly moving of the raiders, is unavoidable.

19. *David recovered everything*: compare the divine assurance
in verse 8.

20. Thus his men proclaim his victory as they return, saying,
'*This is David's spoil*'; what he has rescued belongs to the
king. *

DAVID, THE UPHOLDER OF JUSTICE

When David returned to the two hundred men who had 21
been too weak to follow him and whom he had left
behind at the ravine of Besor, they came forward to meet
him and his men. David greeted them all, inquiring how
things were with them. But some of those who had gone 22
with David, worthless men and scoundrels, broke in and
said, 'These men did not go with us;*a* we will not allot
them any of the spoil that we have retrieved, except that
each of them may take his own wife and children and
then go.' 'That you shall never do,' said David, 'consider- 23
ing*b* what the LORD has given us, and how he has kept us
safe and given the raiding party into our hands. Who 24
could agree with what you propose? Those who stayed

[a] *So some MSS.; others* me.
[b] considering: *prob. rdg., cp. Sept.; Heb.* my brothers.

with the stores shall have the same share as those who went
25 into battle. They shall share and share alike.' From that
time onwards, this has been established custom in Israel
down to this day.

* 22. *worthless men and scoundrels:* again the word *beliʿal* is
used (see on 1: 16). Such men set themselves against justice
and may be thought to be in league with the forces of evil.
retrieved: the reference appears to be limited to what has been
recovered, though the term may be broader.

23. *considering:* although this reading is almost certainly
correct, it may be preferable to keep the words 'my brothers'
(see N.E.B. footnote) as well, for this stresses appropriately
the sense of kinship between David and his men.

24. The legal principle is here set out. The ruling is in
rhythmic form:

    'As the share of the one who goes to battle

      so is the share of the one who stays with the stores

      alike they shall share.'

The same principle is enunciated in Num. 31: 27 and Josh. 22:
8. We should recognize that, as in other instances (compare the
two explanations of the proverb in 10: 12 and 19: 24), more
than one story was handed down purporting to tell how a
particular legal decision came to be made. It is here only rather
loosely attached to the preceding narrative. At the same time,
we may see in this account an illustration of an important
understanding of the king and his upholding of the law.
Ancient rulers would set out their claim to act rightly, in
accordance with the true tradition, by indicating examples of
the principles of justice to which they adhered. Such a statement can be seen in Hammurabi's listing of laws in which
examples of practice are given (for a selection from this, see
The Making of the Old Testament in this series). The law
accepted and proclaimed by Josiah (2 Kings 22–3) offers an
Old Testament instance of the same kind. David here shows
himself to be a true king, a maintainer of law and justice. *

DAVID AND HIS FRIENDS

When David reached Ziklag, he sent some of the spoil to 26
the elders of Judah and*ᵃ* to his friends, with this message:
'This is a present for you out of the spoil taken from the
LORD's enemies.' He sent to those in Bethuel, in Ramoth- 27
negeb, in Jattir, in Ararah,*ᵇ* in Siphmoth, in Eshtemoa, in 28,29
Rachal, in the cities of the Jerahmeelites, in the cities of the
Kenites, in Hormah, in Borashan, in Athak, in Hebron, 30,31
and in all the places over which he and his men had ranged.

* This short note is clearly intended as a direct sequel to the
one event described in this chapter. But the listing of places
covering the whole area in which David and his men were
active suggests that in reality we have a summarizing statement marking the significance of David's activities as leader of
the band.

26. *When David reached Ziklag:* this provides the link to
verses 1–20; it could also be a comment on the whole series of
events indicated in 27: 7–12. Those whom David defeats and
despoils are understood as *the LORD's enemies.*

27ff. The style of these verses is that of a catalogue, a
series of identical formulae. Not all the places in this list are
known, but it is clear that they lie in the southern Judaean
area and the Negeb (see map, p. 169, for some of them).
Ararah: may be identical with Aroer (see N.E.B. footnote);
this place and *Hormah* lie well to the south. For *Rachal* Sept.
has 'Carmel' (see chapter 25), possibly correctly. *Hebron* is a
very important place in Judah; it was David's first capital as
king (2 Sam. 2: 1–4).

By the giving of gifts to the leaders in Judah and the south,
David establishes himself more and more securely, paving the
way for his anointing as king at Hebron (2 Sam. 2: 4). *

[a] *So Sept.; Heb. om.*   [b] *Prob. rdg.; Heb.* Aroer.

THE DEATH OF SAUL

31[a] The Philistines fought a battle against Israel, and the men of Israel were routed, leaving their dead on Mount Gilboa.
2 The Philistines hotly pursued Saul and his sons and killed
3 the three sons, Jonathan, Abinadab and Malchishua. The battle went hard for Saul, for some archers came upon him
4 and he was wounded in the belly by the archers. So he said to his armour-bearer, 'Draw your sword and run me through, so that these uncircumcised brutes may not come and taunt me and make sport of me.' But the armour-bearer refused, he dared not; whereupon Saul
5 took his own sword and fell on it. When the armour-bearer saw that Saul was dead, he too fell on his sword and
6 died with him. Thus they all died together on that day, Saul, his three sons, and his armour-bearer, as well as his
7 men. And all the Israelites in the district of the Vale and of the Jordan, when they saw that the other Israelites had fled and that Saul and his sons had perished, fled likewise, abandoning their cities, and the Philistines went in and occupied them.

8   Next day, when the Philistines came to strip the slain, they found Saul and his three sons lying dead on Mount
9 Gilboa. They cut off his head and stripped him of his weapons; then they sent messengers through the length and breadth of their land to take the good news to[b] idols
10 and people alike. They deposited his armour in the temple of Ashtoreth and nailed his body on the wall of Beth-shan.
11 When the inhabitants of Jabesh-gilead heard[c] what the

[a] *Verses 1–13: cp. 1 Chron. 10: 1–12.*
[b] to: *so Sept.; Heb.* house of.   [c] *So Sept.; Heb. adds* to him.

Philistines had done to Saul, the bravest of them journeyed   12
together all night long and recovered the bodies of Saul
and his sons from the wall of Beth-shan; they brought
them[a] back to Jabesh and anointed them there with spices.
Then they took their bones and buried them under the   13
tamarisk-tree in Jabesh, and fasted for seven days.

✻ This passage appears in a slightly variant form in 1 Chron.
10, where it opens the narrative part of the Chronicler's work.
   1. This verse summarizes the event; the battle itself, the
pursuit and the *dead on Mount Gilboa* as the Israelites escaped
southwards. The verses which follow give some of the details.
   2. Saul's sons appear to have been four in number. Of the
three mentioned here, *Jonathan* is well known for the various
accounts of his heroism (chapter 14) and his close friendship
with David. *Malchishua* is also mentioned in 14: 49. *Abinadab*
appears only here. The fourth son, Ishbaal (Ishyo, Ishbosheth,
see note on 14: 49), was evidently not present at the battle; he
appears again as successor to Saul in 2 Sam. 2: 8, and the
relationship between his claims and those of David forms an
important theme in 2 Sam. 2–4.
   4. *and taunt me:* these words are missing in 1 Chron. The
Hebrew word is the same as that used for *run me through;* it
may have been accidentally repeated or may have this quite
distinct meaning as well. Saul seeks death rather than fall into
Philistine hands; what might then have happened is indicated
by the story of Samson in Judg. 16. The mocking of an
enemy is part of the triumph, and no doubt also is thought to
reduce the enemy to impotence. *the armour-bearer refused, he
dared not:* we may infer that he felt too great respect for 'the
LORD's anointed'. This theme is taken up in what appears to be
an alternative story in 2 Sam. 1, where an Amalekite soldier in
Israel's army relates how he killed Saul. Saul takes the only
course open to him and commits suicide. We may observe

[a] *So Sept., cp. 1 Chron. 10: 12; Heb.* they came.

that no word of condemnation of this appears; the story implies that this is a heroic and courageous action, like that of the rather shoddy character Abimelech in Judg. 9: 54. Suicide is rarely mentioned in the Old Testament, but evidently it was accepted as appropriate in certain circumstances. The case of Ahitophel in 2 Sam. 17: 23 is an important example; when his counsel was overruled, it was as if he had no further reason for living.

6. *as well as his men:* this could mean either 'all the soldiers in his army' or more probably 'all the royal bodyguard'. 1 Chron. has 'his whole house', thus offering an interpretation of the text to deny that there was any successor available in Saul's family.

7. *in the district of the Vale and of the Jordan:* i.e. in the plain of Jezreel and the Jordan valley. The Israelite inhabitants abandoned *their cities* to the Philistines, and presumably crossed into Transjordan. It is there that we find the new kingdom under Ishbosheth established (2 Sam. 2: 8f.), though the area there described also appears to include the central hill-country. The Philistines have thus acquired the whole fertile area to the north and east of the central hill-country, and Israel's position is very weak.

8. The fate of the victims of the battle is described; cutting off the head of a dead enemy appears also in the case of Goliath (17: 51). The Philistines publish *the good news* of their victory to encourage their own people and to intimidate their enemies. The victory is ascribed to their gods, here called *idols*; perhaps we should suppose that they set up a victory inscription in the shrine before the deities. We have an account of such a shrine in 5: 1–5.

10. *his armour:* treated as David did that of Goliath (17: 54, see note). *the temple of Ashtoreth:* the female divinity (see on 7: 3) worshipped alongside Dagon (see 5: 2). We do not know where this particular temple was; it could have been at Beth-shan, for a temple dedicated to a goddess and belonging to this period has been discovered there. *nailed his body on the*

wall of Beth-shan: this important city (see map, p. 212) controlled
the head of the Jordan valley and routes north–south and
east–west; it would be an important element in Philistine
domination of Israel. The exposure of bodies after battle is
attested by Assyrian war pictures. The Chronicler has a
variant here, however; he says that Saul's skull was put in the
temple of Dagon, and this would explain why the head was
cut off. Assyrian pictures also show heads set up on walls or
gates, just as was formerly done in London and elsewhere.
For the exposure of the dead see on 17: 43 f.

11–13. The affection inspired by Saul and his family is again
brought out. *Jabesh-gilead* (see map, p. 212) had been rescued by
Saul from the Ammonites (11: 1–11); this was a debt not to be
forgotten. David subsequently commended them for their piety
(2 Sam. 2: 4–7) and himself had the bodies of Saul and
Jonathan and of others removed from Jabesh-gilead and
reburied in Benjamin (2 Sam. 21: 11–14). The appropriate
rituals associated with the dead are undertaken. *anointed them
...with spices:* the text could mean 'burned them there', but
there is no evidence that Israel practised cremation. *tamarisk-
tree:* such a tree appears in 22: 6 (see the note at 10: 3).

The story ends without comment. The compiler has already
made his view of Saul clear, and the reader will have it in
mind as he follows the narrative. We are left with the impression of a tragic but courageous man. Since there is no real
division between this chapter and the opening of 2 Sam., we
may see that a comment is in fact made, after the relating of
how the news of Saul's death was brought to David. Then
(2 Sam. 1: 17–27), a fitting lament is pronounced by David
over the dead heroes and over the fall of Israel; it is significant
that no word of condemnation appears, but only a note of
sadness at Israel's loss. We have seen this same diversity of
judgement in the case of Eli and his sons (see on chapter 4).
The Chronicler, true to his own interpretation of David,
passes his judgement at the end of the battle narrative; to him,
Saul's 'unfaithfulness' is the cause of his death and of the

transfer of the kingdom to David. Disobedience and the search for guidance from 'ghosts' instead of from God could lead to no other end.

How much did Saul achieve as king? It is very difficult to say. We can detect something of his military prowess; we can see in the David traditions suggestions of his power even in the remote southern part of the country. In 2 Sam. we find his son Ishbosheth established at Mahanaim, east of the Jordan, and able to maintain himself over a kingdom there, with some control to the west of the river. But what area Saul actually controlled is not clear. That David, coming after him, could build on his organization, is likely enough; 14: 47–52 gives some indication of the foundation which was laid. But a changed situation came with David because he was able to contain the Philistines and so exert a fuller control. ✳

✳ ✳ ✳ ✳ ✳ ✳ ✳ ✳ ✳ ✳ ✳ ✳ ✳ ✳

THE MESSAGE OF THE BOOK

Saul and his sons are dead on Mount Gilboa. The sad figure of the first king has come to his tragic end. As a heroic figure he is overshadowed first by his son Jonathan and then by David, but his own abilities and the affection he could inspire still show through the narratives. He is both the divinely chosen leader, picked at the moment of crisis to bring deliverance and hope, and one in whom the demand for absolute obedience to the divine will is expressed, his doom being sealed in his failure. At one level the book provides us with an example of that pattern of obedience and blessing, disobedience and doom, which is written also into the book of Judges and the books of Kings. It provides an example in story form of the demands expressed so plainly in the exhortations of the book of Deuteronomy.

But the book has a wider sweep than this. It is part only of a larger canvas, that which shows the people of God moving from an older tribal organization to be a united nation under a king, from a religious life depicted as somewhat haphazard into a fully organized cult with temple and priesthood. As the books of this part of the Old Testament are now divided, they present something like a series of pictures by Hogarth. The first pictures, in Joshua and Judges, show us the moment of conquest, a conquest not in human power but in the power of God; and of settlement, a chequered and uneven time of fluctuation and change. This book, 1 Samuel, shows the beginnings of the working out of divine promise; the old priesthood begins to be set on one side, the old shrines are no longer adequate, and we are pointed forward to what is to come without this yet being made precise. The old institutions are breaking up, and the new one of monarchy takes its first tentative steps; it seems to end in failure, but we can see that this is not so, for the coming king, David, is already on the stage, ready to step into the leading part when his moment arrives. And the king does not stand alone. Not only will there be a priesthood to guide and direct: there is also the figure of the prophet, here typified in Samuel, but having as his successors Gad, and in due course Nathan and Ahijah and Elijah and a whole host more, named and unnamed.

King and people together are brought into a deeper sense of their relationship with God. For, above all, this book, like so much in the Old Testament, is concerned with the basic questions of life. How does God deal with men? What is the nature of his purpose, and what is human response? Through the variety of its stories, the book invites us to look at questions like these, and to make our own translation of them into the situations in which we endeavour to give our answers.

A NOTE ON FURTHER READING

A fuller commentary on 1 Samuel may be found in H. W. Hertzberg, *I and II Samuel* (S.C.M. Old Testament Library, 1964), based largely on the R.S.V.; shorter but useful commentaries are by W. McKane (S.C.M. Torch series, 1963; paperback 1967) and R. D. Gehrke (Concordia Commentary, St Louis, 1968). Background material for the period may be found in the first two volumes of the New Clarendon Bible (Oxford University Press, 1966 and 1971) and in B. W. Anderson, *The Living World of the Old Testament* (Longmans, 2nd ed. 1967). The reader who is interested in institutions will find much that is of importance discussed in R. de Vaux, *Ancient Israel* (Darton, Longman and Todd, 1961) and in articles in the Bible dictionaries and one-volume commentaries. From these, he may be guided further into the wealth of other literature concerned with history, archaeology, religion and theology which has a bearing on questions raised by the study of this book of the Old Testament.

INDEX